D0712334

DATE			

Red Grange and
the Rise of Modern Football

Sport and Society

Series Editors
Benjamin G. Rader
Randy Roberts

A list of books in the series appears at the end of this book.

Red Grange and the Rise of Modern Football

JOHN M. CARROLL

University of Illinois Press

Urbana and Chicago

© 1999 by the Board of Trustees of the University of Illinois
Manufactured in the United States of America
C 5 4 3 2 1

♾This book is printed on acid-free paper.

Library of Congress Cataloging-in-Publication Data
Carroll, John M. (John Martin), 1943–
Red Grange and the rise of modern football / John M. Carroll.
p.   cm. — (Sport and society)
Includes bibliographical references and index.
ISBN 0-252-02384-6 (cloth : acid-free paper)
1. Grange, Red, 1903–91. 2. Football players—United
States—Biography. 3. Football—United States—History.
I. Title. II. Series.
GV939.G7C37   1999
796.332'092—dc21   99-6056
[B]
CIP

Contents

Preface

RED GRANGE WAS ONE OF the most significant football players of the twentieth century. His name is associated with the rise of the adulated college football hero and the transformation of the intercollegiate game from a mainly plodding, defensive struggle to a more spectacular, offensive-minded pastime. He is also credited as being a catalyst for the growth and increasing popularity of professional football during the 1920s and 1930s. To the people of that time, Grange's name personified football. He is a central figure in football history not only because of his extraordinary athletic ability but also because his football career coincided with events and changes in American society that made him one of the most written about and talked about athletes of his era.

Timing was crucial in Grange's rise from a gifted schoolboy athlete to a sports legend. He started his football career at the end of World War I when the game became increasingly associated with patriotism and fitness. When he began playing at the University of Illinois in the early 1920s, college football was one of the fastest growing spectator sports in the country. It was a time when many Americans sought escape from the grim realities of war and a growing percentage of the population had the means and free time to enjoy sporting events. Grange also benefited from dramatic changes and advancements in the media that occurred in the postwar years. Millions read about Grange and observed his photographs in expanded sporting sections in newspapers, saw him in newsreels, and even viewed him in films and a movie serial. The expansion and intensity of media coverage of sports was vital to Grange's status as a celebrity and football hero in the 1920s but does not fully explain how he became a public idol.

Grange helped claim that position himself. He played his best games as an intercollegiate player at the most opportune times—when a large segment of the nation's sportswriters were focusing on him or his team. Few athletes have been fortunate or skillful enough to give their best performances on the most dramatic occasions. It was also fortuitous that Grange met and befriended Charles C. Pyle in the small college town of Champaign, Illinois. Pyle became Grange's agent and publicized him in an aggressive if not audacious manner. When his football career in the professional ranks began to ebb, Grange remained in the public consciousness for another three decades by working in the media that initially had made him famous.

This examination of Grange's life is not intended to be an intimate study or a psychologically probing account. It is the story of his public and primarily athletic career based mainly on printed sources. Few athletes leave behind enough primary documents such as personal letters, diaries, journals, or in-depth interviews to allow for such a study—certainly Grange did not. In a few instances, for example, concerning his formative years in Wheaton, Illinois, I have attempted to offer some new information on his upbringing and the shaping of Grange's personality and character. I am not suggesting, however, that his early years in Wheaton or his personality were critical to his success or fame.

For some famous athletes, the nature of their personality or character can be important in understanding their impact on sports or their notoriety—Babe Ruth, Babe Didrikson, and Dizzy Dean come to mind. That was not the case with Red Grange. Grange in most ways was down to earth and quite ordinary. In his twilight years, these very traits would fascinate and sometimes confound sportswriters who were intent on portraying him as a larger than life figure. They could not understand why the country's most famous former football star would often rather mow the lawn than watch the game that made him famous. But that was Red Grange.

The importance of Grange in sport history does not revolve around his personality or the inner struggles that he faced. It is doubtful if a probing psychological profile of Grange would tell us much more about why he was such a great athlete or why his fame has been so enduring. Grange, himself, insisted that his athletic ability was God-given. This study of Red Grange and his impact on sport history focuses on how the forces and events of early twentieth century American society intersected with Grange's exceptional athletic ability to make him perhaps the most revered football player of all time. The event that would begin his transformation from a respected midwestern all-American halfback into a sporting legend occurred on a balmy autumn afternoon in 1924.

Prologue:
Comet over the Prairie

★ ★

THE DAY WAS OCTOBER 18, 1924. In many ways, it was an ordinary Saturday in the Midwest. As the sun broke through the haze on the vast prairie extending south from Chicago, farmers and townsfolk were up early attending to their chores and affairs. It was already apparent that it would be an unseasonably mild Indian summer day. By noon the temperature had risen to around eighty degrees and would climb several more degrees by the early afternoon. With the foliage turning bright hues of orange and red and more than a few homeowners already busy with their rakes, the balmy conditions seemed somehow out of place. For the permanent residents of the university towns of Urbana and Champaign, the day was anything but normal. Located 120 miles south of Chicago, the twin cities were besieged by tens of thousands of homecoming guests and football fans anticipating a titanic gridiron clash between the universities of Michigan and Illinois. Few in a throng that jammed the streets of Champaign and the neighboring town of Urbana could have known that they would witness one of the most memorable individual achievements in American sports. It was the day Illinois halfback Harold E. "Red" Grange would run wild against a mighty Michigan team. It was a game Red Grange would never forget, or, more accurately, a game fans and sportswriters would never let the modest Grange forget. Like much about Grange's career, the story of "the game" is shrouded in myth, combined with a number of half-truths and inaccuracies.[1]

The extraordinary excitement surrounding the 1924 Illinois-Michigan game emanated from a number of sources. The University of Illinois was celebrating its annual homecoming, a widespread college event by the end of the decade that had originated at Illinois in 1910. Thousands of alumni from the state and around the country descended on Urbana-Champaign for a weekend celebration and reunion. The festivities began on Friday afternoon with a parade led by ex-servicemen and concluded at a dance on Saturday evening, with the football game being the foremost attraction. All hotel rooms in the twin cities were booked months in advance, and an overflow of some ten thousand overnight visitors roomed at local residences, found lodging in neighboring towns and tourist camps, or slept in their cars or on the cars' running boards. A Chicago *Tribune* reporter may have exaggerated slightly when he estimated that on Saturday "there were almost as many motor cars in Champaign today as there are in all of Europe."[2]

The intense interest in the 1924 Michigan game had a lot to do with the long-standing athletic rivalry between the Fighting Illini and the Wolverines. Since the beginning of intercollegiate football in the Midwest, Michigan and to a lesser extent Chicago had provided the region's strongest teams, and their coaches, Fielding "Hurry-Up" Yost and Amos Alonzo Stagg, were already legends in their profession. Although neither man had posted an exceptional record from the beginning of World War I through 1920, they both fielded powerful teams in the opening years of the new decade. Despite the resurgence of Michigan teams beginning with the 1922 season, however, Yost had come under increasing criticism from students and alumni because of his old-fashioned defensive style of play that included mostly running plays from the short punt formation. He had voluntarily stepped down as head coach after the 1923 season but retained his position as athletic director. Thus, despite some accounts to the contrary, Yost watched the 1924 Illinois game from a box in the stands while the newly appointed George Little coached the Wolverines on the sideline.[3]

It was ironic that Yost had resigned as head coach under pressure in 1923 because his teams had been Big Ten co-champions in 1922 and 1923, sharing the latter title with Illinois. In addition, Michigan under Yost had been undefeated and untied since a 1922 scoreless game with Vanderbilt, and Little had extended the undefeated streak during the 1924 season until it stood at twenty on the eve of the Illinois game. For many fans in both Ann

Arbor and Urbana-Champaign, the 1924 contest was regarded as a play-off game to settle who had been the real Big Ten champion the previous year. Although Michigan had defeated the Fighting Illini in seven out of the nine games played between the two schools, including a convincing 24-0 rout in 1922, Illinois with Grange and the home field advantage was a slight favorite.[4]

An added attraction that helped draw an unprecedented number of football fans to Urbana-Champaign on October 18 was the official dedication of Memorial Stadium. As the fourth-largest university in the nation in terms of enrollment, Illinois joined a number of other leading state and private colleges in a flurry of stadium building in the early 1920s. The Michigan team alone was slated to help dedicate three stadiums in the Big Ten during the course of the season, including Memorial Stadium.[5]

The brainchild of Illinois Athletic Director George Huff, a campaign for the new stadium began in 1921 with a subscription drive targeted at raising more than two million dollars to construct an edifice honoring the 184 Illinoisans killed in the Great War. The stadium was constructed on an eighty-acre site, with initial plans calling for a 150-foot high campanile honoring the war dead at the main entrance, an artificial ice rink under one grandstand, and a ten thousand-seat Greek open-air theater within the structure. University of Illinois President David Kinley predicted that "our Stadium will bring a touch of Greek glory to the prairie." He added that "young men and women spending four years of their lives in the vicinity of such an edifice cannot help absorbing some of its lofty inspiration." When thousands of subscribers failed to meet their pledges, however, the theater, campanile, ice rink, and other extras were jettisoned. Nevertheless, the resulting stadium with its Old World motif was an architectural success and one of the finest athletic facilities in the region. The Fighting Illini had played its first game at the nearly completed stadium against Chicago the previous season before a sellout crowd (60,632), but many students, alumni, and friends of the university awaited the formal dedication of the impressive structure to which so many had contributed.[6]

The convergence of some fifty thousand people on Urbana-Champaign for the homecoming celebration and the Michigan game was overwhelming. The Illinois Central and Michigan Central railroads offered reduced fares and added extra trains. Sixteen special trains of the Illinois Central alone left from Chicago on the morning of the game. The preferred mode of travel, however, was the automobile. Michigan students organized what the Associated Press described as "a curious caravan" that "roared, snorted, jerked and honked its way out of Ann Arbor" on Thursday morning headed for Urbana-Champaign. Tens of thousands of Illini fans motored over newly paved roads to the twin cities. Traffic was so dense in Urbana-Champaign by Saturday morning that the new automatic automobile signals were shut off and scores of special police officers controlled the flow of vehicles. Although estimates of the total crowd vary, the official paid attendance at Memorial Stadium was 67,205, with 11,000 accommodated in temporary bleachers. Several thousand fans who were turned away took up positions on the tops of trucks and peered over the north wall. More than six hundred others gathered at the university armory to view a special grid-graph representation of the game.[7]

Across the state, many high school football games were canceled or postponed to allow Illini fans to attend "the game" or listen to it on radios or crystal sets. In Grange's hometown of Wheaton, the high school game went on as scheduled, but a radio was installed at the football field so everyone could be kept posted on the contest in Champaign. It was not the first radio broadcast of an Illinois football game as many subsequent stories stated. University station WRM and Chicago Westinghouse station KYW had both aired games from the stadium the previous year. The Chicago *Tribune* station WGN under the direction of Illinois alumnus James Cleary selected the Michigan game for its first football broadcast. Quin Ryan, who would broadcast more than two hundred football games during his career, recalled that because the press box was not completed "we simply set up a tent on top of the press box, and worked at a table almost out in the open." Based on letters received from listeners, the *Illinois Alumni News* estimated that more than a hundred thousand fans heard the game on WGN. In later years, Ryan was convinced that "Red Grange did one thing for college football not many people realize—he made it the subject of network broadcasts."[8]

At about 1:30 P.M. after the impressive dedication ceremonies had been completed, the Illinois band, rated by John Philip Sousa as one of the best in the country, marched onto the field 175 strong and "resplendent in new orange and blue military overcoats, presented by the alumni." The Michigan band soon followed, and the two joined forces in playing "The Star Spangled Banner." At precisely 1:45, the Fighting Illini team ran onto the field and was greeted by shouts and howls from thousands of rooters. Moments later, a controversy ensued that delayed the opening kickoff. Fielding Yost, seated with his wife in a box on the far side of the field, quickly noticed that the Illinois men were not wearing woolen socks. As

far as anyone could recall, no college team had played without knee stockings, and Yost suspected a trick from his longtime rival Bob Zuppke, the
Illini coach. The Michigan athletic director sent word to Coach Little to
check the bare legs of the Illinois team for grease or some other foreign
substance. Referee Masker and the Michigan captain, Herb Steger, inspect-
ed the calves of the Fighting Illini players but found nothing but skin,
muscle, and hair.[9]

In later years, Grange credited Zuppke with "a stroke of genius" in or-
dering his players to remove their woolen stockings before entering the field
for the opening kickoff. He became convinced that the "socks episode"
was a psychological ploy by Zuppke, who had taken psychology courses
in college, to distract the Michigan team. Grange maintained that "the
Michigan players were thinking more of the stockings than the game for
the first five minutes. By the time five minutes had passed, the game was
over." In earlier accounts of the game, however, including his autobiography, Grange mentioned the "socks episode" but did not emphasize it as a
psychological ploy. Most contemporary accounts of the game, including
the Chicago *Tribune* report, speculated that Zuppke ordered the woolen
socks removed because of the unseasonably warm temperature or for "stra-
tegic reasons." Like much about that October afternoon, the incident became part of the folklore of the game.[10]

This is not to say that Illinois Coach Robert C. "Zup" Zuppke had not
won the psychological war with Yost and Michigan before the game began. A German immigrant who had been a successful high school coach
in Michigan and at Oak Park, Illinois, Zup was named head coach at Illinois in 1913, and his teams had won or shared five Big Ten championships.
He was an innovative coach and a firm believer in the psychological approach to winning football games. Zuppke had begun to prepare his players for the Michigan game the previous winter after the Michigan student
newspaper left Grange off its 1923 first team all-American selection. The
Michigan *Daily* added insult to injury by declaring that all the otherwise
consensus all-American halfback "could do was run." The *Daily Illini*
responded by noting that "all Galli-Curci can do is sing," a statement
widely attributed to Zuppke in subsequent years. Michigan's Yost, then
still head coach, added more fuel to the fire by stating that Grange and
Illinois would pose little problem for the Wolverines the following autumn.
During spring practice, Zuppke posted the insulting stories emanating from
Ann Arbor in the Illinois locker room, and throughout the summer he sent
out a continuous flow of letters to his players quoting various Michigan

sources on how the Wolverines would crush the Fighting Illini. "By the time
we returned to campus for the fall semester," Grange recalled, "we were
all so mad that beating the Yostmen from Ann Arbor became the most
important issue in our lives."[11]

At 1:55, as the blue-jerseyed Illinois team huddled to receive final instructions at the north end of the field, fireworks burst above the stadium, re-
leasing parachuted banners of "Illinois" and "Michigan" as army airplanes
swooped low to take pictures of the scene. A few moments later, ten cheerleaders turning handsprings led the Illinois faithful in the "Oskee-Wow-
Wow" cry of the Illini. Almost immediately it was answered from across
the field by the inspiring "U. of M., rah, rah; U. of M., rah, rah." Finally,
the referee called the two captains together at midfield, and Frank Rokusek
of Illinois, winning the coin toss, chose to defend the north goal. Michigan Captain Steger, in keeping with the still prominent defensive style of
football, chose to kick off. Grange, wearing number seventy-seven on his
jersey, stood extra deep nearly under his own goalpost because of a 1924
rule change that moved the kickoff from the forty-yard line to midfield.
As the ball soared skyward down the center of the field, few in the jam-
packed stadium could have realized that they were about to witness the
most memorable twelve minutes in football history.[12]

Some erroneous accounts of the opening kickoff maintain that Steger had
asked Rokusek which player was Grange and, being informed that he wore
number seventy-seven, booted the ball directly at him. It was true, however, that past Yost-coached teams had attempted to neutralize outstanding opposition runners by forcing them to carry the ball as often as possible, thus wearing them down. In any case, Grange moved forward a few
yards before catching Steger's kickoff on the five-yard line and raced to
his own thirty before cutting wide right to avoid a mass of tacklers. Dodg-
ing and weaving his way back across the field through remnants of the
Michigan defense, he sprinted down the east sideline for a touchdown.
Pandemonium broke loose in the east grandstand as strangers pounded one
another on the back and sedate businessmen tossed their hats in the air.
In less than thirty seconds, the "Galloping Ghost," as he later would be
called, had electrified the crowd, and Illinois led 7-0 after Earl Britton
booted the conversion.[13]

Despite the stunning effect of Grange's ninety-five-yard touchdown run,
Michigan stuck to its game plan and elected to kick off again. This time
Grange caught the ball in the end zone and, contrary to some fictional-
ized accounts, did not score another long-distance touchdown but ran the

ball out to the Illinois twenty-yard line before being tackled. Illinois failed to move the ball and punted out of danger. The Wolverines advanced to the Illinois twenty-one-yard line before losing the ball on a fumbled field goal attempt at the thirty-two. After halfback Wally McIllwain picked up one yard, Grange took the ball and once more circled and dodged through the entire Michigan team for a sixty-seven-yard touchdown. Britton's conversion gave the Fighting Illini a 14-0 lead. From his box seat behind the Michigan bench, Hurry-Up Yost shouted at Coach Little and his team to lie back for Grange rather than rushing at him.[14]

Undeterred by the commotion, Little ordered Steger to kick off again, and he booted the ball into the Illinois end zone for a touchback. After a few short gains, Britton punted out of danger to the Michigan twenty-yard line. The Wolverines gained only three yards before Tod Rockwell punted to the Illinois forty-four-yard line. After McIllwain failed to gain ground, Grange was off again on a fifty-six-yard run for a touchdown. Veteran sportswriter Paul Gallico, who did not see this particular game but would witness many of Grange's subsequent long runs, recalled that the Illinois halfback "ran with a peculiar sliding motion and wonderfully timed weaving of the hips that always kept his body moving away from the point of impact. He flowed rather than ran, with variable speeds that functioned instinctively with direct relation to the problems facing him, now fast, now imperceptibly slower, then bursting forth brilliantly like a crescendo of music, always in a sweet antirhythm to the thundering phrases set up by the defense. He had likewise," Gallico wrote, "the co-ordination and ability to come to a full stop in mid-flight and change course to start off at another tangent, destroying with one movement the rigid threats to his progress initiated by the enemy." For Michigan the result was a nightmare. After Britton missed the conversion, the score stood at 20-0.[15]

To the amazement of the fans, Coach Little instructed Steger to kick off again, and this time he booted the ball out of the end zone, disappointing the Illini faithful. But they weren't disappointed for long. After Grange lost five yards on the first play from scrimmage, Britton launched a long, high punt across midfield. Tod Rockwell caught it, was promptly hit, and fumbled, with Rokusek of Illinois recovering the ball on the Michigan forty-four-yard line. On the very next play, Grange circled wide around right end, cut back against the grain, and sprinted into the end zone. Britton's conversion increased the lead for Illinois to 27-0. A few plays after a fifth straight Steger kickoff, Illini quarterback Harry Hall called time out. When Illinois trainer Matt Bullock arrived on the field and asked Grange how he felt, the redheaded halfback replied, "I'm so dog-tired I can hardly stand up. Better get me out of here." With three minutes still remaining in the first period, Zuppke complied by sending in substitute Ray Gallivan. As Grange trotted off the field, the crowd erupted in wild cheering that did not subside for several minutes. Grange recalled that "I was grateful for their acclaim, but much too exhausted to fully appreciate the thrill of such a tribute."[16]

After Grange's fourth touchdown run, the excitement and bedlam in the stadium were so great that four girls fell over backwards out of the temporary bleachers on the south side of the field. Fortunately, they were unhurt. In Chicago's White City Stadium where future University of Illinois professor John Schacht was watching a high school game, fans were becoming irritated with an Englewood High School cheerleader who was monitoring the game on a crystal set and proclaiming Grange's touchdowns one by one through his megaphone. Schacht recalled that at first there was cheering but by the fourth announcement "the crowd just giggles incredulously." He remembered thinking, "Either this lad thinks he's kidding us (he's not succeeding!) or the radio announcer has gone crackers—and so let's get back to the game in front of us—it's believable at least."[17]

At the Polo Grounds in New York City where many prominent eastern sportswriters had gathered to watch Army play Notre Dame, Grantland Rice was hunched over a typewriter recording his impressions of the remarkable Fighting Irish backfield of Harry Stuhldreyer, Don Miller, Jim Crowley, and Elmer Layden. In a matter of hours, Rice would write the story of Notre Dame's 13-7 triumph and immortalize the Irish backs in football folklore as the "Four Horsemen of the Apocalypse." Because Rice, Damon Runyon, Ford Frick, and other celebrated sportswriters of the day did not cover the Illinois-Michigan contest and thus had to rely on accounts of the game from the wire services and Chicago newspapers, they tended to speculate about Grange's real abilities and the caliber of "Western" football. That skepticism tended to heighten curiosity about Grange and his incredible performance against Michigan. Eastern sportswriters and fans alike wanted to know if Grange could measure up to the standards of what they smugly considered to be the superior brand of football played in the East.[18]

In Champaign, Grange had not completed his day's work. He sat out the remainder of the first quarter and all of the next period. At the start of the second half, with Illinois leading 27-7, Grange returned to his left halfback position. He broke free for a nifty thirty-five-yard run early in the period and later ran eleven yards for his fifth touchdown. In the final quarter, Grange completed an eighteen-yard pass to Marion Leonard for the Illini's final score in the 39-14 rout of Michigan. Grange's statistics for the game were staggering: He ran for five touchdowns (four in the first twelve minutes) and passed for another, amassed 402 yards rushing, and completed six passes for sixty-four yards. Mrs. Fielding Yost was more gracious than her husband when she admitted to a reporter that "I knew Grange was a star, but had no idea he was a comet."

Over the years, hundreds of thousands of fans would claim to have witnessed "the game" that Saturday afternoon. One who did, George Rockwood, a Michigan alumnus, recalled more than fifty years later that "one thing will always stand out in the memory of those privileged to see it— Red Grange in beating Michigan single-handed that day in October, gave perhaps the greatest performance in memory, and perhaps for all time." As for Grange, he waited for the bedlam to abate outside the Illinois locker room, slipped back to campus, had dinner at an out-of-the-way restaurant with a fraternity brother, took in an early movie, and went straight to bed.[19]

1

An Odd Kind of Family

☆ ☆

RED GRANGE'S EXTRAORDINARY PERFORMANCE in the 1924 Illinois-Michigan game is rightly considered by most sports experts as one of the outstanding single-day athletic feats by an individual in big-time competition. It has been compared with Jesse Owens's record-setting track and field achievements at the Ann Arbor Big Ten Championship meet in 1935, Don Larsen's perfect game in the 1956 World Series, and a number of other singular exploits by athletes in the course of one afternoon or evening. Grange's all-American status earned the previous year and his amazing exhibition of athletic talent displayed before sixty-seven thousand fans that October day in 1924, however, did not in themselves make him into the football immortal he soon would become. Without slighting his achievements in the least, it would be fair to say that of the more than five hundred thousand young men who played intercollegiate football during the 1920s alone, a handful, possibly more, were as good or better than Grange. Ernie Nevers and Bronko Nagurski, to name two, come to mind. Yet neither they, nor arguably any other football player of any other decade, would have the impact on the game or be more tightly woven into the mythology of football than Grange. There are many reasons for Grange's exalted status in the history of the game. A large part of the explanation stems from his interconnection with the vast social, economic, and technological changes affecting American life in the 1920s. Another area of importance is Grange's family background and personality and how the public perceived him in these years of rapid economic and social transition.[1]

When Grange first began to receive national acclaim as a football player during the 1923 season and his photograph appeared in numerous newspapers and magazines, a number of writers commented that he looked much older than his twenty years of age. Although his less than youthful appearance was undoubtedly unrelated to his experiences during his formative years, Grange had a difficult, even traumatic, childhood and adolescence. The circumstances and events he encountered during those years helped shape his personality and character for better or worse. That outward personality as well as his inner character are among the keys to understanding why Grange was ultimately accorded a celebrity status unequaled in the history of football.[2]

Harold Edward Grange was born on June 13, 1903, the third child of Sadie and Lyle Grange, in Forksville, Pennsylvania. A picturesque rural town of about two hundred inhabitants, Forksville was an isolated community more than fifteen miles from the nearest railroad and even further from the closest towns of Williamsport and Wilkes-Barre. Most of the men in town worked in the nearby logging camps. Red's father was foreman at a number of the local camps owned by Sen. Charles W. Sones and spent most of the week working in the rugged forests around Forksville. Lyle Grange was more than six feet tall and weighed more than two hundred pounds. He was a powerful but agile man who was renowned for his feats of strength. When sportswriter Bill Kehoe visited Forksville in the 1960s, residents recalled that Grange was "a man of sinewy robustness, so much so that there wasn't a gent in the whole countryside who could stand up to him. As a log roller he had the footwork of a tap-dancer and as a strong man and wrestler he could toss the lumberjacks around with such great ease it wasn't even a contest." Red remembered his father as "a man for a kid to brag about."[3]

Grange had only a few memories of life in Forksville because his family moved to Illinois a few months after his mother's death in 1908. His recollections of turn-of-the-century Forksville were mainly pleasant boyhood memories of fishing, sledding, attending the county fair, playing with his dog, and visiting the logging camps. He recalled being frightened that the gypsy bands that visited Forksville each summer might steal his dog. In his autobiography and in the hundreds of interviews he gave over the years Grange had little to say about his mother, the circumstances of her death, or how it affected him. He did have some memory of her but pointedly skipped over what he remembered or what his father or other relatives had related about her. Her death created a void in his life that he spent many years attempting to fill. The immediate result of her passing was that Lyle Grange moved the family, which included Red's older sisters, Norma and Mildred, and his three-year-old brother Garland ("Gardie") to Wheaton, Illinois. Many years later, Red recalled that "at first I missed Forksville terribly," but as time passed he realized that Wheaton "offered a more civilized way of life."[4]

By the time the Grange family relocated in Wheaton, a town of some four thousand residents about thirty miles west of Chicago, it was, indeed, more "civilized" than rural Forksville. Settled in the late 1830s by New Englanders Erastus Gary and Warren and Jesse Wheaton, the town began to prosper when the founders enticed a railroad to lay track through the rural settlement by offering a three-mile-wide right-of-way. Wheaton grew up around the Chicago and North Western depot and became the county seat of DuPage County in 1867. Initially an agricultural community with a small but thriving business and manufacturing area fronting the railroad, Wheaton was increasingly becoming a bedroom community for Chicago commuters when Lyle Grange and his family arrived in 1908. The construction in 1902 of an electric railroad, the Chicago Aurora and Elgin Railway, with switching yards in Wheaton hastened the transition of the town into a Chicago suburb. With two railroads serving the town and the time required for travel to and from Chicago significantly reduced, Wheaton would begin to experience an assortment of urban problems that in subsequent years would have a significant impact on Lyle Grange and his family.[5]

Lyle took the family to Wheaton because he had grown up there and had four brothers and a sister living in the town who could provide a network of family support in raising his children. During the next several years the Grange family made a number of moves to different residences in Wheaton, which must have been unsettling for the children. According to Grange's account, his father first rented a small house and went to work with his brother Sumner in the house-moving business. After a short time, the two girls were sent back to Pennsylvania to live with their mother's relatives. Richard Crabb, a long-time Wheaton resident and a close friend of Red's, speculated that the girls may have been sent away because Lyle, given the mores of the era, did not feel qualified to raise them properly. The decision also may have been influenced by financial concerns because Lyle's income was undoubtedly modest. After the girls were resettled, Red and Gardie were cared for part of the day by their Aunt Bertha (Lyle's sister) until she left Wheaton to take a job in New York state. Lyle then hired a housekeeper to supervise the boys during the daytime. A few years later, according to Red's recollection, the family moved in with his Uncle Luther (Lyle's brother), an unmarried lawyer, where they remained for a year or two. Then, in the summer of 1917, Lyle and Garland moved to an apartment over a store on Front Street in the heart of the business district, and Red was sent to live with his Uncle Ernest, who rented a farm outside of town. The series of moves and housing arrangements seem to indicate that Lyle was struggling financially and may have been concerned about his ability to provide a wholesome family environment for the boys.[6]

Throughout his life Grange seldom complained about anything, accepting hard work, injuries, or misfortunes with equanimity. He did register a mild complaint, however, about the year he spent on Ernest Grange's farm. On a typical day, Red remembered, he would arise at five, do two hours of chores, drive the milk wagon to town and back, and then pedal his bicycle the two miles to school. In the evening, he completed another arduous round of chores before retiring. As Grange recalled, "I earned my keep—and then some." According to Red, his father became convinced that Ernest was working the fifteen-year-old too hard and made arrangements for Red to join Gardie and him at the second-story apartment in the business section of Wheaton.[7]

Lyle Grange moved to the second-story flat on Front Street in 1917, not primarily for financial reasons but because his job required him to be in the city's business district for most of the day and night. In 1913 Lyle had taken a job with the Wheaton police department. It is not clear why he left the house-moving business and joined the police force, but, as Richard Crabb explained, security was a natural career for Red's father given his size, strength, and imposing bearing. He was employed by the police department in late 1913 as a $75 a month assistant to Marshal Emil Ehinger, who soon moved on to the position of county sheriff. In May 1914, Wheaton Mayor H. Ward Mills appointed Lyle as "City Marshall," with a salary of $100 per month.

Lyle remained Wheaton's marshal or police chief until 1923 and would hold the position again in the 1930s after serving a number of years as a DuPage County deputy sheriff. Significantly, during Lyle's first tenure as marshal he was usually the town's only police officer because of the difficulty of hiring and retaining qualified deputies given the available city budget. That meant that during part of Red's formative years, from age ten to eighteen, his father was normally on duty twenty-four hours a day. Lyle rented the downtown flat in order to be close to both his job and his family. But given the burgeoning crime wave in the town during the turbulent wartime years, fueled by the process of rapid modernization that acutely affected suburbs such as Wheaton, Lyle Grange was seldom home. During those years, Red and Gardie literally had to run the family household and fend for themselves.[8]

One of the enduring myths about Red Grange that helped add to his appeal as a football and popular hero in the 1920s was that he was a poor country boy who climbed the ladder of success despite his poverty and rural origins. Like many such myths, it was partially true and considerably exaggerated. Although the record concerning Grange's background and upbringing is sketchy, the evidence suggests that he may have been more emotionally than materially impoverished. That is not to say that the Granges were by any means affluent. The family's rapid movement from one home to another and the occasional boarding with relatives during the early years in Wheaton suggest that Lyle may have had financial difficulties in addition to his concern about providing a wholesome home environment for the boys. Once he was employed as a town policeman when Red was ten, however, his financial situation appears to have improved significantly. Lyle's $100 a month salary in 1914 would have placed his income well above the average wage for manufacturing workers, who were the best-paid unskilled laborers in the United States at the time. Counting the overtime pay he earned for working twenty-four-hour shifts, Lyle made $135 per month in 1919, $160 in 1920, and $170 by 1922. The average wage for American manufacturing workers in 1919 was about $97 per month.[9]

It is possible that Lyle had debts or other obligations that consumed part of his monthly income. There is no record, for example, of whether he had invested in the house-moving business with his brother Sumner and perhaps lost money. In addition, he may have partially or fully supported his two daughters who lived in Pennsylvania. We do know that when Wheaton converted from a ward system of government to a commissioner system in 1917 and Lyle was required to post a $500 bond as city marshal he apparently did not have the money. The bond was secured by his brother, A. L. Grange, and Andrew P. Steck. It is also true that in the hundreds of interviews Grange gave from the early 1920s until his death in 1991, his recollection of family history and circumstances was in large part accurate. He consistently maintained that his family had a difficult time meeting expenses when he was young. What appears to be the case is that the family's financial fortunes fluctuated and he primarily remembered the more difficult times. During the summer before Grange entered the University of Illinois, for example, his father earned $170 a month (including overtime) as city marshal and Red earned $37.50 a week as an iceman, a significant monthly income for a family of three in 1922. Gardie most likely also held a job that summer. Although an estimated family income of about $2,500 per year was not a fortune in the early 1920s, especially if one were expecting to have two sons in college within two years, it was well above the median family income in the United States at that time. Presumably, Lyle Grange would not have even encouraged his boys to attend college if the family's financial circumstances were as consistently grim as Red sometimes later claimed.[10]

Grange once described himself as a "green country punk" when he entered the University of Illinois in 1922. The assertion is credible but like the family's alleged poverty needs to be qualified to some extent. There is little doubt that during the 1910s and early 1920s Wheaton had many of the characteristics of a rural Illinois town. Outside the busy business district there were open spaces, muddy country roads, and numerous small farms like the one rented by Red's Uncle Ernest. Elmer Hoffman, one of Red's closest boyhood friends and four years ahead of him in school, remembered living on such a farm near Wheaton around 1914 and riding one of several "western broncos" to school in town. He recollected Grange's delight at being allowed to ride one of these horses while Hoffman attended football practice after school. The football field itself was a converted apple orchard that Judge Elbert Gary allowed the high school to use for practice and games. One of the stories that Grange enjoyed telling in later years was how the boys first had to pick up the apples before a Saturday game.[11]

Despite these rural trappings, however, it is important to note that Wheaton was less than an hour away from Chicago by rail and a little longer by automobile. Grange, an avid baseball fan, frequently attended Chicago White Sox games even if it meant skipping school to do so. He often recollected watching the talented but infamous "Black Sox" team of 1919 play at Comiskey Park. Grange undoubtedly had more than a passing familiarity with the city and its customs. Beyond that, Wheaton was close enough to Chicago to be influenced by its trends and values. Even if one rejected big city mores as Grange may well have done, it seems unlikely that he could have remained uninfluenced by these forces. Although he was clearly no man of the world in 1922, Grange was just as certainly not a country bumpkin. His humble, withdrawn, almost self-effacing bearing that impressed both friends and strangers alike seems to have had less to do with poverty or rural upbringing than with other family circumstances.[12]

What appears to have been at the root of Grange's sometimes difficult childhood and an apparent shaping force in his personality was the absence of a consistent female influence in his family. Almost everyone who knew Grange remarked about his modest and reserved nature, especially given his later spectacular career and national acclaim. Elmer Hoffman explained that "Red was always very shy, bashful, and an unassuming person. Today," Hoffman wrote in the 1950s, "he has lost some of the shyness and bashfulness but is still the same unassuming Red Grange that I knew as a youngster in Wheaton." He attributed some of the change in Grange's demeanor to the influence of Margaret Grange, whom Red married in 1941. In his written statement, Hoffman also alluded to some of the forces that may have contributed to the shaping of Red's personality. After mentioning Red's father as a powerful man and an excellent chief of police, he noted significantly that Lyle "raised his family as best he could." Hoffman then added that "a great deal of Red's success can be credited to Mrs. Dollinger, the wife of a druggist in Wheaton. She often took Red in and saw that he had everything that a boy needed and followed his athletic career very closely."[13] The clear implication is that Lyle, although undoubtedly a fine man, could spare little time for his family and that Red needed and sought love, support, and care from a family friend, Emma Dollinger.

In his autobiography, Grange surprisingly devoted only a single paragraph to the Dollinger family. He stated that Charles "Doc" Dollinger owned the corner drugstore and served free sodas and sundaes to all members of Wheaton High School teams after games and that Charles, Jr., was a close friend and teammate on the football and basketball teams. Charles's mother Emma Dollinger, "Ma" as the members of the Wheaton High School football team called her, Grange continued, was the boys' biggest fan and patron. In the Wheaton High School yearbook of 1922, the senior football players praised her as a "Good Samaritan, general advisor, faithful nurse, and aid to success." Ma Dollinger clearly devoted extra attention to Grange, who had little in the way of a traditional family life and yearned for the warmth and comfort of a motherly touch. Neverthe-less, Grange had little to say about her in his autobiography, or for that matter in any of his numerous interviews. He recalled in 1953, "Whenev-er I wasn't cooking at home, I ate my meals at their house. Mrs. Dollinger was a kindly, gentle woman who gave me the mothering a boy of my age needed." It is significant that Red said and wrote so little about a woman who one of his childhood friends considered one of the important shap-ing forces in Grange's early life. At minimum, it appears that Grange lacked a mature female figure in his formative years and recognized that inade-quacy. It is also possible that this void, only partially filled by Emma Dol-linger, increased his insecurity and reinforced his shy, humble, almost self-effacing personality.[14]

Grange's shy and self-conscious demeanor was particularly evident with regard to girls and dating. Although that characteristic is not all that un-usual for teenage boys, Red's discomfort around girls seems to have been acute. Charles "Dink" Weldon, Grange's teacher and football coach dur-ing his last two years at Wheaton High School, was sufficiently struck by this aspect of Red's schoolboy career to emphasize it above other seem-ingly more noteworthy events in a statement to an interviewer in 1974 when Grange was being honored in Wheaton. "Red wasn't much inter-ested in fair girls much in high school," Weldon began and then related a story about how Grange had jumped out a back window of the locker room to avoid three who wanted to walk home with him after a high school basketball game at the Wheaton College gymnasium. "Girls had a hard time to get a date with Red," Weldon concluded in a follow-up letter to the interviewer. "They used to try many schemes but very few worked." Weldon may have been in a position to know and appreciate Grange's feelings on the subject. When he died later in 1974 at the age of eighty, Grange noted that "not only was he our coach but many of us took our problems to him." When he addressed the subject of high school dating in his autobiography, he said, "I never went out on dates with girls, be-cause I didn't have any money or a decent suit of clothes to wear." The evidence suggests, however, that the lack of money and dress clothes may have been only part of the problem. It appears that Grange was particu-larly uncomfortable around girls because of a paucity of experience in dealing with women and a perceived lack of social skills stemming from a male-oriented and unusual family environment.[15]

Beginning in 1918, after Red completed a year's residence on his uncle's farm and rejoined Gardie and his father at the second-story apartment on

Front Street, the two boys were responsible for running the entire household. Grange remembered that he did all the cooking, Garland did the shopping, and they took turns washing and wiping the dishes. "We also did the house cleaning ourselves," he added, "since Dad was generally too busy to help with any of these chores." Starting in 1914 when he was appointed city marshal, Lyle patrolled the downtown area on foot and only infrequently had the assistance of a deputy. He was usually on duty twenty-four hours a day and was paid overtime beginning in 1917 when the crime rate increased in Wheaton and it became even more difficult to hire qualified deputies due to wartime mobilization. Had Wheaton been a sleepy rural town, Lyle might have safely set aside sufficient time to attend to family needs while maintaining peace in the community on a round-the-clock basis. That was not the case.[16]

By the time America entered World War I, Wheaton was plagued by an increasing number of criminal acts caused in part by its proximity to Chicago, easy access to and exit from the town by either railway or motor car, and the turbulent social conditions related to mobilization. It is not surprising that the Grange boys saw little of their father. Lyle's only relaxation, according to Red, was to attend all Wheaton High School football and basketball games, which he considered an official police duty. As Richard Crabb related an often told story, when the football games at the apple orchard became exciting Marshal Grange "would walk up and down the sideline saying to everybody: 'get back, get back, give the boy [Red] a chance to run.'" At most other times the young Grange boys were on their own.[17]

There is no question that Grange loved, admired, and respected his father. When asked in 1981 to list some of his heroes for a film to be shown at the DuPage Heritage Gallery in Wheaton, Grange named his father first, commenting that "he simply did not know fear." On another occasion, he described his father as "the toughest man I ever knew," adding that "when the drunks got off the Chicago, Aurora & Elgin, they'd all run for home instead of raising Cain downtown. I don't think anything in the world scared my father." He emphasized that his father was a fair man but imposed rigid discipline on both boys. When asked what it was like growing up as the son of the police chief, Grange quickly replied, "I never tangled with him, if that's what you mean." Yet despite his size and reputation for toughness, Lyle Grange was a humble man and expected his sons to conduct themselves similarly. Red explained that "around my dad you could never be a big shot, even if you wanted to be, because he wouldn't stand for it." He added, "We're kind of an odd family, I guess. Things don't impress us that much. I'm not impressed by too many people, and I don't feel that I impress very many people. I think it's a good way to live."[18]

On the list of heroes he dictated to Richard Crabb, an important promoter of the DuPage Heritage Gallery, in 1981, Grange ranked the legendary western marshal Wyatt Earp seventh. In a note beside the selection Crabb wrote, "You did personal research even to photocopying the Arizona pool hall where he was murdered." Standing out on a list that primarily contained schoolboy friends, teachers, coaches, and famous athletes, Earp's name appears to be out of place until one considers that Lyle Grange was a kind of modern day Wyatt Earp in Wheaton. Among their many responsibilities, concerns, and anxieties, Red and Garland had to face the real danger that their father might be injured or even killed in the line of duty on any given night. Grange, although not dramatizing the situation, acknowledged tersely in a 1985 interview that "I was always afraid he'd get shot." He quickly added that "he did, once, in the foot." Although Wheaton was not exactly nineteenth-century Tombstone, by the wartime years the small city was experiencing a surge in crime, particularly robbery, which menaced not only larger American cities but also many bedroom communities of similar size and location as Wheaton. The fact that the Wheaton police department was understaffed put considerable strain on the city and also on the Grange family. As Wheaton's only police officer, Lyle was stretched to the limit in his effort to protect the community and raise his sons at the same time.[19]

The pace of modernization accelerated during the era of World War I and could be gauged by a number of changes, including an increase in fast motor cars, paved highways, and high-speed commuter trains. Communities such as Wheaton were affected by these forces of modernization in many ways, one of the most noticeable and disturbing being an increase in crime, primarily perpetrated by outsiders who used the improving transportation system to prey upon the town. Up until 1895 Wheaton had no police department at all and relied on Chicago detectives who visited the city once a week or so to investigate complaints. In the opening decades of the new century, Wheaton mainly employed only one police officer due to budget constraints and a lack of qualified candidates to assist the city marshal. By the time America entered World War I, Marshal Grange, operating on foot, faced the increasingly difficult task of combating mobile thieves and hooligans who raided Wheaton stores and residences and then sped off into the night on the electric railway or in motor cars on newly paved roads connecting DuPage County with Chicago.[20]

Wheaton was ideally situated as a potential target. Most of the city's important businesses were on Front Street facing the railroad tracks and less than a mile from the Roosevelt Road. This highway, which was under construction between 1917 and 1921, was the best partially paved road heading west out of Chicago and slated to become part of the transcontinental Lincoln Highway. Marshal Grange succeeded in foiling a number of attempted burglaries in 1917 and early 1918 but seldom apprehended the suspects, who usually fled in automobiles. Praising his efforts, the Wheaton *Illinoian* began a campaign in early 1918 to get the city to procure a motorcycle for the marshal, who hardly could pursue the motorized criminals on foot. City commissioners responded by purchasing a used motorcycle for the police department in early 1919, but the crime wave in Wheaton increased rather than abated. By the fall of 1920, after the previous year's devastating and unsettling Chicago Race Riot, the *Illinoian* suggested that the mayor and commissioners take action by hiring more policemen to protect the city properly. The newspaper editorialized that because Wheaton is located "but a few miles from the heart of all cussedness, Chicago, it seems reckless for the city to attempt to get along with but one policeman and expect him to be on the job twenty-four hours a day. No one questions Marshal Grange's ability," the article concluded, "but there is a limit to any man's endurance."[21]

Increasingly distressed by the postwar economic and social turbulence and the escalating crime wave, the *Illinoian* became more critical of Marshal Grange and predicted extreme action if city commissioners did not expand the police force. Under the headline "Night Marauders Raid City Stores and Residences," the *Illinoian* warned on October 8, 1920, that "if the city cannot act in the matter there is very likely to be a citizen's vigilance committee organized to patrol the city after dark." The crime spree in Wheaton continued into early 1921 before the burglaries tapered off. Pressed by the *Illinoian*'s threats and sometimes sarcastic criticism, city commissioners hired a night watchman and a part-time motorcycle officer and had a light installed in the alley behind the Front Street businesses. The crime wave abated without resorting to vigilantism, but the crisis almost certainly caused additional strain and anxiety in the Granges' already tenuous family life.[22]

By relating how Lyle Grange was compelled to neglect his family during the boys' important teenage years and why Red and Garland were concerned over their father's safety is not to imply that the boys suffered permanent psychic damage. In fact, Red in later years usually pointed to his family background with pride, emphasizing the self-reliance and confidence it fostered in him. During a 1974 interview, he noted that his upbringing was remarkable "because without a mother, who generally has the rule of the house, kids don't generally turn out that well." Grange was serious when he said his father "was a man for a kid to brag about."[23]

Lyle Grange was both a tower of strength and a paragon of humility. He exemplified the West African proverb that Theodore Roosevelt made popular: "Speak softly and carry a big stick, and you will go far." A story Richard Crabb related about Lyle when Grange was a DuPage County deputy sheriff in the 1920s speaks to both the quiet confidence of the man and the force of his character. When Sheriff Emil Ehinger noticed that Lyle never locked the jail cells after attending to the prisoners, he asked his deputy what he would do if the prisoners rushed him. According to Crabb, Grange "was reported to have stood up to his full height with his arms spread wide, and said, 'I would smother them.'" Whether or not the story was true, few in Wheaton doubted that the deputy could do it. In his autobiography, Red almost casually describes a fight his father had during his lumberjack days in Pennsylvania in which Lyle fought a larger man for six hours before beating him unconscious. Red seemed to internalize these traits of frontierlike, rugged individualism that were highly valued in the transitional decade of the 1920s, when individuals appeared to be increasingly overwhelmed by the expanding forces of an encroaching industrial society.[24]

Described often during his life as a maddeningly humble man, Red Grange associated this quality with his father. He once described him as a man who "hated anybody who got cocky about success. If I'd gotten cocky," Red added, "he would have paddled me." Lyle also had a softer side both in dealing with police business and his sons. The Wheaton *Illinoian* occasionally noted that the burly marshal could be sympathetic in dealing with young petty criminals. In one instance in 1920 he freed two Chicago youths he had arrested for stealing a basket of cherries when no one appeared to arrange their release the following day. The newspaper explained that the boys "heeded some fatherly advice and made themselves scarce." When he was around, Lyle could also be sympathetic and supportive with regard to his boys' concerns. In many cases, however, Red and Gardie had to seek support or counsel elsewhere. One of the few exceptions was their athletic endeavors, which Lyle encouraged and supported unswervingly. In discussing his high school days, Grange recalled, "I don't think Dad ever missed a football game—or basketball game. There were a lot of Saturday afternoons," he added, "when anybody could have robbed the bank." It is little wonder that Red and Gardie spent most of their free time engaged in athletic competition.[25]

During the 1924 football season on the eve of an important game between the University of Illinois and the University of Chicago (possibly deciding the conference championship), a Chicago sportswriter, after interviewing Grange, focused on some of the qualities of Red's personality and character that fascinated commentators and fans in the 1920s and still do today. Under the headline, "What, Ho Grange Says He Doesn't Like Football," the uncredited reporter quoted Grange as saying: "I wish this was over." The perplexed writer interpreted Red's simple statement with the following uncomprehending, overblown flourish: "—which phrase in politeness he refers to the football season, to the wild huzzahs which will be stifled so soon, to the unthinking adulation which is as tight as thistledown in quality." Struggling to understand how one of the most acclaimed football players of the time could utter these words on the eve of such an important game, the sportswriter attempted to analyze Grange. "The boy dismisses himself," he began, "—dismisses his qualities as a man as well as his brilliance as a football player. Grange, with his quietness, his gentleness, his beneath-the-surface strength of body and mind tucks himself into the heart as well as intrigues the passing fancy." In a crude way but to a greater extent than many of his contemporaries, the sportswriter illuminated certain aspects of Grange's personality and character that helped make him the most captivating football hero of the era.[26]

Grange's formative years helped shape his sometimes perplexing personality and character. On the one side, his youthful experience of frequent uprooting and movement from home to home, his mother's early death and the lack of a stable feminine influence in his life, and his father's regular absences from home and dangerous occupation combined to promote a basic insecurity. Lindsey Nelson, Grange's television broadcasting partner during the 1950s, alluded to that side of Grange's persona, perhaps unknowingly, when he mentioned that Red believed his greatest achievement in life was the success he made in the insurance business during the 1940s and 1950s. He felt that way, Nelson said, because "he did that by himself. Everything else was God-given and team work."[27] That insecurity often dovetailed with his other noticeable traits of shyness and humbleness, hallmarks of his father's influence. Many reporters interpreted Red's seeming diffidence toward his athletic accomplishments and growing fame as the reaction of a rawboned country youth awed by the bright lights and glamour of urban America. Grange did nothing to discourage that view, and it worked to his advantage in an era in which rural and urban values were often in conflict. Thus, Grange, knowingly or not, became a symbol of older rural American values, a curiosity for some urbanites to be sure but a person who held values that were still firmly entrenched in diverse areas of the nation.

The other side of Grange encompassed an inner strength of pride, fearlessness, and combativeness that his father epitomized. The driving energy that lay just beneath the surface mystified observers who tried to reconcile Grange's outwardly humble and self-effacing manner with his fierce determination to compete and succeed. The combination of these seemingly opposing forces understandably perplexed analysts such as the Chicago sportswriter who after posting the aforementioned story would watch Grange play one of his finest games against Chicago the following day. The apparent incongruities of Grange's personality and character, which fascinated fan and sportswriter alike, spoke to one of the overriding concerns of post–World War I Americans. How could the rural-born, usually soft-spoken, and unpretentious rugged individual so celebrated in American history and culture make a mark in a society increasingly dominated by machines, vast corporations, and stifling bureaucracies? Of all the American heroes of the 1920s, perhaps only Charles A. Lindbergh dramatized that paradox more than Red Grange.

2

Football and the Emergence of Red Grange

★ ★

WHEN RED GRANGE WAS BORN IN 1903, American football as an organized sport had been in existence for less than thirty-five years. Derived from the British school games of football (soccer) and rugby, the first intercollegiate game in America was played in 1869 by teams from Princeton and Rutgers, and it soon became a popular pastime on eastern college campuses. It was, from the beginning, primarily a sport of the elite. In comparing baseball with football, paleoethnologist and sports enthusiast Stephen Jay Gould has written that football "until recent years, largely flourished within an institution that catered to a tiny minority of the population: colleges and universities." Football was attractive to the youth of the elite because it was exciting, promoted campus community, and, in the beginning at least, it was student-controlled. Beyond that, it was a violent and virile sport for gentlemen who were concerned about their manhood in an increasingly sedentary society and questioned their ability to measure up to the past generation that had been tested in combat.[1]

By the early 1890s, football had replaced baseball as the most popular intercollegiate sport. From its casual beginning on eastern college campuses, football thrived in a nation that embraced laissez-faire economics and whose leaders were fascinated with the doctrine of Social Darwinism. In the eyes of the social elites, early football seemed to mirror those economic and social tenets. One of the landmarks of increasing popularity was the inauguration of the Thanksgiving Day game. Beginning with a game between Princeton and Yale at Hoboken, New Jersey, in 1876, the holiday contest, featuring the best teams in the East, afforded the backdrop for a kind of spectacle that appealed to New York's social elites. From an audience of about a thousand in 1876, the game moved to the Polo Grounds in 1880 and drew upward of forty thousand fashionable fans by the 1890s. The New York Thanksgiving Day game, Michael Oriard maintains, was also "the engine that drove football's early economic development and demonstrated the financial bonanzas that might be realized on a regular basis by building one's own fifty thousand-seat stadium." Although football spread rapidly by the mid-1890s to include a wide variety of college, preparatory school, high school, and club teams, the sport retained its association with the elite strata of American society well into the twentieth century.[2]

The rise of college football as a major American sport was not achieved, however, without opposition. Beginning in the 1880s, some college presidents, trustees, professors, and others questioned the legitimacy of football in an academic setting. The list of complaints was long, and most of them have been echoed periodically over the course of the twentieth century. Critics condemned the emphasis on football over academics, the win-at-all-costs mentality, the poor scholarship of many players, the commercialism and professionalism associated with the game, and the brutality and lack of sportsmanship on the field. In addition, they said, the game provided an atmosphere in which students gambled, drank, and were unruly. Some colleges, in what Ronald A. Smith has called the "football crisis of 1894," threatened to ban football if reforms were not instituted. At least two colleges did drop football altogether during the decade. As a result of the crisis, some changes were implemented. The New York Thanksgiving Day game was abandoned, a few eligibility requirements were adopted, and the flying wedge and other mass-momentum plays were banned. But little else was done before the early years of the next century to address other problems, especially those concerning the increasing number of players who were maimed or killed during football games.[3]

Although the early history of college football has been fairly well documented, little has been written about the development of the game at the private preparatory school and high school level. Benjamin G. Rader speculates that the popularity of Thomas Hughes's *Tom Brown's School Days*, a novel about life and sports at an English public school that was widely read in the United States after its publication in 1857, provided the impetus for a number of New England academies to take up football enthusiastically during the 1860s. "The school boys played without rules," Rader concedes, "but they brought a measure of respectability to the sport and reintroduced it into northeastern colleges." From that point on, colleges took the lead in refining and popularizing football, but prep schools provided a ready source of trained players that the "Big Three" football schools, Yale, Harvard, and Princeton, as well as other elite northeastern colleges, eagerly tapped. Toward the end of the century, a number of high schools in metropolitan areas began to organize teams. The pool of available talent was also augmented by town and club teams formed at about the same time.[4]

During the last two decades of the nineteenth century, football spread rapidly to other parts of the country, with the North Central states in the lead. The first professional coaches at numerous midwestern colleges were former players from the Big Three who carried the game westward with a missionary zeal associated with Muscular Christianity. As in the East, football at the secondary level quickly began to take root at prep schools and high schools in the larger cities. Frequently, town or club teams that competed against their counterparts in nearby communities or with college teams predated the formation of interscholastic leagues.[5]

In the case of Chicago, competitive interscholastic sports began in 1889, when the Cook County Athletic Association sponsored a field day at South Side Park (later Comiskey Park). The competition included bicycle races, baseball throwing, and track and field events but no team sports. By the end of the 1890s, the Cook County association formed an interscholastic league that featured contests in track, baseball, football, and later basketball. During the early years of the Cook County Athletic League, Amos Alonzo Stagg, a Yale graduate and former Eli end who had been coaching at the University of Chicago since 1892, practically adopted the nearby Hyde Park High School squad as his own farm team. Just as Harvard and Yale recruited heavily from Andover and Exeter academies and Princeton from Lawrenceville, Stagg did the same with Hyde Park. The Chicago Maroons not only scrimmaged the high school team but Stagg also offered handsome inducements to the best Hyde Park players, such as future Chicago all-American quarterbacks Walter Eckersall and Walter "Butch" Steffen, to attend the university on the Midway. Under his indirect influence, the quality of football at Hyde Park High School and in Chicago generally improved dramatically. In 1902 Hyde Park, led by Eckersall and Sam-

uel Ransom, defeated a Brooklyn, New York, high school team 105-0 in
the first national interscholastic championship game. Within a few years,
the Cook County football league was one of the strongest in the nation,
providing talented players for area colleges as well as for some of the best
eastern collegiate teams.[6]

By the early years of the twentieth century, football nationwide continued to expand at both the collegiate and secondary school level. A 1905
study of 555 cities showed that 432 of them had football teams. At the
intercollegiate level, more schools were fielding teams, especially in the
Southwest and West; there were more intersectional contests; and although
the sport was still dominated by elite eastern colleges it was moving in the
direction of becoming a national pastime. Even more impressive was the
large number of high schools taking up football. Although that process
began well before the turn of the century, the wide publicity given to the
early success of the Public Schools Athletic League (PSAL) established in
New York City in 1903 inspired other cities to organize similar schoolboy athletic leagues that included football. The brainchild of Luther Gu-
lick, a pioneer physical educator, the PSAL was financially independent of
the city school system but depended on New York's 630 schools to implement its programs. Along with other public and private backing, the endorsement and financial support of the PSAL by such prominent men as
John D. Rockefeller, Jr., Pierpont Morgan, and Andrew Carnegie went a
long way toward popularizing the concept of interscholastic sports for
secondary school children. In this era, however, interscholastic athletic
leagues were largely confined to urban areas where adequate funding and
transportation were available. Thus, in the early 1900s, football outside
the college ranks was substantially a city game, with the exception of some
prep schools, club teams, and a few high schools.[7]

Despite the growth of football in the early 1900s, particularly at the high
school level, the game faced another period of crisis. The football controversy of 1905–6 focused on the college game, specifically on what appeared
to be increasing levels and incidents of violence, unsportsmanlike conduct,
and brutality on the playing field. Critics were also concerned about the
continuing commercialization and professionalization of the game. Criticism concerning those issues had been building for more than a decade.
The dramatic behind-the-scenes intervention by President Theodore Roosevelt, who called for the reform of football, put this controversy in the
national spotlight. An ardent football enthusiast, Roosevelt feared that the
brutality and unsportsmanlike behavior associated with the game might

bring about its banning, as had been the fate of prizefighting in many parts of the country. For many historians, the 1905–6 football crisis, which had been sparked in part by muckraking journalists, was a typical sociopolitical conflict during an era in which Progressives attempted to reform and rationalize an institution (football) to make it conform to the public interest. Standing against the Progressives, presumably, was the Old Guard, who represented laissez-faire and the dog-eat-dog philosophy of Social Darwinism.[8]

The football controversy abated in early 1906 after a new Intercollegiate Football Rules Committee met in New York and adopted a number of changes designed to open up play and prevent the large number of serious injuries and deaths on the gridiron. To curtail brutal play, the committee prohibited backs from hurdling the line, created a neutral zone at the line of scrimmage, required six men on the offensive line, banned tackling below the knees, increased the number of officials to four, and assessed larger penalties for infractions. In order to open up play, teams were required to make ten yards in three plays for a first down, and the forward pass was legalized within strict limits. The National Collegiate Athletic Association was also established as a supervisory agency over college sports. As Ronald A. Smith has shown, the future of college football during the 1905–6 crisis was in greater jeopardy than previous historians believed, primarily because Harvard, a Big Three power, seriously considered dropping the game.[9]

The major eastern schools adopted the new rules, with Columbia, Union College, and the Massachusetts Institute of Technology being the only colleges of note in the region to drop football. More important, the number of deaths attributed to the game dropped from twenty-three in 1905 and to fourteen, fifteen, and ten in the following years. Although the number of serious injuries fluctuated, the public seemed satisfied with the "new football." During the 1909 season, however, a series of widely publicized fatal football injuries at prominent eastern colleges reopened the debate on the future of the game. The Washington *Post* inquired if the public needed "any more proof that football is a brutal, savage, murderous sport? Is it necessary to kill many more promising young men before the game is revised or stopped altogether?" Although coaches and most college presidents wanted to continue with the existing game if the number of serious injuries and deaths could be decreased, the outcry against the present state of American football was as strident as it had been in 1905 and 1906. William Reid, a former Harvard coach, wrote to Walter Camp, a former

Yale player and coach who was largely responsible for shaping the early game, to explain that in California there was much talk of replacing American football with rugby. David Starr Jordan, president of Stanford University, referred to football as "Rugby's American pervert" and counseled that "the farce of 'football reform' of five years before should not be repeated." On the East Coast, Woodrow Wilson, president of Princeton, observed that the sideshows had "swallowed up the circus." In addition, Georgetown University, the University of Virginia, the U.S. Military Academy, and Loyola University in Baltimore all canceled the remainder of their football schedules by mid-November 1909.[10]

Commentary on the 1909–10 football crisis has focused on the nation's colleges, but its impact at the high school level is also significant. By mid-November 1909, the *New York Times* reported that in response to the outcry over the estimated twenty-six players killed and seventy seriously injured as a result of football up to that point in the season, "Many of the city High Schools in various parts of the country have been forced to give up the sport." On November 18 the board of superintendents of New York City voted to ban football. The *Times* estimated that more than a half-million public school students in New York City alone were affected by the abolition of football and listed four other cities that had either suspended the game for the rest of the season or banned it entirely. "It is not considered improbable," the *Times* claimed on November 19, "that some of the other public school systems, following the example of New York City, will also abolish the sport in their respective communities." In an editorial printed the day after the New York City board terminated football, the *Times* castigated college officials for their laxity. Noting that there had been no deaths attributed to football in New York City during 1909, the writer remarked sarcastically that the board of superintendents was "not following the fashion. Would it not have been better for the Superintendents to withhold their decree, as the institutions of higher learning have done and are doing, until some mother's son actually gets his neck broken or his skull crushed in." On December 9, after the superintendents voted to ban football in the PSAL, New York lawyer Frederic R. Coudert may have expressed some of the public's hostility toward football when he referred approvingly "to Col. John S. Mosby's characterization of football as 'murder.'"[11]

As local school boards or city officials debated the future of football in their communities, coaches and college presidents scrambled to devise a set of rule changes that would be acceptable to the collegiate football fraternity and also convince the public that safeguards were in place to reduce the number of deaths and serious injuries on the gridiron. In May 1910 the American Intercollegiate Football Rules Committee adopted a set of new regulations: Seven men were to be positioned at the line of scrimmage on offense; pushing, pulling, and interlocking interference were outlawed; and the time-span of a game was reduced to four fifteen-minute quarters. The forward pass was readopted, but with some still stringent restrictions.[12]

From available evidence it appears that the rule changes of 1910 were a success in restoring football to or near its 1908 level of participation. Despite criticism and predictions that the new rules would fail to lessen deaths and injuries, most colleges resumed their schedules for the 1910 season. Only Georgetown among major eastern colleges failed to recommence football that year. A few West Coast schools continued to play rugby and were joined by the University of Southern California and a couple of smaller western colleges in 1910 and 1911. Much less is known about the high school game. The board of education in New York City reinstated football in mid-September 1910 under the new rules with the proviso that "if it is found that accidents continue to occur the Committee on Athletics will prepare new rules, under which the boys will be allowed to play." There is no data concerning how many high schools that had suspended schedules or abolished the game the previous year fielded teams in 1910.[13]

In terms of opening up the game and making it safer and more exciting, the 1910 rules had only a limited immediate impact. According to John S. Watterson, "The new football was duller, lacking scoring and usual excitement" and "despite fewer restrictions, the forward pass was not widely used by eastern schools." The Brown University passing combination of Bill Sprackling and Russ McKay in 1910, however, led the Bruins to their first ever victory over Yale, made Sprackling an all-American quarterback selection, and provided a foretaste of the memorable passing displays by Gus Dorais and Knute Rockne of Notre Dame after passing rules were further liberalized in 1912. In addition, midwestern teams used the pass more frequently, beginning in 1910. The death rate among football players did decline in 1910, but only marginally. A Chicago *Record-Herald* survey listed twenty-two fatalities and 499 injuries during that season. The following year, however, the same newspaper reported only nine deaths and 177 injuries related to football by the last week of November. With the exception of the 1901 season (seven deaths), it was the fewest number of fatalities since the turn of the century. For those who took a wait-and-see attitude on the 1910 rule changes, the 1911 season seemed to repre-

sent a vindication of the intercollegiate officials who had set out to allevi-
ate the more brutal aspects of the game.[14]

Like many institutions that came under public scrutiny during the Progressive Era, football was likely never in serious danger of being abolished,
but only reformed so its most offending aspects might be eliminated. In
the next few years there were a number of signs that the game had not only
survived its two early-twentieth-century crises but was also expanding its
grip on American sports fans. Although most teams continued to play
conservative, defensive football, the liberalization of the forward passing
rules in 1912 added a new and exciting element to the game. At about the
same time, Jim Thorpe of the Carlisle Indian School, after winning two
gold medals at the 1912 Olympic games in Sweden, capped his extended
collegiate football career by racking up 198 points in 1912 and being
named a consensus all-American halfback. Thorpe came closest in the pre-
1920 era of being acclaimed as a national football hero. With the entertaining Carlisle Indians under Coach Glenn "Pop" Warner playing as many
as sixteen games a season, mostly on the road, Thorpe was a major gate
attraction in the East, and his name and reputation were known to football fans around the country. In addition, Princeton and Yale dedicated new
football stadiums in 1914, with the Yale Bowl seating more than seventy
thousand fans. Two other major universities were optimistic enough about
the future of the game to lay plans for new and larger football arenas before World War I interrupted the projects. As the war engulfed Europe,
the major California colleges abandoned rugby and returned to football,
making the game the undisputed autumn pastime.[15]

If football had survived its time of trial in the early twentieth century,
critics by no means had been silenced. Numerous complaints were registered about the game, but the most persistent focused on the brutality of
play and the unsportsmanlike behavior of players and coaches. During the
1913 season, high-ranking officers of the U.S. Army and Navy assailed
football as the cause of unnecessary serious injuries and for shortening the
careers of men who had played for the service academy teams. Col. Clarence P. Townsley, superintendent of the U.S. Military Academy, asserted
that injuries due to football were so severe at West Point as to "make it a
question of whether football is of sufficient value to the corps to warrant
its continuance." The same year Surgeon General Charles Frances Stokes
of the U.S. Navy conducted a study of more than 1,200 Naval Academy
graduates from the classes of 1892 through 1911 to evaluate the impact
of football and other strenuous sports on them. He found that midship-

men who had been star athletes were less healthy than the less athletic men and recommended that "endurance contests dependent upon brute strength be eliminated from the category of Academy sports." As the European war evolved into a stalemate by 1915, the *Journal of the American Medical Association* added its condemnation of highly competitive athletics, concluding that "exercise is intended to benefit, not to injure, the individual."[16]

Criticism of football and other highly competitive sports continued into the early wartime period while Grange was entering his teenage years. A number of high school principals, headmasters, and college presidents complained about the excesses and evils associated with athletics that stressed a win-at-all-cost philosophy and accepted unsportsmanlike behavior as part of the game. As the United States moved closer to entering the Great War in 1916 and 1917, however, American attitudes concerning competitive athletics as reflected in the popular press became increasingly positive. One factor was British propaganda. Having initially built their athletic structure on the English model, Americans were susceptible to British claims that good athletes made good soldiers and that athletic events raised morale and fighting efficiency and helped reduce idleness and vice. Once America entered the war in April 1917, however, organized athletic activity was curtailed. By the start of the football season that year, tens of thousands of college men had already joined the armed services, and others reported late to their institutions after spending the summer on farms in response to a government request for the nation's youth to help boost agricultural production. Most colleges fielded football teams during the 1917 season, but, significantly, two of the perennial powers, Harvard and Yale, canceled their usual varsity schedules.[17]

In the fall of 1918, when Red Grange began his first varsity football season at Wheaton High School, a number of colleges had followed Harvard and Yale's lead by disbanding their teams. Some schools had little option when the Railroad Administration under William G. McAdoo took control of the nation's railways and restricted nonessential travel. Although the war appeared to represent a setback for spectator sports, including football, nothing was farther from the truth. The biggest boost for athletics came from the armed services, whose medical leaders had criticized highly competitive sports as recently as 1913. Secretary of War Newton D. Baker set up the Commission on Training Camp Activities under the direction of Raymond Fosdick, who had earlier cleaned up the vice-ridden camps on the Mexican border during Gen. John J. Pershing's punitive expedition against Pancho Villa in 1916. Under Fosdick's guidance, army camps organized broad-based recreational programs under the control of physical directors as well as base teams in various sports, including football, which competed against other camps and college teams. When the navy appointed him to head a similar commission, Fosdick extended these athletic activities to naval training stations. With Walter Camp and Professor Joseph Raycroft of Princeton as athletic directors for the navy and army, respectively, all-star service teams became a popular attraction during the 1917–18 seasons. James Mennell has observed that the rise of service teams during the 1917 season was "one of the most dramatic developments ever in American football."[18]

On the high school level, the war also provided a major boost for physical education and competitive interscholastic athletics. Between 1915 and 1917, educators engaged in a vigorous debate over how to prepare American youth for war if the United States entered the European conflict. One group favored mandatory military training in the nation's high schools, whereas another advocated compulsory physical education. By the time America entered the war, the physical education advocates were in the ascendancy and had won the support of most of the nation's military men. The most telling arguments of the physical education faction stressed the fear that military training in secondary and high schools might foster the kind of "Prussian" militarism against which America was fighting and that the dismal state of fitness among America's youth, as revealed by prewar army medical rejections and the wartime draft physical examinations, could be best corrected by a broad-based physical education program. Football was one of many sports that would benefit from the wartime and postwar emphasis on physical education in public schools.[19]

In terms of timing, Red Grange was fortunate to have begun his formal football training at Wheaton High School in 1918. Two forces, public realization of how exciting the "new football" produced by the earlier rules changes had become and the stimulus that war gave to the game, were converging to generate one of the greatest growth periods in the history of football. Grange had first played football when he was in grammar school. He recalled that it was "not really football, but a game the kids used to call, 'Run, Sheep, Run.' I used to get my pants and socks all torn up." Grange also remembered that during the summers he would go over to a vacant lot on the eastern edge of town not far from his home and near where Wheaton's only African American families lived. "There'd be about twenty guys, and I'd be the only white kid. They took me in, we got along fine, and they probably taught me more baseball and football than any-

one else. They were great athletes—they just never had the opportunity."
From the start, his exceptional speed, agility, and coordination made him
a standout in football and nearly any other game he tried. When asked in
later years about his running ability, Grange replied, "It was God-given; I
couldn't take any credit. Other guys could make 90s and 100s in chemis-
try. I could run fast. It's the way God distributes things."[20]

By the time he was twelve, Grange was a budding athletic star in
Wheaton. "I don't remember ever losing a footrace as a kid," he remembered in 1985. "I'd go to those church picnics and I'd win a baseball, and
then my father would give me a quarter every time I won. Hell," Grange
said jokingly, "I was a pro when I was in the sixth grade." Lyle's encour-
agement of his sons in athletics was especially important. With the family
living under unusual and stressful circumstances, the attention and approv-
al the elder Grange gave to the boys' athletic achievements must have been
eagerly sought and reinforced their natural inclination toward sports.
Grange recalled that he, "like any other kid," hated elementary school and
that "the more important part of living came after school when I was able
to play football, basketball and baseball with my pals." Besides his father,
Grange had a number of role models who encouraged his love of athletics. His boyhood hero in Wheaton was Elmer Hoffman, whom he watched
play on the high school team. Outside the city, Red's two "special heroes"
were Bart Macomber and Potsy Clark of the University of Illinois football team. Thus, when he tried out for the Wheaton High School football
team in 1918, Grange, a fifteen-year-old freshman who had apparently
started school late or stayed back a year, was highly motivated to make
his mark as an athlete.[21]

In 1918 the Wheaton High School football program was only in its ninth
year. As was the case in many secondary schools in the early part of the
century, students organized the first football team at Wheaton High School.
Beginning in 1910, the school assumed some of the costs, provided a supervisor who had some knowledge of athletics, and organized a regular
schedule of games. In evaluating Grange's high school athletic career it
should be noted that Wheaton was in the second wave of communities that
organized high school football teams. From the late 1880s into the early
twentieth century, mainly larger cities such as Chicago, New York, Cleveland, and Detroit had the means, organizational ability, and, most important, the transportation facilities to support teams and interscholastic
leagues. Because of its proximity to Chicago, which had one of the earliest interscholastic football programs in the country, and the excellent trans-

portation provided by two railroads, Wheaton joined larger Illinois cities
such as Elton, Aurora, and Rockford in organizing formal football programs before 1914. Most cities of Wheaton's size in Illinois, and, for that
matter, in many areas of the country, could not effectively engage in interscholastic team sports until the late 1910s or the 1920s when the automobile became a more reliable mode of transportation. In Oregon, Illinois,
for example, a rural town about half the size of Wheaton in 1918 and
lacking convenient railway connections, the effort to inaugurate high
school team sports during the 1910s quickly collapsed because of the excessive travel times to and from nearby towns. High school team sports
were not reorganized in Oregon until the early 1920s.[22]

The quality of high school football in Illinois varied widely in the late
1910s, ranging from solidly established teams in Chicago and other large
cities to what were basically sandlot teams in smaller cities and towns. The
Illinois State High School Athletic Association, one of the oldest in the
nation, did classify schools by size (Wheaton, with fewer than five hundred students, was in Class B) but did not organize leagues; schools scheduled their own games on the basis of proximity, rivalries, and reputations.
In 1918 Wheaton ranked well below the elite teams in terms of size, funding, and organization. The Wheaton Tigers did not have a trained coach
when America entered the war in 1917, relying on a teacher-volunteer to
supervise the team. They practiced and played home games on a field in
an apple orchard a mile and a half from school. The boys picked up the
apples before Saturday games but invariably missed a few, which, during
the heat of battle, made for soggy landings or a squirt in the eye for players of both teams. There was no seating at "the Orchard," and no admission was charged at games. Grange remembered that the fans walked up
and down the sidelines with the movement of the ball, and a hat was passed
among the spectators, which may have provided the team's primary source
of revenue. He also recalled that each player had to provide his own football shoes and helmet, which proved to be a financial hardship for Red,
who borrowed shoes from a non-playing teammate during his freshman
year. The team was generously supported by a few boosters, particularly
the Dollingers, who often provided transportation for the boys and made
it possible for the 1921 squad to conduct preseason training at their summer home in Powers Lake, Wisconsin. On balance, Wheaton's 1918 football team was a cut above the largely sandlot high school teams that were
beginning to spring up in rural and suburban Illinois, but the Tigers could
barely hold their own against the teams on Chicago's western rim. The

emergence of Red Grange, however, would put Wheaton High School football on the map.[23]

At his first day of practice in 1918, Grange remembered that Coach Ray Puckey, a manual training teacher and the only male faculty member, who doubled as the supervisor of all athletic teams, asked him what position he played. Red immediately inquired about which positions were open. When informed that all the boys were returning from the previous year except the right end, Grange claimed to play that position. He played end his entire freshman year. In the last wartime year, Wheaton had a disappointing season. The Tigers managed only two victories against five defeats and were shut out four times. They were routed by a U.S. Marine Corps team from West Aurora 45-0 and had a late-October game against Downers Grove canceled, most likely because of the influenza epidemic. Grange recalled that despite his slight build (138 pounds), he was tall enough to be "able to reach up high for passes, although no one ever threw any at me during the games." The Wheaton *Illinoian,* however, cited Grange a number of times during his freshman season for his outstanding defensive play. In his autobiography, Grange remembered sprinting seventy yards for a touchdown on a kickoff return in the last game of the season, which caused him to try out for left halfback the following season. Although he clearly got the game wrong (Wheaton was shut out by Riverside that day), his transfer to the backfield in 1919 would begin one of the most remarkable careers for a ball carrier in football history.[24]

During his last years in college and well into his professional career, sportswriters and the public alike would refer to Grange frequently as the "Wheaton Iceman." The symbolism the moniker conveyed to the public can only be guessed at. Thousands of posed photographs showing Grange lugging seventy-five-pound blocks of ice appeared in newspapers and magazines around the country. The image may have represented Grange as a throwback to an earlier, simpler era in an age of rapid modernization or it may have personified his humbleness or coolness under pressure while running with a football. Regardless of the symbolic meaning, Grange firmly believed that his job hauling ice for L. C. Thompson and Company, which he began in the summer of 1919, was a major factor in his athletic conditioning and success. "I only thought of it that way afterward," he told an interviewer, "because there's no doubt it made me stronger. But I did it for the money." Grange conceded, however, that each fall "I would be tough as nails and at least four weeks ahead of the other boys in conditioning. My iceman's duties made my arms, shoulders and legs strong and developed my wind."[25]

Beginning with the 1919 season, Grange went on a running and scoring rampage that would not be equaled in Illinois high school football until the 1930s. Under the direction of Coach Bill Castleman, the new manual training teacher, Wheaton posted an impressive 5-1-1 record that included an early-season defeat at the hands of the alumni team. Taking advantage of his additional weight, strength, and endurance gained in part by his summer on the ice wagon, Grange used speed, agility, and an impressive stiff arm to register fifteen touchdowns and add nine extra points. He did all that while playing most of the season with a badly sprained ankle. A glance at Wheaton's schedule reveals that the schools the Tigers played were small ones from Chicago's western suburbs and had enrollments equal to or less than Wheaton's approximately two hundred students. One of these teams from nearby Glyn Ellen managed a 19-19 tie with Wheaton, which resulted in a county co-championship for the two schools. In addition to the alumni contest, the only other difficult games for Wheaton were against two larger schools, Chicago Austin and Elgin High School, the latter featuring Grange's future University of Illinois backfield mate Earl Britton. Grange and Wheaton decisively defeated these teams by scores of 21-0 and 38-6, respectively. The Wheaton *Illinoian* named Grange to the all-county team, calling him "the star of the selection." Remarking on his stiff arm, the writer added that "his gains would be considerably less if deprived of this asset as in every game this year he has spilled from three to seven men in his long runs, all with his right arm."[26]

Before the 1920 season, Wheaton High School hired Charles "Dink" Weldon as a full-time coach and athletic director. A former Wheaton quarterback, he played on the school's first organized team in 1910. After serving in the U.S. Marine Corps during World War I, Weldon completed his studies at Western Michigan College, where he played football. The Wheaton *Illinoian* endorsed the employment of Weldon, noting that "Wheaton High has finally taken the right step to bring back the prestige that local teams once enjoyed." In later years, Grange praised Weldon as one of his three great coaches, but one suspects that it was more for training other members of the team rather than Grange himself. Grange was always thankful that none of his coaches ever tried to change his running style. Although 1920 would prove to be Grange's best year as a high school player in terms of yardage gained and scoring, he almost did not play. During his summer job as an iceman, he fell from the side of the truck and was accidently run over by his co-worker and football teammate Herman Otto. With the truck filled with three tons of ice, Grange was fortunate that the rear wheel caught him two inches above the knee and not lower or his knee would have been shattered. As it was, Grange remained in bed for almost a month, his leg in a sling, before recovering with no apparent ill-effects.[27]

When the season began, Grange was once again in fine form. Playing quarterback in the first game against Wauconda, Red ran for more than three hundred yards and three touchdowns in a 41-13 victory. The following week, however, Wheaton ran into a stone wall, the perennial Chicago-area powerhouse LaGrange, and lost 38-0 despite the fact that Grange gained 259 yards. From that point on, the season was like a track meet for Grange. With freshman Vic Gustafson, a future all-Big Ten player at Northwestern, at left halfback, he returned to right halfback and literally ran wild. Wheaton shut out its next six opponents, registering 42, 70, 51, 83, 46, and 73 points on successive Saturdays. In those games, he scored an incredible thirty-three touchdowns and booted an equal number of extra points. Against Batavia, he rushed for 504 yards in twenty-one carries, recording fifty-two of his team's seventy points. He bettered that mark by scoring fifty-nine of Wheaton's eighty-three points against Naperville a few weeks later. In the wake of Grange's touchdown blitz, a reporter for the *Illinoian* made one of the understatements of the day when he wrote that "we firmly believe that this young star is the greatest player Wheaton has ever had." Wheaton lost its Thanksgiving Day game with the alumni team 20-12, with both Grange and quarterback William Frazer sitting out with injuries. In all, Wheaton ended the season with seven victories and two defeats. Grange recorded thirty-six touchdowns and thirty-nine extra points.[28]

In Grange's senior season, Coach Weldon put together a tougher schedule that helped reduce Grange's offensive output a bit, but he still scored twenty-six touchdowns and made thirty-four conversions. Weldon apparently tried to schedule a number of Big Seven teams (high schools in large cities west of Chicago) but only managed a game with Freeport, which the Wheaton yearbook described as a team not living up to its reputation in a 21-0 loss to the Tigers. Equally impressive were Wheaton's wins over Riverside (47-6), a close Chicago suburb, and Chicago Austin (21-0), the 1921 runner-up for the Cook County league championship. After Grange scored four touchdowns in a 47-0 win over Hinsdale, the Wheaton *Illinoian* observed that Red "simply floated away from opponents whom he didn't get with his stiff arm." Reflecting on the substandard playing conditions of the day, Grange remembered that at Hinsdale the field was so uneven that when he played defensive safety he could not see either team. As in the previous season, Wheaton demolished DuPage County schools, averaging more than thirty-five points per game. Grange scored seemingly at will. In recalling Wheaton's 63-14 Thanksgiving Day victory over Downers Grove for the county championship, Grange remembered it as a track meet. "We were so exhausted from making long runs," he wrote, "that we considered the possibility of pulling the tackles back to carry the ball for a while."[29]

Wheaton's only defeat of the season came at the hands of Scott High School in Toledo, Ohio. The circumstances of the game are clouded in that the Wheaton *Illinoian* suggested that the Ohioans were laying for Grange and may have used illegal players. In his autobiography, Grange mentioned that he was kicked in the head early in the first quarter, was carried unconscious from the field, and did not come to for almost forty-eight hours. He added, "It was the only time I was ever seriously hurt playing high school football." The *Illinoian* reported that early in the game a Scott player decked Wheaton's Charles Moore with a punch and then apologized, saying, "He mistook him for Grange." According to the newspaper's account, Grange was then kicked in the head after catching a pass in the second period with the game still in doubt. Scott went on to overwhelm Wheaton 35-0. The *Illinoian* also remarked that some of the Scott players looked a little old for high school boys. Wheaton ended the season with seven wins and one loss and another DuPage County championship.[30]

In four varsity football seasons, Grange scored seventy-five touchdowns for Wheaton and booted eighty-two extra points for a total of 532 points, an average of nearly fifteen points per game. With his father agreeing to pay him a quarter per touchdown, Grange had earned $18.75 by the end of his senior season. No schoolboy in Illinois approached Grange's scoring prowess until Bill De Correvont of Chicago Austin High School surpassed many of Red's records in the late 1930s. If he had just played football at Wheaton, Grange would have been an Illinois high school legend. He was, however, a star performer in four sports and earned sixteen varsity letters. Grange played four seasons of basketball and earned numerous all-sectional honors. Incredibly, he considered basketball his best sport in high school. In the spring, Grange divided his time between track and baseball. As a sprinter and broad-jumper, he set several records in 1922 at the newly organized Little Seven Conference meet at St. Charles, Illinois, that would stand for almost twenty years. In addition, he won the 220-yard dash and broad jump in 1921 and the 100-yard dash in 1922 at the state interscholastic track meet at the University of Illinois. Although baseball was not considered as important as other sports at Wheaton High, Grange played whenever he could and was good enough to be offered a major league try out with the National League Boston Braves while in college.[31]

That Red Grange was a great athlete or even a phenomenal athlete there can be little doubt. To rank him among the millions of young men who have played high school football during the twentieth century, however, is more difficult. One must consider the caliber of the players he faced and the relative training they received. The population of the United States was nearly one hundred million in 1918. High school enrollments had increased by more than 700 percent between 1890 when numbers of urban schools took up football and 1918 when Grange first played at Wheaton. Despite these important gains, Timothy O'Hanlon has pointed out that "most children dropped out after grade school, and the majority of those who went to high school left before graduation." In 1918 a government bulletin reported that a third of grade school students went on to high school and about one in nine graduated. Although there is no reliable data on how many high schools fielded football teams in 1918, it is safe to say that Grange competed against only a fraction of his peer group.[32]

Stan Grosshandler, a football historian, has addressed the question of why have we never seen another Red Grange. Although he primarily analyzes Grange as a college football phenomenon, some of Grosshandler's remarks also apply to the training and skill of high school players when Grange played. After World War I, most high school football teams had one coach, occasionally two. As in the case of a smaller school like Wheaton, the coach might have some football expertise, as did Dink Weldon, or have been drafted from the male faculty as his predecessors were. Grosshandler observes that not only do most high schools now have large coaching staffs but the coaches are also usually highly skilled. He maintains that although some athletes, like Grange, "have greater natural talent than others, good coaching will help decrease the gap" and promote parity. Grosshandler assumes that many high school players in the 1910s had a minimum of skilled coaching, and "this enabled a player with Grange's vast talent to stand out. Today," he adds, "most coaches can design defenses and coach their players to contain the big star or at the least, minimize the destruction."[33]

Grosshandler's analysis appears to be consistent with the foregoing survey of Grange's high school career. During his junior and senior years when

Wheaton played teams from within DuPage County or nearby areas, most likely Class B schools, the Tigers usually won by forty or more points, with Grange making numerous long runs and touchdowns. Against Chicago teams such as Austin or teams from the Big Seven Conference such as Freeport, presumably Class A schools with larger enrollments and better coaching, Wheaton triumphed by three touchdowns or less. These statistics do not demean Grange's records or athletic ability because Coach Weldon put together a football team from a group of about ninety-eight potential players, the male enrollment at Wheaton High in January 1919. In fact, it is a tribute to Grange's athletic ability that he was able to lead an undermanned and probably less skilled Wheaton team to victory over larger and probably better coached Class A schools.[34]

Moreover, Grange was not the only superior athlete at the time to dominate high school football on Chicago's western rim and to the northwest of the city, where many high school football programs were less than a dozen years old. In October 1920 the Wheaton *Illinoian* reported that Ralph "Moon" Baker of Rockford High School led his team over Joliet, 100-0, by scoring seven touchdowns, converting eight extra points, and booting a thirty-five-yard field goal for a total of fifty-three points. Baker would be Grange's freshman football teammate at the University of Illinois. To a lesser degree, backs Frank Wickhorst of Aurora High School and Earl Britton of Elgin High School, both of whom were also on the 1922 Illinois freshman team, posted impressive marks, especially against some of the newly formed or poorly coached teams west of Chicago. Unlike in the past, when metropolitan Chicago was the major source of high school football talent in the state and the city's major universities, Chicago and Northwestern, shared most of the college-bound players with the University of Illinois, Coach Bob Zuppke at Urbana-Champaign would begin to tap an increasing stream of talent from Chicago's western rim and the northwest section of the state by the 1920s. Red Grange would be his prize recruit.[35]

The farmhouse in Forkesville, Pennsylvania, where Harold "Red" Grange was born in 1903. (Red Grange Collection [SC-20], Special Collections, Buswell Memorial Library, Wheaton College)

The 1920 Wheaton High School football team, with Grange third from the left on the front row. Coach Charles "Dink" Weldon is wearing a cap. (Red Grange Collection [SC-20], Special Collections, Buswell Memorial Library, Wheaton College)

Grange as a sophomore at the
University of Illinois, 1923.
(Courtesy of University of Illinois)

(Below): Grange and Illinois coach
Bob Zuppke discussing a play
before practice. (Courtesy of University of Illinois)

The nearly completed Memorial Stadium with the famous Michigan game in progress, Homecoming 1924; a sea of automobiles appears at the top of the photograph. (Courtesy of University of Illinois)

Grange breaks loose against Michigan in the Homecoming game, October 18, 1924. (Courtesy of University of Illinois)

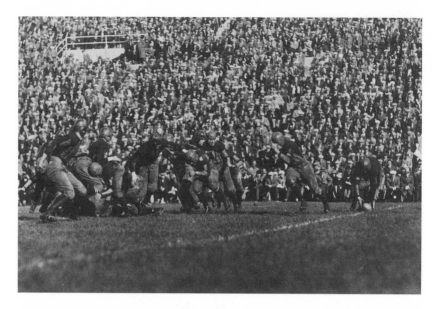

Even Grange fumbled, as in this game at Memorial Stadium. Note the excellent blocking in the Illinois single-wing formation. (Courtesy of University of Illinois)

Grange catches a pass from Earl Britton in their final college game against Ohio State in 1925. (Courtesy of University of Illinois)

Grange shows his power as he breaks through center in a 1924 game. (Courtesy of University of Illinois)

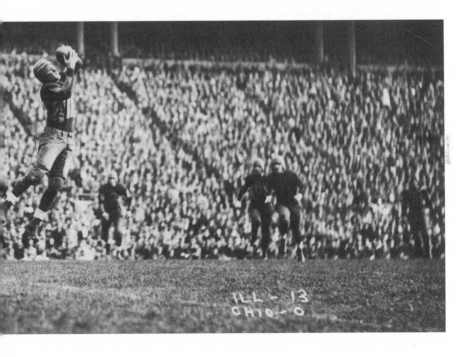

A close-up of Grange on the Illinois practice field shows why many in the media thought he looked much older that his actual age. (Courtesy of University of Illinois)

Grange heads for the goal line in one of his touchdown runs against Michigan in 1924. (Courtesy of University of Illinois)

"RED" GRANGE STARTS FOR THE GOAL LINE
ILLINOIS 39 · MICHIGAN 14
1924

The Fighting Illini football team, 1924, with Grange in the second row, far left. (Courtesy of University of Illinois)

Grange also played for the Illinois baseball team. Although he claimed that he could not hit, he was offered a major league tryout. (Courtesy of University of Illinois Athletic Public Relations)

Famed sportswriter Grantland Rice interviewing Grange during the 1925 season. Writers like Rice were important in making Grange a national sports celebrity. (Red Grange Collection [SC-20], Special Collections, Buswell Memorial Library, Wheaton College)

Grange and his famous number 77 jersey after his final college game against Ohio State in 1925. (Courtesy of University of Illinois)

3

Grange and the Golden Age of Sport

★ ★

IN 1974, WHEN SPORTSWRITER Myron Cope asked him what accounted for the golden age of sport of the 1920s and all of that decade's exciting
sports personalities, Red Grange replied, "Each sport had a number of outstanding individuals, really stars. And they were publicized to death. The
First World War was just over; they had been trying times for everyone,"
and many people had good jobs and money to spend by the early 1920s.
"Everyone seemed to let their hair down after World War I."[1] Although
most historians would argue that he did not touch on all the factors that
led to the takeoff of sports during the 1920s, Grange did focus on perhaps
the most important single stimulus: the impact of World War I.

Sport historian Guy Lewis maintains that "the catalyst for the sudden
burst of popular interest in sport [in the 1920s] was the activity of the
United States government during World War I." Raymond Fosdick, head
the government's Commission on Training Camp Activities, organized
broad-based athletic programs in all military training camps and extended those activities to facilities in France as U.S. troops arrived there. Referring to the army's sporting activities at camps in 1918, a newspaper
sports editor remarked that "never before in the history of this country
have so large a number of men engaged in athletics. Every kind of sport is
involved—football, baseball, basket ball, volley ball, push ball, medicine

ball, soccer, track and field athletics, and particularly boxing." The military's emphasis on competitive athletics also rekindled an earlier notion that sports training made for better soldiers. What impressed Lewis most, however, was that for the first time the American government assumed "responsibility for encouraging the constructive use of free time" of its citizens. Government attempts to shape public behavior before 1917 came largely through restrictive legislation such as blue laws and Prohibition. The wartime sports boom that began at military training camps under government direction and extended throughout the nation marked a watershed in government policy toward recreation and leisure time.[2]

The high point of the military's involvement in athletics came after the Armistice when Elwood S. Brown, director of the Athletic Department of the YMCA, proposed that the American Expeditionary Forces (AEF) engage in an extensive program of athletic competitions. During the first five months of 1919, most of the two million men of the AEF participated in the sports events as either participants or spectators. Gen. John J. Pershing, commander of the AEF, remarked enthusiastically that "the results of this type of athletics are sure to create a higher type of athletics at home." The culmination of Brown's athletic program was the staging of the Inter-Allied Games in the summer of 1919, with 1,500 athletes representing eighteen nations participating at sites in and around Paris. Because one of the objectives of the "military olympics" was to "arouse universal interest in sports," the American organizers arranged for extensive press coverage of the games. According to Lewis, "Never before had so much information about a sports event reached so many publications in so many countries."[3]

As Americans followed the progress of the Inter-Allied Games in the press they also read about the poor physical condition of the nation's youth. During the war, 30 percent of the men who underwent draft medical examinations had been rejected as physically unfit. Because some had been disqualified earlier as obviously unfit and were never examined by military doctors, Gen. Leonard Wood estimated "that 50 per cent. of our men were unfit for field-service in war." During the wartime mobilization, Wilson administration officials such as Secretary of War Newton D. Baker and Secretary of the Navy Josephus Daniels had encouraged "athletics for all," both in and out of the services, and educators began a campaign to expand recreational facilities and physical education programs at colleges and secondary schools throughout the country. The number of students enrolled in physical education classes increased from a few thousand in 1914 to a majority of the nation's high school students by 1934. Government officials such as Baker and Daniels were also supportive of intercollegiate athletics, which, Daniels stated in 1918, "stimulate interest and should be encouraged. The stimulus both in improved morale and in improved body is everywhere recognized." The wartime emphasis on athletics would escalate during the 1920s and contribute to the sports craze associated with the postwar decade.[4]

As he worked toward completing his final year in high school in 1922, Grange, like most teenagers, was largely unaware of these and other forces that would boost public interest in sports during the 1920s. Incredible as it may seem now, Grange was not heavily recruited by colleges. "Toward the end of my senior year at Wheaton," he recalled, "I was officially contacted by a college for the first time during my high school career." Grange explained that "Carl Johnson, one of Michigan's all-time track greats came down to Wheaton with a few Wolverine alumni to sell me on the idea of going to their school." The Wheaton senior was flattered by the interest but had not made up his mind about going to college. It was Lyle Grange who insisted on it. "I'd still be delivering ice, probably," Red told a reporter on the occasion of his seventy-seventh birthday, "if my father hadn't made me go to college. But we had no choice." Given his athletic ability and superlative football record in high school, one might assume that Grange was enticed to attend the University of Illinois by some sort of scholarship offer. But as he would explain numerous times, "There were no scholarships then, and I wouldn't have taken one if it had been offered. We were taught to earn those things." Illinois may not have offered Grange a scholarship—and, indeed, he might not have accepted one—but colleges, including Big Ten schools, did pay or compensate athletes in a number of ways during the 1920s.[5]

In his autobiography, Grange listed three reasons, in ascending order of importance, why he decided to enroll at the University of Illinois. First, it was the least expensive school for him to attend as a resident of the state. Second, his neighbor and former football teammate George Dawson played football for Illinois and constantly talked to Red about going to school there. Finally, Grange was impressed by Illini coach Bob Zuppke when he spoke with him at the state interscholastic track competition in Urbana-Champaign. Grange had no idea that Zuppke was well aware of his athletic exploits at Wheaton and had come to the track meet with the intent of speaking with him. On May 25, 1922, Grange won the 220-yard dash event and finished third in the hundred-yard dash at the state track meet on the Illinois campus. After the competition ended, he recalled, "Coach Zuppke came over and asked me my name and I told him. He walked around with me and talked to me. He said that if I came down to Illinois 'I think you have a good chance of making the football team.' That," Grange emphasized, "made a big impression on me. He called me Granche. Zuppke never pronounced anything except Germanwise."[6]

Robert C. Zuppke was born in Berlin, Germany, in 1879 and emigrated with his family to the United States in 1881, where they settled in Milwaukee. After high school, Zuppke attended Milwaukee Normal School, beginning in 1902. He played for the freshman football team but was too small to make the varsity eleven. At Milwaukee and later at the University of Wisconsin in Madison, Zuppke served three grueling years on the scrub team, an experience he would find beneficial. After graduating from the University of Wisconsin in 1905, Zuppke, a talented artist, went to New York City to pursue a career but was only able to gain employment as a sign painter. Returning to the Midwest, he was hired the following year as a gymnasium director, history teacher, and coach at Muskegon High School in Michigan. From 1906 to 1909 he coached track and football at Muskegon High and also directed a second football team at the nearby Hackley Manual Training School. According to Grange, it was during these years that Zuppke "began developing the open type of game for which he was later to become famous and which was a major factor in the evolution of football from massed movement to the modern, exciting style of mixed aerial and running assault." After a successful tenure at Muskegon High and the Hackley School, during which his football teams became known as "adding machines" because of their offensive prowess, Zuppke was hired to coach football at Oak Park (Illinois) High School, where his teams would enjoy even greater success.[7]

At Oak Park, Zuppke became one of the nation's most successful high school coaches and was recognized for his innovative style of play. From 1910 to 1912 his teams won the Cook County league championship each season, piling up top-heavy scores against the best Chicago teams. Not content with the county championship, Zuppke took his 1910 team to Portland, Oregon, and defeated two of the best West Coast high schools. The following two seasons the Cook County champions routed two Massachusetts teams, St. Johns (1911) and Everett High School (1912), reputed to be among the best prep teams in the East. As a high school coach, Zuppke was best known for using the forward pass as an offensive weapon rather than a third down desperation measure, as most teams employed it. When reminded of the popularly held notion that the forward passing era began with the combination of Gus Dorais and Knute Rockne at Notre Dame in 1913, Zuppke often remarked, "That is perfectly true—except that seventy thousand forward passes had already been completed by that time." Among Zuppke's other innovations were the spiral pass from center to the backs (Muskegon); the screen pass (Oak Park); and the forward and backward lateral passes, or "flea flicker" play (Oak Park).[8]

University of Illinois athletic director George Huff, a former star athlete and football coach at the school, hired Zuppke in 1913 to coach the Illini at a salary of $2,700. With one assistant coach and only thirty men out for the team that first season, Zuppke would initiate a remarkable turnabout in Illinois football fortunes. From 1896 through 1912 the Illini had shared in only one Big Ten conference championship. During Zuppke's first decade as coach, however, Illinois won four championships, three outright and one as conference co-champions. With a record of forty-five wins, twenty-one defeats, and five ties and the development of further innovative techniques such as the guards back protecting the forward passer (1914) and the institution of the modern "outdoor" huddle (1921), Zuppke was widely recognized as one of the foremost college football coaches in the nation.[9]

In referring to the fact that he had not been heavily recruited, Grange told an interviewer in 1974 that widespread recruiting "came along in the 1930's. The great college coaches when I was playing—men like Bob Zuppke [Illinois] and Knute Rockne [Notre Dame] and Alonzo Stagg [Chicago], and Fielding 'Hurry Up' Yost [Michigan]—they would not recruit. It was beneath their dignity. You held those fellows in awe." He added, "If you wanted to come to the campus and talk to them, they were available, but they would not recruit. It was an honor to play for them."[10] His assessment had some basis in fact but clearly understated the extent of recruiting and player subsidization that prevailed during the early 1920s.

In October 1925 the *Literary Digest* carried a critical commentary on a series of articles that had appeared in sixty-five U.S. newspapers and focused on the state of college football. Most were written by college presidents, who either called for the abolition of the game or "for sweeping investigation and reform as prerequisite to the 'saving' of college football," which, they all agreed, was "in a precarious state of health calling for desperate remedies."[11] Most of the alleged evils and abuses they listed were familiar to those conversant with turn-of-the-century football crises: scholarships and other inducements as a reward for athletic ability, professionalism, commercialization, recruiting and bidding for high school athletes, alumni interference, excessive injuries, and raiding high schools and other colleges for superior players. The college presidents and a graduate manager of a large eastern university provided specific examples to support their case, and a few of the colleges represented had abandoned football or were considering doing so in the near future.

During the ensuing weeks, supporters of college football came forward to defend the game. In the lead was Grantland Rice, one of the nation's foremost sportswriters, who maintained that "the case for football is much stronger than the case against it." He argued that the revenue from football supported other college sports and allowed a large percentage of students to participate in some form of athletics. Citing the Western Conference (Big Ten) schools as an example, Rice stated that "no student can play football who has a single condition in any study." He maintained that "football to a certain extent puts a premium on scholastic ability" and that "in 90 per cent. of the universities to-day there are no football employees." Although "there was a time when football 'employees' were entirely too common in college life. But constant pressure has been brought against this practise, and the 'large offers' you hear about to-day are mostly fairytales. There is still room for improvement along this line in certain isolated colleges or universities," Rice noted cautiously, "but they are being dropt by their rivals."[12]

The periodic attacks against and defense of college football continued during the second half of the decade. After the 1926 season a number of spirited criticisms of the game, including one by West Virginia Wesleyan president Homer E. Wark, led New York *Sun* sportswriter John B. Foster to label football as "the goat of college sports." As in the past, the criticisms were deflected by partisans of the game, this time including officials representing some of the most prestigious schools in the East. The ongoing attacks coincided with a study of American college athletics undertaken by the Carnegie Foundation for the Advancement of Teaching in 1926 that yielded a 347-page report published in 1929. Singling out football, the Carnegie Report was a stinging indictment of intercollegiate athletics, focusing on the recruitment and subsidization of athletes. The report concluded that "the subsidized college athlete of to-day connives at disreputable and shameful practices for the sake of material returns and for honors falsely achieved. Arguments in support of such practices are specious, calculated to mislead, and fundamentally insincere. Viewed in the light of common honesty, this fabric of organized deceit constitutes the darkest single blot upon American college sport."[13]

As in the case of other attacks against college football during the 1920s, the Carnegie Report was assailed by some college officials and sportswriters, but the study, the result of a three-year investigation, was too thorough and comprehensive to be taken lightly. Of the 112 colleges and universities the Carnegie team investigated, "in only twenty-eight did they fail to find evidence of subsidizing athletes by individuals and groups." The New York *Evening Post* estimated, as a result of the report's findings, that "one out of every seven varsity athletes in the United States, considering all major sports, is, in some form or other, a subsidized athlete." The proportion rose to between 25 and 50 percent when football alone was considered. Two Big Ten universities, Chicago and Illinois, were on the list of schools at which there was no evidence of subsidized athletes. At some of these colleges, the report cautioned, "There has been subsidizing in the past. Of any one it is impossible to say that there will not be subsidizing in the future. Possibly, also, at the time of the field visit subsidizing existed without being discovered, but in our enquiry an apparent absence of subsidizing inevitably occasioned the closest scrutiny."[14]

The Carnegie Report stated that up to World War I the basis of recruiting and subsidizing athletes was primarily associated with students. Around 1919, "older hands," presumably townsfolk and alumni, began to become involved and made it a more "businesslike procedure." Howard J. Savage, the primary investigator, noted that the new methods spread quickly through the East and South and along the West Coast. He added that "the result is that to-day, notwithstanding many statements to the contrary, the colleges and universities of the United States are confronted with acute problems of recruiting and subsidizing, especially with respect to intercollegiate football." Focusing on the Big Ten, the report stated that the conference, "regarded by many as the most thoroughly controlled of all conference bodies, has repeatedly called recruiting and subsidizing its most serious problem."[15]

During the early years of the Western or Big Ten Conference, Illinois, like Chicago and other member schools, engaged in recruiting and subsidizing practices that were common at the time. In 1905, for example, a writer for *Collier's* quoted Illini coach George Huff as saying, "There are 'more liars and hypocrites than amateurs made through the efforts of colleges to keep within the boundaries of the conference rules.'" He added that he "had seen but few college athletes of any ability that were willing to study and do honest work to sustain themselves in school after a position on the team has been assured, and he asserted further that victory in the west today depends upon the ability of the colleges to maintain men by devious means." During the 1905–6 football crisis, however, Frederick Jackson Turner, a prominent historian at the University of Wisconsin, led a movement that resulted in more faculty control over athletics in the conference and an effort to stamp out abuses such as brutality, professionalism, and corruption. The reform movement made some headway but did not fully eliminate the evils of intercollegiate football as Turner had envisioned. One historian who examined the 1906 Big Ten reforms has concluded that "without question, after 1910 big-time football in the Midwest was more carefully supervised than it had been before and subject to faculty oversight much more frequently than its southern or western counterparts. But in the Big Nine as elsewhere, the regulation of sports would be a matter of countless compromises and concessions."[16]

As a result of the Big Ten reforms, many coaches in the conference began to comply with most of the established rules with regard to recruitment and subsidization of athletes. By the wartime era, Chicago's Amos Alonzo Stagg, who had earlier engaged in blatant recruitment of high school athletes, abandoned some of his former practices but continued to recruit through more subtle methods. Other conference coaches such as Northwestern's Dick Hanley and especially Michigan's Fielding Yost, who, like Stagg, had earlier blatantly violated amateur standards, especially with regard to recruitment, were not as vigilant in enforcing Big Ten regulations. Thus Grange was at least partially right in asserting that by the early 1920s a number of Big Ten coaches did not actively recruit football players, at least in the bold fashion that had been common in earlier years. He was also largely correct when he asserted that Bob Zuppke believed that recruiting was beneath his dignity. By the early 1920s, it was widely known that Michigan and other Big Ten schools were actively recruiting high school football prospects. In Urbana-Champaign, however, Zuppke remained adamant. He would not "go around kissing babies and talking to mothers of poor boys to persuade them to send their sons to Illinois." He remained opposed to recruitment and subsidization as he understood those practices for the rest of his coaching career. Ultimately, it was a string of poor teams in combination with his refusal to budge on such issues that would cost him his job in 1941 after twenty-nine seasons at Illinois. Shortly before his death in 1957, Zuppke explained the reason for his sub-par seasons during the 1930s: "The quality of Illinois football became less and less when other schools began to subsidize and we did not."[17]

Although the University of Illinois was not cited for infractions with regard to recruitment and subsidization in the 1929 Carnegie Report, there is evidence that during Grange's collegiate career the school was in violation of some of the standards the Carnegie team later used as a yardstick in its study. The report noted, for example, the regrettable practice of college coaches using the occasion of high school tournaments and championship meets for "spying out" promising schoolboy athletes. Specifically, the Carnegie team cited the track and field competitions sponsored by the universities of Chicago and Pennsylvania as spectacular events conducive to collegiate athletic recruitment. Zuppke clearly used the Illinois interscholastic track and field competition held annually in Urbana-Champaign as a recruiting forum, just as Stagg continued to use a similar event staged on the University of Chicago campus in his recruitment efforts.[18]

It is also likely that Grange's eventual college fraternity, Zeta Psi, helped recruit the Wheaton schoolboy star and partially underwrote his living expenses at Illinois. Although he admitted that his neighbor, Illini football player and future fraternity brother George Dawson, influenced his decision to attend Illinois, Grange did not elaborate on the nature or degree of that influence or how it happened that he moved into the Zeta Psi fraternity house a few days after arriving on campus. In his autobiography, Grange recounts how he originally intended to go out for basketball and track at the university but was persuaded by fraternity members to try out for the football team: "I planned to go out for those two sports at college, but the Zeta Psi's had other plans for me. They figured that since I also had a pretty good record in football at Wheaton High, it would be much more desirable, prestige-wise for the fraternity, if I were to concentrate on football." Grange went to the first freshman football practice but returned to the fraternity house without checking out a uniform because nearly 120 men were out for the team, and most of them were bigger than he was. "I didn't believe that a yokel halfback from Wheaton had a chance," he later stated. When he explained the situation to his fraternity brothers, they got out a paddle and had him bend over. Grange immediately agreed that "football makes a lot of sense to me." The following day he reported for practice and was issued his later famous number seventy-seven jersey. Asked how he had gotten such a high number, Grange replied, "The guy in front of me got seventy-six; the guy in back got seventy-eight."[19]

The question of whether Grange was recruited by the Zeta Psi fraternity or subsidized by that organization is difficult to determine. According to the Carnegie Report, both practices were fairly common during the 1920s. Of the two allegations, it appears less certain that the fraternity recruited Grange in any systematic way. There is no evidence, for example, that he visited the Zeta Psi house for any reason before the fall of 1922. George Dawson's conversations with Grange about Illinois and its football team and his passing on information about Red's football talent to his fraternity brothers may have been incidental. On the question of subsidization, there is more reason to believe that some of Grange's living expenses were absorbed by his fraternity. He often complained about how poor he was while attending the University of Illinois and once recalled that he "stagged most of the time in college because I seldom had 15 cents to buy a girl a soda." Grange's friend Richard Crabb recalled that Grange "went into the fraternity because there were older students ahead of him that were in that fraternity and they just made it possible for him to be there. Now we don't know the details," he added, "but that's the way it was." Crabb's statement and Grange's immediate residency at the Zeta Psi house his freshman year open the possibility that at minimum the fraternity underwrote some of his expenses.[20]

When Grange arrived on campus in 1922, the University of Illinois was beginning its fifty-fifth year. Originally known as Illinois Industrial University, the school was founded as a result of the Morrill Land Grant College Act of 1862 and had an initial class of fifty students who were taught by two professors. By 1922 the University of Illinois enrolled 9,084 full-time students, tripling its student population of 1919 and making it the fourth-largest university in the nation and second-largest in the Big Ten, slightly behind the University of Michigan. The growth in size of state-supported universities during the years immediately after the war not only changed the face of American higher education but also altered the balance of power in college football.[21]

State-supported universities were emerging from an era when elite private colleges routinely scheduled them as early-season tune-up opponents into a period when they would begin to dominate college football. In the Midwest, on the Pacific Coast, and in parts of the South, private colleges did not dominate intercollegiate sports for very long. There were relatively fewer of them and the private preparatory schools that traditionally provided a pool of athletic talent for them. Although state-supported universities in the Midwest developed into football powers more rapidly than in most other regions for a number of reasons, major factors included the rapidly increasing population and wealth in these mainly industrial states combined with superb secondary school football leagues in some of the larger cities such as Chicago, Detroit, and Cleveland. Soon after the war, when recruiting was less of a factor than it would soon become, young men who had football talent usually attended their state-supported university for financial reasons and also as a matter of state pride, as Grange did. He estimated, for example, that during his four years at Illinois only two football players on the team were from out of state; roughly the same ratio held at other Big Ten schools. With four Big Ten institutions ranked among the top seven universities nationally in terms of enrollment by 1922, it is not surprising that the conference turned out fine football teams. It is more difficult to explain, however, why so many outstanding football prospects enrolled at Illinois in 1922.[22]

The University of Illinois freshman team of 1922 was undoubtedly one of the most talented first-year teams in college football history. Out of the some 120 candidates who reported for tryouts, freshman coach Bert Ingwersen selected a squad that eventually would produce three all-American players and two others who would become prominent Big Ten performers. The starting lineup for the freshman team included Grange at left halfback, Ralph "Moon" Baker of Rockford at quarterback, Earl Britton of Elgin at fullback, Paul Cook at right halfback, and Frank Wickhorst of Aurora at tackle. Looking back on that group, Grange recalled, "Three of us went on to make All-America our sophomore year—except that Moon Baker made it at Northwestern and Frank Wickhorst at Navy after they transferred." He added, "Earl Britton should have made it. What a player—our fullback for three years, the best blocker I ever saw." Although he was incorrect about Baker and Wickhorst being all-Americans in their sophomore seasons (they were consensus all-American selections in 1926 their senior year), Grange might have added that Paul Cook, who transferred to Michigan, had an outstanding career in the Big Ten.[23]

Even after his fraternity brothers persuaded him to return to the Illinois gymnasium and check out football gear, Grange still doubted that he could make the team. At five feet, eleven inches and 166 pounds, he was convinced that he was too small to compete against the beefy candidates he saw on the practice field. After winning a few wind sprints and surviving several cuts, however, he began to realize that "although most of the aspirants were much bigger than I, they couldn't run as fast nor handle a football as well." By the end of the first week of practice, Coach Ingwersen had culled the freshman team down to sixty players. Grange had not only made the team but was also the starting left halfback. Shortly thereafter, Zuppke scheduled a regulation game between the varsity and the freshman team. The varsity barely defeated the underclassmen 21-19, and Grange was the star of the game. He scored two touchdowns, including a sixty-yard punt return. "The first time Grange attracted my attention," Zuppke recalled, "was when the redhead, then a freshman, returned a punt through the Varsity for a touchdown." From that day on, Grange said, "I was 'made' as a freshman."[24]

During the rest of the season Zuppke had the varsity scrimmage the freshmen twice a week. Grange recalled that Ingwersen prepared for those games as if they meant the conference championship. With the freshman team outweighing the varsity by about ten pounds per man and lining up with Grange, Britton, Baker, and Cook in the backfield and Wickhorst at tackle, it is little wonder that the underclassmen handily won most of the scrimmages. As the season progressed, Grange recalled, "Coach Zuppke became so enthused with our potentialities he spent more time with us than he did with the varsity. It is an accepted fact," Red added in something of an understatement, that "the 1922 freshman team was one of the strongest Illinois ever had." With his varsity team struggling through a 2-5 season, its worst since 1906, Zuppke eagerly looked forward to the future. In the spring, the Illinois coach drilled the candidates for the 1923 varsity team for nine weeks of what Grange described as "hard, serious work." When the spring semester ended, Grange returned to Wheaton, still relatively unheralded, to begin his summer job at Luke Thompson's ice company.[25]

How good the 1923 Illinois football team might have been had Moon Baker, Frank Wickhorst, and Paul Cook not transferred to other colleges before the beginning of the fall semester is a matter of speculation. As it was, the Illini swept through the season with an 8-0 record, a Big Ten Conference championship, and only three touchdowns scored against them. Grange started quickly in the preseason drills of 1923 and made spectacular long runs in the early scrimmage games, gaining local notoriety. A few days before the university's opening game with Nebraska, the Urbana-Champaign *Courier* reported that "the debut of Zuppke's new back will be anxiously awaited. Harold Grange has trotted through the freshmen ever since practice opened." Grange, before some eighteen thousand fans at Illinois Field, lived up to his preseason buildup. He scored all of the Illini touchdowns (three) in a 24-7 victory over Nebraska, recording 202 yards rushing, including touchdown runs of thirty-five and sixty yards. Earl Britton, also making his varsity debut, recalled that Red "was an easy man to pass to and we all liked to block for him. We played the single wing and I passed from the punt formation. The blocking was good. You know we had a very good line—one of the best in the country." Walter Eckersall, former all-American quarterback at Chicago and referee that day against Nebraska, wrote in the Chicago *Tribune* that "it was a spectacular piece of work, the sort expected of a player with the speed of the former Wheaton star who has all the earmarks of developing into a wonderful player."[26]

After a relatively easy 21-7 victory over Butler University the following week with Grange scoring two touchdowns in twenty-eight minutes of play, Illinois traveled to Iowa to face a strong Hawkeye team that had gone undefeated the previous season and shared in a Big Ten championship. Grange later told sportswriter John Underwood that Earl Britton's field goal in the Iowa game "gave me my biggest thrill in football. . . . It was our first big game before a big crowd, at Iowa City, thirty-five or forty thousand people. I held for him, and I just sat there watching the ball go, fifty-two or fifty-three yards, as I remember. I knew immediately he had it." Underwood remarked, "Typically, Grange didn't mention that the Illini were losing 6-3 until he scored the winning touchdown with two minutes to play" in a 9-6 Illinois victory.[27]

Grange and the Illini rolled on the next week at Cubs Park in Chicago with an easy 29-0 victory over Northwestern. The game was decided early when Grange stifled a Wildcat scoring drive with an interception on his own ten-yard line and raced ninety yards for a touchdown. "Northwestern seemed to become so demoralized after that run," he recalled. "They appeared to lose their fight." In nineteen minutes of play, Grange scored three touchdowns and accumulated 247 total yards, his season high. "The last two periods were more even," the *New York Times* reported. Grange was on the bench for most of the second period and the entire second half to guard against injury. The Northwestern contest provided a suitable tune-up for the all-important game against the University of Chicago the following Saturday in Memorial Stadium, which was still not fully completed. With Chicago, Illinois, and Michigan still undefeated in Big Ten games and the Wolverines not scheduled to play either of the other two schools in 1923, the game would likely determine the conference championship.[28]

The 1923 Homecoming game against Chicago was like a dress rehearsal for the Memorial Stadium dedication contest with Michigan the following season. Illini graduates and boosters from around the state and the Midwest gathered to attend Homecoming and view the first game in the new, much-heralded stadium. A number of towns in the state, such as

Benton in far southern Illinois, hired special trains to aid fans in attending the event, and the Illinois Central Railroad offered special rates and put on extra cars to accommodate the more than six thousand University of Chicago fans who had purchased tickets and numerous others from that city who supported the Fighting Illini. The *New York Times* reported that a few fans came by airplane, and "some youthful enthusiasts, lacking carfare, started from their home last night and walked all night." Most of the 60,632 paying customers, the largest crowd ever assembled in central Illinois, used America's preferred means of transportation, the automobile. More than twelve thousand parking places near the stadium were easily filled, and thousands of overflow cars were parked on side streets in the twin cities. The entire Illinois state trooper force was stationed on major paved highways leading into Urbana-Champaign to deal with the record number of cars that would descend on the Illinois campus. To ease congestion, the major Chicago newspapers as well as the St. Louis *Post-Dispatch* published detailed road maps the week before the game, outlining primary and secondary routes to Urbana-Champaign from various points in the Midwest. Fans planning to stay overnight were warned that local hotels were "loaded to the guards" and were urged to seek accommodations in private houses or in nearby towns. Local residents were requested to leave their cars at home and walk to the game.[29]

As game time approached on November 3, radio station KYW in Chicago, one of the three largest in the country, went on the air with a play-by-play account of the Homecoming contest. A crew of more than thirty-five men was needed to assure a continuous signal from Urbana-Champaign to the station's towers in Chicago. Urged to communicate their reaction to the broadcast, thousands of fans responded to the University of Illinois Athletic Association. Walter Evans, chief engineer for the Westinghouse station, later reported that the game "met with more favorable reaction from radio listeners than any other feature that has been broadcasted from KYW." The editor of *Memorial Stadium Notes,* a university publication, wrote that since the station "broadcasts everything from Galli-Cursi in grand opera to addresses by Lloyd-George . . . , this statement is impressive." With commercial radio broadcasting only in its fourth year in the United States, football programming may have had a greater impact on the growing interest in college football during the early 1920s than previously thought.[30]

With a persistent rain falling throughout the day, the game was primarily a defensive battle. The stadium was a riot of colors as fans not protected by the upper decks fashioned slickers out of oilcloth of various shades. Despite the slippery field, Grange did not disappoint the thousands who had come to see the man whom Chicago *Herald and Examiner* sports editor Warren Brown would nickname the "Galloping Ghost." In a game otherwise characterized by straight-ahead plays for small gains, Grange reeled off spectacular runs of sixty, forty-two, thirty, and twenty-three yards. The *New York Times* reported that "the Chicago defense was unable to solve his twisting advances and he frequently shook off five men or more before being stopped." It was Grange's third-quarter, five-yard touchdown plunge and Britton's extra point, however, that gave Illinois a hard-fought 7-0 victory over the Maroons. After five games, the Fighting Illini were undefeated. Grange had scored ten touchdowns and gained an average of almost 4.6 yards per minute that he played.[31]

The following week, controversy surrounded the university's home conference game with undefeated but once-tied Wisconsin. Hours before game time, Big Ten authorities declared Erving Gerber, the star Badger tackle, ineligible because he had played professional baseball the previous summer. Angered by the midseason ruling, Wisconsin players were determined to spring an upset. Grange, however, scored the game's only touchdown on a twenty-eight-yard end run early in the first period. Britton kicked the point after and added a thirty-five-yard field goal in the same quarter for all the scoring in a 10-0 Illinois victory. Grange was tackled hard in the second period, became light-headed, and sat out the entire second half. Zuppke also kept him on the bench the next Saturday and played most of his other regulars sparingly in a lopsided, non-conference victory over Mississippi A&M, 27-0. The season came to a close in Columbus, Ohio, on November 24. An underdog but inspired Buckeye team outplayed Illinois for three periods and threatened to score on a number of occasions, including three consecutive unsuccessful line plunges from the Illinois one-foot line. At the beginning of the final quarter, however, Britton and Grange came to life and tallied nine points in the space of a few minutes. Britton kicked a thirty-eight-yard field goal, and Grange, behind excellent interference, broke away for a thirty-two-yard touchdown run to give Illinois a 9-0 win.[32]

The victory in Columbus combined with Michigan's 10-0 triumph over Minnesota the same day to make the Fighting Illini and the Wolverines co-champions of the Big Ten Conference. Illinois ended the season with an 8-0 record, the best Zuppke would post in his long tenure as coach at Urbana-Champaign. Grange tallied twelve touchdowns in seven games, which led the conference and accounted for two-thirds of his team's points in those games. In mid-December, Walter Camp named Grange to a half-back position on his prestigious all-American team. The selection was by no means a foregone conclusion. In his thirty-four years of choosing the nation's best football players, Camp clearly had an eastern bias. From 1889, when his selections began, through the turn of the century, he selected only one non-eastern player to his first team. After the war he began to recognize talented players in other regions more frequently, but eastern performers continued to dominate his teams. Camp's 1923 first team included seven players from eastern schools, one from the South, and three players from the Midwest, all representing Big Ten schools.[33]

In commentary on his all-American selections for 1923, Camp, who had not seen Grange play, described the Illinois halfback as "not only a line smasher of great power, but also a sterling open-field runner." He added that Grange was "one of those runners who always seem destined to get loose at the psychological moment," a remark that would aptly character-ize Grange's college football career. In the Midwest, some coaches who at-tempted to devise defenses to contain Grange described his success by us-ing the term "the Grange Eye." The expression, which referred to Grange's seeming ability "to see possible tacklers on either side of him and even behind him while still keeping his eye on the goal line," would remain part of popular football jargon for several decades.[34]

Coach Zuppke later wrote that "Grange was a genius of motion. I saw that and made a team-picture with him at the focal point. He ran with no wasted motion, like Eddie Tolan, Michigan's Olympic sprint champion of '32." Not satisfied with his description, Zuppke related, "I once made a trip to the Kaibab Forest on the edge of the north rim of the Grand Can-yon, and as a deer ran out onto the grass plains, I said: 'There goes Red Grange! The freedom of movement was so similar to Red's.'" In later years Grange modestly tried to account for his success on the gridiron as fol-lows: "I was blessed with one thing you don't just grab—you either have it or you don't—and that's speed. Speed, instinct, and one other thing. I've seen a lot of players who shy away from contact, but I liked it. In my day, the badge of a good football player was if your two front teeth were gone. If you didn't have that, you weren't much of a football player" he added as he pulled out two false front teeth to show a stunned interviewer.[35] Whatever the keys to his success, Grange was on his way to becoming one of the memorable athletes of the golden age of sport.

4

Football and Mass Society

★★★★★★★★★★★★★★★★★★★★★★★★★★★★★★★★★★★★

In 1936 Willa Cather commented in a note introducing a collection of her essays, "The world broke in two in 1922 or thereabouts, and the persons and prejudices recalled in these sketches slide back into yesterday's seven thousand years." According to Warren Susman, a cultural historian, Cather's world did not break apart only because of World War I but because "by 1922 an exceptional and ever-growing number of Americans came to believe in a series of changes in the structure of their world, natural, technological, social, personal, and moral." They were made constantly aware that they were living in a new kind of society. "Communications was key to this, and no more dramatic instruments of total change had come along than the automobile and the motion picture." Commenting on Cather's assertion about 1922, William Leuchtenburg has written that "the year may not be accurate, but the observation is. The United States had to come to terms with a strong state, the dominance of the metropolis, secularization and breakdown of religious sanctions, the loss of authority of the family, industrial concentration, international power politics, and mass culture."[1]

In the field of athletics, the impact of the emerging middle class could be seen in a number of ways, none more vividly than in the frenzy of stadium-building during the 1920s. It was in these massive temples of sport that Red Grange and many other athletic heroes of the decade would display their talents before throngs of spectators. Because major league baseball developed earlier as the nation's premier spectator sport, most of the sixteen franchises had built modern steel and concrete stadiums before World War I. One of the exceptions was the New York Yankees, who, after purchasing the popular and multitalented Babe Ruth from the Boston Red Sox in 1920, constructed the mammoth Yankee Stadium, which opened for play in the Bronx in 1923. As of World War I, only a few universities had built large football facilities. The first college football stadium was the University of Pennsylvania's Franklin Field, constructed in 1895 with a relatively small seating capacity. It was followed by Harvard Stadium (originally Soldiers' Field, 1890) in 1903, which was the first steel-reinforced football stadium in America accommodating more than forty thousand fans with temporary seating; Chicago's Stagg Field (thirty thousand seats), originally built in 1893 but refurbished to seat more fans in 1914; and, both ready for play in 1914, the Yale Bowl (sixty-one thousand seats, expanded to more than seventy thousand) and Princeton's Palmer Stadium (forty-two thousand, expanded to fifty-two thousand).[2]

Several universities had plans to erect football stadiums as the war began, but only Michigan completed a forty-six-thousand-seat wooden structure during the late 1910s. From 1921 though 1925, however, more than a score of colleges built football structures that had more than twenty thousand seats and would accommodate overflow crowds. Beyond that, a number of municipalities erected huge athletic stadiums. The most spectacular were the Rose Bowl (1922) in Pasadena, the Los Angeles Memorial Coliseum (1923), and Soldier Field (1924) in Chicago, all of which would eventually seat more than a hundred thousand spectators. In the Big Ten Conference alone, eight schools built new stadiums or expanded existing ones during the 1920s. One of the most elaborate and expensive was Memorial Stadium at the University of Illinois.[3]

Like most other universities, the University of Illinois planned the construction of a new football facility to increase its athletic revenue and enhance its prestige. Paul Gallico, commenting on the collegiate stadium building boom of the 1920s from a cynical perspective during the Great Depression, maintained that the universities, too, "thought that prosperity would last forever, and, as a result, dipped into their treasuries, or floated bonds, or mortgaged the statue of Alma Mater, to erect bigger and roomier stadiums to accommodate the ever-increasing throngs of customers who were parting with three or four dollars apiece each Saturday during the season for a look at football teams that cost the colleges nothing but maintenance, equipment, and the salary of the football professor engaged to instruct them." From 1900 to 1923 the Fighting Illini played home football games at Illinois Field, which seated about twenty-two thousand and was not improved after 1915. When more than twenty thousand people could not obtain seating for the 1920 Ohio State game, George Huff, Illinois athletic director since 1901, Coach Zuppke, and alumnus Elmer Ekblaw suggested the idea of a new stadium and saw the project through to completion. "I haven't the slightest doubt," Huff stated in 1921, "that we could have sold more than forty thousand tickets, and possibly fifty thousand for the Ohio State game if we had had the seating facilities. With the growing interest in our athletics, it is no idle guess to prophesy that every one of the seventy-five thousand seats in the new Stadium will be sold for the big games of the next few years."[4]

In the spring of 1921, the university received permission from the state legislature to construct a stadium as a memorial to the 184 Illinoisans who had died in the Great War. Under the direction of Huff, a fund-raising drive was begun that spring in which more than twenty-one thousand students, alumni, and friends of the university would eventually pledge more than $2 million for the project. Due to defaults on subscriptions, however, the Illinois Athletic Association collected only $1,735,000 from the pledges, but that organization as well as the football program provided additional funds to complete the stadium. Even at that, Memorial Stadium was never built to the specifications or grandeur that Huff and university president David Kinley had envisioned. As in the case of other massive stadiums being constructed on college campuses during the 1920s, including those at the universities of Kansas and California, the Illinois structure would link academics and athletics to the recent war. As Patrick Miller has described the relationship, "Consuming hundreds of tons of poured concrete, elaborately inscribed, dominating the campus landscape, vast memorial stadiums became the foremost patriotic symbols of the twenties, solidly establishing the bonds between muscular and martial values, cementing the relationship between the war effort and the academy, Mars and Minerva."[5]

For President Kinley at least, the stadium would also provide a link between American culture, which many intellectuals of the day warned was dissipating under the assault of an encroaching mass society, and the classical Greek civilization upon which modern education was based. "Perhaps my greatest interest in the Stadium," he wrote in 1921, "is its cultural effect. Our Stadium will bring a touch of Greek glory to the prairie. Young men and women spending four years of their lives in the vicinity of such an edifice cannot help absorbing some of its lofty inspiration." The original stadium plans called for a ten-thousand-seat, open-air Greek theater to be set in an Italian-style garden that would have a proscenium arch at one end and colonnades, archways, and shining towers at its entrance. Kinley was convinced that the setting would "bring an appreciation of old-world beauties, of fine and eternal traditions, which, blended with the ruggedness and shrewd intelligence of our people, will help us to realize the greatness which is our birthright."[6]

Given the reverence and central place that Kinley and others bestowed upon the college football stadium, the rituals associated with the Saturday afternoon contests, the public's mania for the game, and the popular perception that the great players were modern day supermen, it is not surprising that some commentators began to view football as a secular religion. In an article entitled "The Great God Football," sportswriter and social analyst John Tunis suggested in 1928 that the great intercollegiate game "is at present a religion—sometimes it seems to be almost our national religion." Somewhat whimsically, he noted, "The religion of football has its high priests (prominent coaches) and acolytes (players), its saints (great players and coaches who have passed on), and sanctuaries (stadiums), as do other religions." Focusing on the central role of the stadium, Tunis wrote that "with fervor and reverence the college man and the non-college man, the athlete and the observer approach its shrines; dutifully and faithfully they make their annual pilgrimage to the football Mecca, be it Atlanta or Urbana, Cambridge or Los Angeles, Princeton or Ann Arbor."[7]

Despite Kinley's vision of a stadium encompassing the Platonic ideal of a sound body and a sound mind, the failure of the Illinois Athletic Association to collect all of the stadium drive pledges and higher construction costs than expected meant that original plans for the facility had to be modified. It came as no surprise perhaps that the first features to be excised were Kinley's Greek amphitheater and Italian-style garden. The second wave of cutbacks eliminated an extensive complex of basketball, handball, and tennis courts as well as an intramural ice-skating rink that Huff had proposed be built underneath the stadium stands. As in the case of other Big Ten schools, Illinois spent relatively little of its football profits to enhance and expand intramural athletics that benefited the entire student body. Although Huff was more committed to the concept of intramural sports than many other athletic directors in the conference, the university plowed most football receipts for 1923, more than $147,000, back into the stadium. Less than $7,000 of that sum was spent on intramural athletics. The same emphasis on intercollegiate sport over intramural athletics was evident at Ohio State University, where a $1.6 million stadium had opened in 1922. At Columbus, football receipts for 1924 amounted to nearly $275,000—of which $127,000 was expended on the stadium and $13,000 on intramural athletics.[8]

A massive football stadium not only became a symbol of big-time intercollegiate athletics in the 1920s but also put more pressure on coaches, athletic directors, and college presidents to produce competitive if not winning teams. One of the major effects of the stadium-building boom was the pressure on a growing number of colleges to devise more effective ways to recruit and subsidize players. At Illinois, where Zuppke, Huff, and Kinley remained adamantly opposed to most forms of recruitment and subsidization, Memorial Stadium still created a tendency toward blurring the line between the "amateur ethic" and athletic expediency. Although, like many university administrators, Kinley routinely extolled college amateur athletics, he just as certainly helped erode their foundation. Beginning in 1923 and continuing through 1930, when his tenure as president ended, he annually sent hundreds of complimentary season's tickets to state legislators, prominent alumni, and other distinguished citizens of the state. The object, of course, was to capitalize on the stadium and the university's football success to ensure a favorable image and generous appropriations.[9]

One factor that made massive football stadiums feasible was the emergence of the automobile culture during the 1920s. The automobile and the road system that supported it were fundamental to America's rapid economic growth during the 1920s and played a major role in the increasing popularity of college football and in the construction of large stadiums to showcase its heroes. It was fitting perhaps that Grange, when he began to make large sums of money as a professional player, bought his father an expensive automobile. He himself owned two or three cars at a time.[10]

Despite the origin of the good roads movement during the Progressive Era, by World War I American highways remained primitive and were poorly planned. Local road districts, townships, and counties were responsible for road-building and maintenance. Surfaced highways in the United States increased from about 154,000 miles in 1904 to 276,000 miles in 1915 but were inadequate for the nearly 2.5 million registered motor vehicles in the nation by the latter date. In 1916 the passage of the Federal Aid Road Act provided national funds for highway construction on a matching-grant basis. By 1917 all states had organized highway departments to supervise and coordinate bridge and highway construction. Immediately after the war, the U.S. Army helped popularize motor travel by organizing the First Transcontinental Motor Convoy of 1919, which sent eighty-one military automobiles and trucks from coast to coast along the Lincoln Highway. Two years later, Congress appropriated $75 million, almost four times the previous year's allocation, to help plan and build a nationwide network of key roads. By the time Illinois played its first game in Memorial Stadium in 1923, the state had more than a million registered motor vehicles, more than forty thousand miles of surfaced roads, and plans to surface another thousand miles of roads that year—which the Wheaton *Progressive* proclaimed as a world's record.[11]

Beyond the rapid increase in cars and surfaced roads after the war, public acceptance of closed automobiles was a major factor in the athletic and recreational boom of the 1920s. Families took to the road for scenic holidays of various kinds as well as to attend sporting events. Because many rapidly expanding public universities were located in largely rural areas, as was the University of Illinois, closed automobiles made it convenient for alumni or football enthusiasts from throughout the state and beyond to make a weekend excursion to an intercollegiate game. Only about 10 percent of automobiles manufactured in the nation in 1919 had closed bodies, but 43 percent had them by 1924 and 85 percent by 1927.[12]

President Kinley and other university officials were keenly aware of the automobile's potential impact upon the stadium in terms of financial success for the athletic program and positive public relations for the university. In 1923 Ellis Kriekhaus, writing in the university publication *Memorial Stadium Notes,* observed, "When the good roads program is finished in Illinois, five million people will be within five hours drive of the Stadium and Illinois." He added that "the Stadium is to be one great agency in putting the University before the state of Illinois." The following year, the *Illinois Alumni News* appealed to local boosterism by claiming that "as an advertisement of the University and the twin cities, the value of the stadium is realized by everybody." The article went on to point out that "the stadium has hastened the development of real estate in south and southeast Champaign, and has made possible much new pavement in that area which otherwise would not have come for several years."[13]

Illinois fans remember the 1924 season as the year of the stadium dedication game in which Grange ran wild against Michigan, but many overlook the fact that the 1924 squad was probably stronger than the 1923 Big Ten Conference champions and the best team on which Grange played in his three varsity seasons. Realizing that he had one of the nation's top teams returning, Zuppke scheduled a tougher slate of games for 1924, replacing weaker 1923 opponents Northwestern and Wisconsin with Michigan and Minnesota, much stronger teams. The Fighting Illini had lost three starting linemen to graduation, but Zuppke easily filled those positions with experienced players from the previous year's team. Grange, Harry Hall, Wally McIlwain, and Earl Britton were all returning as backfield starters. Zuppke did make some changes, however, switching Britton to wingback and putting McIlwain at fullback, Britton's old spot. He also inserted light, fast backs into the line at guard to run interference downfield on Grange's famous sweeps. The backfield changes were to allow Grange to both run and pass from the tailback position he took over from Britton, making it difficult for opponents to gang up on him by playing him only for the run. As tailback in the single-wing formation, which looked something like the modern shotgun formation, Grange would no longer be a potential receiver, but Zuppke calculated that he would more than make up for his pass-receiving yardage of 1923 by completing passes, which he did. Under instructions from Zuppke, Grange spent part of the summer practicing passing. "I started winging baseballs to my brother Garland for hours at a time," he recalled, "until I developed near perfect control and the ability to throw on the run. Then I switched to throwing a football. It got so I could pass with a high degree of accuracy at twenty or thirty yards."[14]

Illinois got off to a slow start in the 1924 season, barely squeaking out a 9-6 victory over a solid University of Nebraska team. Before a crowd of a little more than seventeen thousand at Lincoln, Zuppke's new offensive alignment was mainly held in check by a rugged Cornhusker defense. He later claimed that he had kept his run-pass offensive formation centering around Grange under wraps. Earl Britton provided the margin of victory with a second-half field goal. Although he was held scoreless in sixty minutes of play, Grange ran for 116 yards and completed six passes for another 127 yards. As was the custom of the day for many top-flight football programs, Zuppke had scheduled two tune-up games with weaker opponents, one early in the season and one near the end. On October 11, Illinois faced a badly over-matched Butler University team at Memorial Stadium. Only 9,135 fans turned out to watch the Illini maul the hapless Butler eleven. In sixteen minutes of play, Grange rushed for 104 yards and two touchdowns and completed two passes for forty-two yards. Referring to his scoreless performance the previous week against Nebraska, the *New York Times* reported that "Grange proved conclusively that he had not gone back by scoring two touchdowns." The second team played most of the way in the 40-0 Illinois victory. Grange and the Illini were now primed for the stadium dedication game against Michigan—a game that would alter his life immeasurably.[15]

Many sports experts agree with Jerome Brondfield, who wrote in 1973 that beginning with his spectacular performance against Michigan in 1924, "Red Grange became a folk hero, a sociological phenomenon of his time." Beyond question, the fact that Grange scored five touchdowns and passed for another against Michigan was remarkable. What was even more extraordinary for 1920s fans, not far removed from the defensive-oriented, ball-control football that prevailed during the game's first half-century, was the rapidity with which Grange scored his first four touchdowns and the distances from which he ran to cross the goal line. How many modern fans, moreover, could comprehend why Michigan chose to kick off four straight times to Illinois after each of Grange's touchdowns in the first period. Fans of the 1920s were fully familiar with the Michigan strategy, which emphasized the "kicking game" with the objective of forcing opponents to operate from poor field position. Many coaches believed that one offensive mistake by their opponent—a broken play, a poor punt, a fumble, or an intercepted pass—might be enough to decide a game. In fact, most games between the best teams in the Big Ten during the 1920s were decided by one touchdown or less. That Grange reeled off consecutive touchdown runs of ninety-five, sixty-seven, fifty-six, and forty-five yards against one of the nation's best teams—and in less than twelve minutes—was stunning to fans and most football experts alike.[16]

In later years Grange remembered the 1924 Michigan contest as "the most perfect football game that I ever had the chance to play in." He might have added that it was one of the most publicized games in the Midwest in the immediate postwar years. The game was given more coverage than usual by regional newspapers and the wire services because of the elaborate dedication ceremonies for the new stadium and an anticipated record crowd for a football game in the Midwest. In the East, where Big Ten games usually rated only three or four inches of type in major newspapers, the *New York Times* printed a column-long Associated Press game account in a prime position on the first page of its sporting section. Reflecting the provincial nature of football at the time, only one major New York sportswriter, Henry Ferrell of United Press, attended the game. Many of the city's top reporters, such as Grantland Rice of the New York *Herald-Tribune,* would cover the Army–Notre Dame game or other important contests in the East. After the Michigan game, however, Grange and Illinois would receive expanded coverage in eastern newspapers, whose sportswriters routinely depreciated what they called "Western football." Even the doubters among the eastern sporting fraternity had to address the Grange phenomenon: How good was he, and could he measure up to eastern competition? As would be the case several times during his collegiate career, Grange could not have selected a better occasion to play one of his greatest games.[17]

Grange's spectacular performance against Michigan by itself does not fully explain his rise to celebrity status over the coming weeks and months. Numerous great football players have had superb single-day, season, or career achievements, but few have been as enduring as Red Grange in the public mind. In Grantland Rice's view, what distinguished the athletic heroes of the golden age of sport was that "they had something more than mere skill or competitive ability. They had in record and quantity that indescribable asset known as color, personality, crowd appeal, or whatever you call it." Interpreting Rice's words, Gilman Ostrander, a social historian, has suggested that "the period was distinguished not so much by the skill of the athletes as by the record quality and quantity of the romanticizing of them by the American public." He maintains that "the triumph of sport in the twenties was fundamentally a triumph of the sports media, mainly the newspapers and radio. The national sense of athletic prowess was by necessity a technological accomplishment in communications above all else."[18]

By the 1920s American newspapers had become increasingly standardized, and many stories and columns were carried nationally. The content of newspapers had changed dramatically during the first quarter of the century. Space allocated to editorials, letters to the editor, and society news had been reduced by more than 50 percent, and sporting news and illustrations (including photographs) were up by 47 and 84 percent, respectively by 1923. As the fastest-growing major spectator sport, college football was a prime beneficiary of the trends. Expanded sports pages were partly due to the recently developed technique of transmitting photographs by wire. Two hours after the completion of a Saturday football game, pictures as well as reports of the gridiron action were available to readers of early Sunday editions nearly everywhere in the country. Grange's friend

Richard Crabb recalled, "I grew up on a farm near Macomb, Illinois, and we never had a Sunday paper until Red Grange played football." Most of the larger Sunday newspapers included a rotogravure section. Crabb maintained that "one thing that was extremely important, probably more important than any other phase of communication at that time were those brown Sunday sheets, the rotogravures. All during the football seasons there were big things in there about Grange." Printed on a rotary press, the pictures were close-up and lifelike. "You could hold them in your hand and look at them for five minutes or a half hour," Crabb remembered, "and you could pass them around." The rotogravures, Crabb believed, were "the single biggest factor in Grange's fame. We don't even yet understand it quite."[19]

Although newspapers were still the dominant sources of sporting news during the 1920s, national magazines, both weekly and monthly, had a long tradition of covering athletics. After the war, *Collier's*, the *Saturday Evening Post*, and the *Literary Digest* were among a number of weekly periodicals that devoted space to sports. After the Michigan game, Grange became the subject of great interest for magazines and their readers. In November 1924, the *Literary Digest*, a publication that capsulized current newspaper and literary opinion, ran a feature on Grange. Entitled "The First All-American Iceman," the article not only solidified Grange's sobriquet as the "Wheaton Iceman" but also helped fix in the public mind a number of perceptions about him that made Grange an appealing sports celebrity. The article identified Grange with the traditional Protestant work ethic by pointing out that he preferred the rigorous summer job of being an iceman over other, more genteel positions and that he planned to keep the same job the following summer. It emphasized Red's humility by mentioning that he kept no scrapbook of his achievements and assigned credit for his success to his blockers and his God-given ability. The writer also focused on Lyle Grange's modest job as Wheaton's "city jailer" and Red's long-standing and continuing efforts to sustain the family financially. In addition to assigning Grange these basic values, much admired in a nation undergoing a transformation from a rural to an urban culture, the article placed him among the legends of the game by referring to him as "this twenty-two-year-old Jim Thorpe of football." Supporting that view, the writer asserted that Grantland Rice, who had not seen Grange play, had called him "one of the few real All-American football players to ever come along." Within a month after the stadium dedication game, many of the important elements of the Grange legend were already in place.[20]

In addition to the more obvious factors contributing to Grange's mounting fame were more subtle but important characteristics. One concerned the color of his hair. His red hair identified him as a typical, small-town American youth who had made good. It also gave him a moniker that alluded to his explosive running style and speed. The press loved the nickname and used it incessantly until "Red" became almost synonymous with Harold Grange. In 1974 Grange maintained that his hair "never was red, but more auburn. I was called Hal in high school and I didn't pick up 'Red' until I came to Illinois." As Richard Crabb observed, however, "the thing would have been greatly different if his hair had been black. Red, Red, Red. It wasn't even that red either, but it was red. If it had been blond, he would have been 'Whitey' Grange. But nothing like Red Grange."[21]

The image of Red Grange as an evasive "streak of fire, a breath of flame, . . . a gray ghost thrown into the game," as Grantland Rice lyrically described him in 1925, was enhanced by newsreels, a staple of the movie business. By 1924 an estimated sixty million Americans attended motion picture theaters each week. In addition to the feature film, the standard fare for movie-goers might include a Mickey Mouse cartoon (after 1928), a travelog or Grantland Rice sports reel (after 1925), and a nine- or ten-minute newsreel. Audiences found the visual presentation of news exciting and unique. After newsreels were introduced in American theaters in 1911, sporting events became a popular subject in news summaries and accounted for more than 20 percent of the newsreel footage by the late 1920s. Athletic competitions were ideally suited to the motion picture medium because they were pre-planned events that were highly visual, filled with action and movement, and not controversial. With five newsreel companies competing in the market, major sporting events received ample coverage. Because of the existing technology, the silent, visual football clips preceded by captions had an eerie quality—a slightly speeded-up, jumpy, black and white image that flickered. It is perhaps not surprising that sportswriters and other viewers perceived Grange as an elusive, gray, ghost-like figure as he weaved through the opposition on long touchdown runs. Beginning in 1925, Grantland Rice teamed up with John Hawkinson to produce Sportlight News, a weekly series of one-reelers for Pathe News. Red Grange, of course, was a popular subject in these films for the rest of the decade. Although it is difficult to determine the impact of newsreels on his growing fame, one student of the medium, Raymond Fielding, maintains that "for many people, especially the illiterate, it [the newsreel] was a principle source of news until the coming of television."[22]

The impact of radio on the creation of sports celebrities such as Red
Grange is also difficult to assess. Radio or wireless technology was in use
before World War I but remained primarily under government control in
the United States until after the conflict. One of the earliest broadcasts of
a football game for a radio audience came in November 1920, when station WTAW used Morse Code signals to air a play-by-play description of
the Texas–Texas A&M Thanksgiving Day game. Earlier that month,
KDKA in East Pittsburgh had become the first station to schedule regular
programming, beginning with the 1920 election returns. From that point
on, radio became one of the fastest-growing industries of the decade. By
1922 there were thirty broadcast stations, and nearly sixty thousand
American families owned receivers. Seven years later, those figures had
grown to 606 stations and more than ten million families. The fact that
Jim Cleary, manager of Chicago *Tribune* station WGN, the largest in the
Midwest, decided to inaugurate football coverage at his station with the
1924 Michigan game clearly advanced Grange's notoriety in the region.[23]

Over the next decade, WGN would broadcast at least one and often two
or three Illinois games a year. Anecdotal evidence indicates that fans in the
Chicago broadcast area gathered around radio sets at high school football games, gas stations, or at home to hear announcer Quin Ryan's play-
by-play description of the 1924 Michigan game and subsequent Illinois
contests. It is more difficult to determine whether Grange's fame in the
Midwest prompted many people to buy radio sets as some commentators
have claimed or whether the dramatic increase of radio sales and the beginning of play-by-play football broadcasts in the early 1920s contributed significantly to Red's growing prominence as a sports celebrity. Perhaps
both were true. Admittedly, sports broadcasting was in a primitive stage
of development during Grange's college years. By 1926, however, the beginning of network broadcasting by the National Broadcasting Company
(NBC)—the Columbia Broadcasting System (CBS) followed suit the next
year—paved the way for the promotion of national football stars. Public
interest in games transmitted around the country helped sponsors sell products. By the late 1920s, and especially during the 1930s, radio broadcasting of college football games had a major impact on popularizing the game
and promoting football celebrities. In 1937 Quin Ryan claimed that
Grange's popularity as a national sports figure convinced the major net-
works to air college football games each Saturday. Radio, like the print
media and the movies, helped bring about a more homogenized, consum-
er-based culture and usher in the age of the athletic celebrity.[24]

The impact of the Michigan game and the aura surrounding Grange's spectacular performance entered the public consciousness in stages around the country. In Illinois and the rest of Midwest, the immediate reaction was one of euphoria, and the descriptions of Grange's feat contained much hyperbole. Lamenting the fact that twelve thousand fans had to be accommodated in temporary seating and several thousand more failed to get into the stadium at all, the *Illinois Alumni News* discussed the possibility of holding two homecomings so all fans could see the games. A correspondent to the same magazine claimed that with Grange's heroics the deeds of all other football luminaries from Nat Poe and Willie Heston to Walter Eckersall and Jim Thorpe faded into oblivion. "When histories are written on the feats of redheaded warriors," the Detroit *Free Press* enthused, "Grange must be given his place with those old heroes, Richard the Lionhearted, Frederick Barbarossa, and Eric the Red." In the East, the cradle of football, where there remained a skepticism of the western game and its star performers, the Red Grange phenomenon was slower to take root. The *New York Times* and other eastern newspapers did, however, increase coverage of Illinois football and Red Grange.[25]

After their devastating defeat of Michigan, the previous season's Big Ten co-champions, the Fighting Illini were poised to capture their second straight conference title and a possible national championship. With Grange watching the game from the sideline, the Illinois second team pulverized a weak DePauw University eleven 45-0 at Memorial Stadium on October 25. The following weekend, Iowa, projected as a contender for the conference championship, fared little better. Before forty-five thousand fans at Urbana-Champaign, Grange reeled off two first-period touchdowns to lead Illinois in a 36-0 rout. Zuppke had Grange sit out the final period to avoid injury and preserve his strength for the upcoming pivotal battle with Chicago.[26]

In later years Grange described the 1924 Chicago game as "the toughest football game I ever played in college." It was also one of his three best college performances. Endowed by John D. Rockefeller in the 1890s, the University of Chicago quickly became one of the leading universities in the nation. Under the direction of Amos Alonzo Stagg, a disciple of Yale's Walter Camp, Chicago also established itself as a premier football power in the Midwest. Since the beginning of their football rivalry in 1892, Chicago dominated Illinois with seventeen wins, eight losses, and two ties. Chicago had a good team in 1924 but was installed as a three-to-one underdog in the game on the basis of a 3-1-1 record and the strength of its previous opponents. The keen rivalry between the schools, the fact that it was Chicago's Homecoming, and the presence of Grange, however, had made the game a sellout for several weeks. More than thirty-two thousand fans jammed Stagg Field for the game, while outside scalpers were asking and getting from $20 to $100 for $2 or $3 tickets. As game time approached on a cold and blustery November day, students perched themselves on the walls of Stagg Field, prepared to relay the details of the game to those below through megaphones.[27]

Stagg, the dean of Midwest football coaches, and his assistant coach and scout Fritz Crisler had prepared a strategy designed to stymie the potent offense of Grange and Illinois. Realizing that Zuppke had inserted small, fast guards into his lineup to assist Grange in his open-field running, Stagg and Crisler worked out a ball control offense using Chicago's larger linemen (outweighing Illinois linemen by about fifteen pounds per man) and big backs. The Maroons planned to jam the ball up the middle, through and over the small, speedy Illinois guards who under existing rules were required to play both offense and defense while in the game. Although common wisdom has held that he only thought one game ahead, one football analyst has suggested that Stagg may have recruited the large linemen a year or two before in preparation for this game. If Chicago could successfully control the ball on short runs throughout much of the game, Zuppke's explosive offense might be stifled. "Did you ever see Grange score without the ball?" Stagg asked before the game.[28]

Chicago's strategy worked perfectly in the first period. The Maroons won the coin toss and elected to defend the south goal. Illinois opted to kick off. It is not clear whether Zuppke chose to kick off because of the wind disadvantage or the still-prevalent tendency toward defensive football, but in either case it played into Stagg's hands. Chicago quickly drove to the Illinois five-yard line before fullback Austin McCarty fumbled and the Illini recovered. Earl Britton immediately punted in the only possession of the first period for Illinois. McCarty then began a series of successful line plunges through the middle of the Illinois line, earning himself the nickname "Five-yard" McCarty and resulting in the first touchdown and a 7-0 Chicago advantage. Inexplicably, Zuppke elected to kick off again, and the Chicago backs marched through the Illinois guards on a long drive culminating in an early second-quarter touchdown and a 14-0 Chicago lead. Dazed by the Chicago onslaught, Zuppke changed tactics and chose to receive the kickoff after the Maroons' second touchdown. Suddenly Grange sprang into action. With a series of short runs and pass completions, he moved the Illini to the Chicago four-yard line before circling right end for a touchdown. After a Britton placement, Chicago led 14-7. "Up to now Illinois had not carried the ball once," Stagg recalled. "Where is Grange? Here he is and there he goes!"[29]

Illinois again received the kickoff, but this time failed to gain and was forced to punt. Chicago began another drive that featured a rare pass that gained seventeen yards to the seventeen-yard line of Illinois. A few plays later the Maroons scored and extended their lead to 21-7. At this point, the game seemingly slipping away, Zuppke changed his offensive game plan. He began to vary his offense from the run-pass formation centered around Grange to a number of different fronts, including the 1923 offense that featured Britton passing to Grange and other receivers. The Dutch Master, as the press nicknamed Zuppke, also sent in a number of trick and razzle-dazzle plays for which he was famous. After taking the kickoff, Illinois moved the ball from its own twenty-six-yard line into Chicago territory on three outstanding runs by Grange. With the drive apparently stalled, Britton dropped back to punt but instead passed to Grange for twenty-five yards and a first down inside the Chicago twenty-yard line. In probably the most spectacular play of the day, Illinois executed a quadruple pass. Receiving the center pass, Grange lateraled to Britton, who passed to right end Chuck Kassel, who lateraled back to Grange, sweeping left end. The play gained Illinois thirteen yards and moved the ball to the three-yard line. From there Grange raced around end for his second touchdown, which, combined with Britton's conversion, made the score 21-14 in favor of Chicago. A few moments later the half ended.[30]

During half-time, Zuppke brought to bear all his powers as coach, salesman, and psychologist to reverse his team's fortunes. He installed a back-field box defense, a formation Ohio State had used successfully two years in a row against Chicago, to contain the Maroons' pounding running attack. Zuppke also ordered his quarterback to show as many offensive fronts as possible, similar to Dallas Cowboy teams of the 1970s and 1980s, in order to loosen up the Chicago defense. Grange remembered that his coach alternately berated and cajoled the players, making "us ashamed, sore, and determined." Zuppke was particularly critical of the usually dependable fullback Earl Britton. "You looked just like a guy standing up on the field playing a piano," Zuppke assailed Britton. "Instead of hitting those guys hard you were pushing them away with your finger tips." Grange remembered that Britton was so angry about the remark that "he almost fractured the first Maroon who came his way at the start of the second half."[31]

Zuppke's late-second-period and half-time adjustments paid some dividends in the second half, but the pace of play slowed as both teams showed the effects of the furiously contested opening periods. In the third period the teams exchanged punts, after which Illinois drove to the Chicago forty-five-yard line. Britton attempted a field goal, but it went wide of the goalposts. The Maroons failed to gain and quick-kicked fifty-five yards over Grange's head to the Illinois twenty-yard line. On the next play, the Wheaton redhead, aided by well-executed downfield blocking, snaked eighty yards for his third touchdown. Britton's placement tied the score at 21-21. During the latter stages of the third and the beginning of the fourth periods, both teams failed to convert field goal opportunities; Britton's fifty-five-yard attempt was on-line but about ten yards short. Midway through the final period, Chicago mounted a sustained drive to the Illini twenty-yard line. Then, with time running down, Illinois end Chuck Kassel intercepted an ill-advised Chicago pass on his own eleven-yard line. Grange immediately responded by breaking away on a fifty-yard run to the Maroons' thirty-nine-yard line, but it was all for naught. The run was nullified by an Illinois holding penalty, an infraction one commentator has described as "one of those mysterious penalties that visiting teams seem to suffer once a game on key plays." Britton renewed the attack from his own one-yard line but was forced to punt as the final seconds of the game ticked away.[32]

The Chicago game proved to be the turning point of the season for Illinois and the beginning of the end of what Zuppke hoped would be a dream season. Had the Illini defeated Chicago, the way seemed clear for another conference championship and a likely invitation to the Rose Bowl for a fabulous confrontation between Grange and Stanford's sensational fullback Ernie Nevers. With Illinois as Big Ten champions, Rose Bowl officials could hardly turn down such a match-up. As it was, Notre Dame and the Four Horsemen would play against Stanford in Pasadena on New Year's Day. After the battle at Stagg Field, Illinois with a 5-0-1 record, was still within reach of the Big Ten title and a possible national championship. Two relatively weak opponents (Minnesota and Ohio State) remained on its schedule. The Chicago game, however, had taken a toll, both physically and psychologically. Grange recalled that he and "the entire Illinois team took a terrific beating" in Chicago. "I don't believe the Illini in my day had ever been in such a ferocious football game." What was worse, the effect of the game carried over to the following week. Stagg and Crisler, moreover, had not only out-coached Zuppke for most of the first half but also provided a blueprint for future Illini opponents to contain Grange and the explosive Illinois offense. Admittedly, Zuppke had made some important adjustments to salvage a tie with Chicago, but at a cost to his lighter and badly battered players. After the game, he instructed Milt Olander, his assistant coach and recruiter, to "voik on the beeg boys. The little ones are no good."[33]

For Grange, the Chicago game added to his growing reputation as the season's and decade's premier football player. The aura associated with the "Galloping Ghost" that began with the Michigan game increasingly seeped into the national consciousness. Coach Stagg, reviewing what he called "one of the greatest football dramas ever played on any field," praised "Grange's magnificent response in which he brought the Illinois score from 0 to 21 virtually single-handed." Walter Camp, who viewed the classic battle at Stagg Field, would select Grange for a second time to his all-American team and remarked that "Harold Grange is the marvel of this year's [1924] backfield. His work in the Michigan game was a revelation, but his performance in the Chicago game went even further when by his play—running and forward passing—he accounted for some 450 yards of territory. He is elusive, has a baffling change of pace, a good straight arm and finally seems in some way to get a map of the field at starting and then threads his way through his opponents." Grange's offensive performance against Chicago turned out to be his second best as a collegiate, gaining only thirty yards fewer than in the Michigan game.[34]

On November 15 what Grange described as "a battered, weary band of Illinois athletes traveled to Minneapolis to play Minnesota." Despite a first-period touchdown by Grange on a ten-yard sweep and an early 7-0 Illinois lead, the Illini were no match for the Gophers that day. Hammering away at the interior of the Illinois line Chicago-style, the large Minnesota backs led by Clarence Schutte rolled up a 20-7 lead midway through the third period. Grange was thoroughly bottled up by the big Gopher linemen. He gained only fifty-six yards rushing and completed three passes for forty-one yards before a severe shoulder injury late in the third period sent him to the sidelines and ended his season. By that time the outcome of the game was not in doubt as Minnesota maintained the 20-7 margin to the final gun. "The Minnesota encounter was just too much for us after what we had been through against Michigan and Chicago," Grange remembered. With Grange on the bench, Illinois managed to edge Ohio State 7-0 in the season finale at Memorial Stadium, but it was not enough to keep pace with Stagg's Chicago Maroons, who won what turned out to be their last Big Ten championship on the basis of a win and a tie in their final two games.[35]

The conclusion of the 1924 season was a bitter disappointment for Zuppke and the Illinois team despite an overall record of 6-1-1. Grange, however, had a spectacular season, scoring thirteen touchdowns and seventy-eight points in only six games to lead the conference in scoring. More important, he played his two best games against the most respected teams in the region on days when even the eastern media was casting an eye toward these midwestern football contests. As he settled into his off-season routine and awaited the Christmas break and a return to Wheaton, Grange had but a vague idea of the attention he was generating in the national media. He was summoned home prematurely on November 28 for a testimonial banquet in his honor attended by 250 townspeople and special guests in Wheaton. According to the town newspaper, he sat "rather bored and fatigued" as the master of ceremonies read letters heaping praise on him from such notables as George Huff, Bob Zuppke, Alonzo Stagg, and Walter Eckersall.[36]

By December, Grange's exploits and fame became a national phenomenon. The *New York Times* reported, "It is seldom that a player's fame spreads so rapidly and so definitely throughout the country. Grange is known and his deeds are followed from coast to coast with almost the same interest as in his own section of the country." Referring to a Philadelphia *Ledger* story expressing incredulity that Grange was working his way through college peddling ice, the *Illinois Alumni News* remarked, "The papers and magazines continue to explore Red Grange; he is referred to in speeches, automobile ads, and in learned committee meetings." As part of a year-end review of major events in 1924, the Boston *Globe* featured Grange and a paragraph about the Michigan game alongside commentary on the visit of the prince of Wales to America, the fall of the labor ministry in England, and the deaths of Woodrow Wilson, Florence Harding, and Samuel Gompers. Grange became a focus of the emerging national media apparatus of the 1920s. The postseason media blitz was just the beginning of his nationwide exposure and fame.[37]

5

A Media Frenzy

DURING THE EARLY MONTHS OF 1925 the media continued to focus on Grange. He received several trophies commemorating his extraordinary season, including one from former football players at the University of Pennsylvania recognizing him as the "most valuable player in the country." In a Chicago *Journal* poll to determine the world's greatest athlete, he finished fourth behind Jack Dempsey, Johnny Weissmuller, and Jim Thorpe. He easily out-polled other luminaries of the decade, including Babe Ruth, Ty Cobb, Walter Johnson, and Bill Tilden. Throughout the winter and spring, numerous rumors circulated that Grange had received and declined various movie contract offers ranging from $25,000 to $300,000. He did make a trip to Milwaukee in May to meet with producers from Universal Studios and take a screen test. In later years, however, Grange could recall turning down only one substantial offer in his junior year, and that from Illinois alumni who wanted him to sell insurance. "I could have made quite a bit of money in Chicago selling insurance that summer," he stated in 1974, "but I would have been out of shape, and maybe I'm crazy, but I've always disliked anything that isn't fair."[1]

In February, Grange contracted the mumps in Richmond, Michigan, while on a "speaking tour." What he was doing in Michigan during the school term and on whose behalf he was speaking remain a mystery, but

as captain-elect of the football team one might speculate that it had something to do with university business and perhaps recruiting. Grange was
ill for about six weeks, and, as an off-campus student newspaper later
explained, he "slipped up a little" in his studies. At the end of the semester he made passing grades in four courses but failed a class in transportation. Under university rules, he was required to maintain a C average or
above and complete fifteen hours of study in any given semester to remain
eligible for varsity athletics, and the failing grade put him below that standard. Fortunately for Grange and Illini fans, the university allowed athletes to take a "special" examination at the end of the semester in any class
failed in order to try to reestablish eligibility. Grange would do so in July
and pass. It was not the first time that he had run into academic difficulties at Illinois. During the spring of 1924 he failed a course in economics
and attended Wheaton College that summer to make up the class while
taking a break from the ice wagon between eleven and one o'clock. When
he left Illinois in November 1925, Grange had completed 85.5 hours out
of the 130 required for graduation and had a 3.14 grade point average on
a five-point system, slightly below the university average (3.22) for the years
between 1920 and 1925.[2]

While Grange began what would turn out to be a difficult semester, the
attention of many Americans was riveted on the plight of Floyd Collins, a
young man who had become trapped in a cave in western Kentucky. Had
he followed the drama surrounding efforts to rescue Collins, Grange might
have learned something about the powerful forces of the media that were
about to engulf him and also about the fickleness of the public who followed this and other sensational stories during the 1920s. Few people
would have ever heard of the accident or Collins had it not been for W. B.
Miller, a reporter for the Louisville *Courier-Journal*, who daringly wormed
his way through a deep, dangerous, slippery passageway to interview
Collins, whose foot was trapped under a rock. Miller vividly described
Collins's heroic struggle to reach freedom and, much to his amazement,
discovered that the wire services had picked up his stories. Much of the
nation became engrossed by the drama, which became front-page news.[3]

When he first arrived at the accident site, Miller found only three men
at the cave entrance, calmly speculating on how soon their friend might
free himself. Soon a city of more than one hundred tents had sprung up,
along with milling crowds who had to be restrained by barbed wire and
the drawn bayonets of state troopers. After he died in the cave in mid-
February after more than two weeks, Collins and the drama he had creat-

ed were soon forgotten. A North Carolina mine disaster that claimed fifty-three lives the following month drew little national attention. Frederick Lewis Allen has written that the Collins incident "was an exciting show to watch, and the dispensers of news were learning to turn their spotlights on one show at a time. It was the tragedy of Floyd Collins, perhaps, which gave the clearest indication up to that time of the unanimity with which the American people could become excited over a quite unimportant event if only it were dramatic enough."[4]

After the school term ended at Illinois, Grange returned to Wheaton, still dogged by persistent rumors that he had or would accept a film contract or some other lucrative job offer. Even Wheaton and his familiar job at Luke Thompson's ice company were not quite the same, however. Thompson had begun using Grange's name to advertise his store and its relocation the previous year, and Red became a bit of a celebrity on his delivery route. He posed for photographs with customers and their children, and frequently a photographer from a national newspaper or magazine would turn to capture the Wheaton Iceman in action. When he began his summer job in mid-June, a *New York Times* correspondent reported from Wheaton that Grange, although earning only about $30 a week, "likes his job because, he says, it's real work and keeps him fit." During that summer Grange spent only about six weeks toting ice; he took time off to go to Panama with friends. While in Wheaton, he often tried to avoid situations that might draw attention to himself. On one occasion at Hiatt's Drug Store, Grange spied Col. Robert McCormick, owner of the Chicago *Tribune* and part-time Wheaton resident, for whom he had caddied as a youth. Grange tried to avoid the Colonel, but McCormick sought him out before leaving the store. He congratulated Grange for being selected as an all-American and related that he had a member of the *Tribune*'s sports department scout Grange during his sophomore year with an eye toward arranging for Red to attend and play football at Yale, the Colonel's alma mater. McCormick explained that the sportswriter's report was negative. Then, pausing for a moment, he said, "I want you to know that man isn't with us anymore."[5]

By September, Grange was looking forward to returning to school and his final football season as a collegian. He was particularly excited about the prospect of playing alongside his brother Gardie, who had a fine season at halfback for the Illinois freshman team in 1924 and was expected to see some action with the varsity in 1925. Red did not look forward to the long, grueling practices that Coach Zuppke favored, however. Throughout his career he disliked practice and especially loathed the three-and-half-to four-hour drills Zuppke routinely scheduled. The 1925 squad was considerably weaker than the previous Illinois teams on which Grange had played. As a result of graduation, Zuppke had lost starters Frank Rokusek at end, Dick Hall at tackle, Roy Miller and Lou Slimmer at guards, Gil Roberts at center, and backs Wally McIlwain and Emil "Heinie" Schultz. The loss of wingback and blocker McIlwain was critical because in the single-wing formation the lack of an experienced player at that position often affected the performance of the entire offense. To make matters worse, quarterback Harry Hall, a two-year starter, had been injured in the 1924 Minnesota game and his status was questionable. Zuppke had not had an exceptional recruiting class since 1922 and did not have adequate blockers to complement Grange and Britton. In desperation, he experimented by shifting Britton from fullback to guard at the start of the season. It was perhaps not surprising that Illinois got off to a poor start in a season that football experts would remember as "the year of the big mud."[6]

In later years Grange sometimes said that he had played his best college football in 1925, but, he would quickly add, "Sometimes I looked terrible." Before the regular season began Zuppke and Grange received another blow when Gardie Grange suffered an injury in practice and decided to withdraw from school. A record-setting early-season midwestern crowd of nearly thirty thousand turned out at Memorial Stadium to watch the Illini open their campaign against Nebraska. Grantland Rice, covering the game for the New York Herald-Tribune, predicted that it would take "great football to beat this Nebraska team, and Illinois will run into heavy trouble, even with Grange, unless the somewhat green Zuppke forwards can face the pressure without caving in." He added that "Grange will be tested to-morrow up to any human limit and if he can make any notable headway against this rival in his first contest he will add another fresh supply of laurel branches to his large collection of the same." Zuppke had informed Rice before the game that the team was overconfident and he was unable to wake them. "Grange won't make a first down," he predicted.[7]

Grange failed to do so, and the Cornhuskers decisively outplayed Illinois on the way to a convincing 14-0 victory on a rain-soaked field. All-American tackle Ed Weir and the Nebraska line bottled up Grange all afternoon, holding him to fifty-seven yards rushing and one pass completion. The following week Illinois managed a 16-13 home victory over a weak Butler team. Grange scored two touchdowns, one on a seventy-yard run. He continued his resurgence at Iowa on October 17 by running the opening kickoff back eighty-five yards for a touchdown and posting more than 250 yards in total offense, but the team failed to generate enough scoring to prevent a 12-10 Iowa victory. The opening phase of the season was a disappointment for Illinois and Grange despite preseason speculation that the Illini would be hard-pressed to measure up to their performances of the previous two seasons.[8]

The most obvious reason for a lackluster start in 1925 was the lack of experienced players (especially blockers) due to graduation and a few key injuries. Football historian James Mark Purcell has argued, however, that Grange did not play up to all-American standards after his memorable performance in the 1924 Chicago game. From that game through the end of the 1925 season, Illinois posted a record of only six wins and four loses, and Grange averaged 179 yards per game in total offense as opposed to 238 in his first twelve varsity games. Purcell maintains that Grange's offensive statistics for 1925 were "the good sound stats one expects of a great offensive star on a mediocre team," but Eddie Tryon of Colgate and Johnny Mack Brown of Alabama had better seasons than Grange and deserved first-team all-American consideration ahead of him. Grange, who in later years at least was not impressed by all-American selections, would not have been impressed by Purcell's analysis. "There weren't any one man teams," he stated emphatically in 1984. "I carried the ball, but I wasn't more important than the guys doing the blocking or anybody playing in the line or the backfield. We never thought of it as anybody being a star. You were one of the cogs."[9]

Part of the reason for Grange's substandard performance during most of the 1925 season may have been the inordinate amount of publicity being focused on him. As Purcell has noted, "Promoters and the crowds were after a shy smalltime boy who didn't like fuss or being isolated in the spotlight as a celebrity freak." The heightened public awareness may have been intensified by the opening of a new Harold Lloyd film, *The Freshman* (1925). Premiering just before the start of the college football season, *The Freshman,* a burlesque-style spoof featuring college football heroes, frivolous flappers, hip flasks, and raccoon coats, was an instant sensation around the country. Although the bespectacled Lloyd was a bumbling football hero at best, the film focused attention on college and football, a world unfamiliar to many. The film was so popular that by the end of the decade it had helped spawn more than thirty motion pictures that also had football themes. It is not far-fetched to assume that movie audiences somehow associated the film's comic hero Harold Lamb (Lloyd) with Harold "Red"

Grange. Over the years Grange commented sparingly about the pressures the fanfare placed on him. There is little doubt, however, that by 1925 he was an object of hero worship and being pursued by publicity-seekers. "My last season was all confusion," he acknowledged in one of his few comments on the subject. "I had no privacy. Newsreel men were staying at the fraternity house two and three days at a time. I wasn't able to study or anything." How the circuslike atmosphere affected Grange's concentration and performance on the football field is a matter for speculation.[10]

Another burden may have been an agreement Grange made with Charles C. Pyle, a Champaign theater owner. In the numerous statements and interviews he gave over the years, Grange provided slightly varying accounts of his first meeting and agreement with Pyle, but the essential facts were the same. He had first became acquainted with Pyle in September 1925 while attending the Virginia Theater in Champaign to watch a movie (which he sometimes said was *The Freshman*). An usher handed Grange a free pass to attend the Virginia and Park theaters, explaining that Mr. Pyle, who owned both movie houses, wanted him to have it. When Grange attended another movie at the Virginia a few days later, Pyle met him in the lobby and invited him to his office. How, he immediately asked, would Grange like to make $100,000? "I thought he was crazy," Grange recalled. "That was like saying how would you like to make a million today. I said 'naturally, anyone does.' He said, 'sit down, I've got an idea. I'll get back to you inside of a few weeks.'"[11]

Throughout his life, Grange staunchly admired and defended Pyle, who he once called "the most impressive man I ever met." In the fall of 1925, however, Grange seemingly knew very little about Pyle except that he appeared to be nearly six feet, one inch and 190 pounds, had a close-cropped mustache, wore spats and carried a cane, and was "the most immaculate dresser I have ever seen." Pyle, the son of a Methodist minister, was born in Delaware, Ohio. His mother wanted him to become a preacher like his father, but young Pyle had little interest in the ministry or school. He did inherit his father's talent for preaching, however, and put it to good use as a promoter, huckster, booster, and businessman. According to Alva Johnston's overblown account of his career in *The New Yorker* in 1928, Pyle promoted his first event at the age of sixteen, a bicycle race between a local youngster and future auto racer Barney Oldfield. Oldfield received $25 for his part in the race, Pyle netted $7, and the local boy, an amateur, received nothing. From then on, Johnston wrote, Pyle was partial to amateurs. As he vowed, "I will never desert professionalism. There isn't enough money in the world to induce me to turn amateur."[12]

After dropping out of Ohio State University, Pyle went west, where he became involved in an astounding variety of money-making schemes, promotions, con games, and business ventures. For Pyle, being in on the action was often more important than how much he gained or lost. Grange once remembered that "money meant nothing to Pyle." But "he liked to hear his name mentioned. . . . He'd ride the 20th Century Limited between Chicago and New York and whenever one of the waiters would say, 'Mr. Pyle, How are you.' He'd give him a ten dollar tip. If he didn't know his name he wouldn't give him a nickel. He loved that acclaim." In the West, Pyle sold Western Union time-service clocks, ran a modest travel bureau using the free railroad passes Western Union provided him, and, when his funds ran low, promoted a boxing match between himself and an elderly miner. He temporarily hit his stride as an advance man for the Margarita Fisher Stock Company and gained useful experience in the art of barnstorming. According to Johnston, he "posted the bills, painted, repaired and shifted the scenery, blew a plugged tuba in the band, took tickets, did a drunk act, made the hotel and stagecoach arrangements, and engaged opera and implement houses for the performances."[13]

Pyle eventually acquired his own stock company and became a master of efficiency in staging productions. He put on *Uncle Tom's Cabin* with a four-member cast and *The Three Musketeers* with only one musketeer. Actors routinely played four or five parts. When there was dialogue between two characters that were being played by one actor, he talked to himself. In 1908 Pyle became involved in the movie business. He bought a projector and some films and had some success on the road before he went broke. After acquiring an amusement park and vaudeville theater in Idaho, Pyle sold his assets for $750 in 1910 and moved on to Illinois, where he entered the movie theater business. From then until he met Grange, Pyle had led a relatively humdrum life while building up a chain of three movie theaters, two in Champaign, where he made his home, and one in Kokomo, Indiana.[14]

After the meeting with Grange at the Virginia Theater, Pyle contacted Edward "Dutch" Sternaman, co-owner of the Chicago Bears professional football team, and then traveled to Chicago, where he negotiated a tentative deal with him and the team's other owner, George Halas. Under the eventual agreement signed in November, Pyle, as Grange's agent, would provide the services of the Illinois halfback to the Bears immediately after his last college game for the remainder of Chicago's National Football League (NFL) schedule and for a postseason barnstorming tour that Pyle would help arrange. In return, Halas and Sternaman agreed to split the gate receipts for all games approximately fifty-fifty with Pyle and Grange. As negotiations progressed and throughout the remainder of the college season, Grange maintained that he signed nothing. "Although a lot of people and a lot of papers claimed that I had signed a contract," he explained, "I hadn't. No, I never talked to Halas, never met Halas or Sternaman in my life until two days after I played my last [college] football game."[15]

When he concluded negotiations in Chicago, Pyle left immediately on a trip to the South and the Pacific Coast to book exhibition games for the proposed postseason tour. When Pyle met with Grange again, he outlined the arrangements he had worked out with Halas and Sternaman. That may have been the meeting at which Pyle and Grange agreed to split their half of the gate receipts 60-40 in Red's favor. Grange approved the deal with Pyle and the Bears by shaking Pyle's hand, and both men agreed that he would not receive any compensation from Pyle or the Bears until after he finished the college season.[16]

Pyle, by shaking Grange's hand and later signing the formal agreement with him in November, became one of the first true player agents in sport history. Grange later explained, "I signed a contract with him as a manager or an agent [in November]—they call them agents today—it was the same thing—they called them a manager then. He handled my personal stuff at that time." Managers were common in some sports by the 1920s, notably in boxing. Doc Kearns (John Leo McKernan), for example, had been Jack Dempsey's manager since 1917, and the practice of engaging managers in that sport had been common since before the turn of the century. In team sports such as baseball, however, the use of managers or player agents had been rare. Team owners were reluctant to deal with them, and the reserve rule gave baseball owners nearly complete control over players. Babe Ruth had engaged the services of sportswriter Christy Walsh as a ghostwriter in 1921 and over the years he became Ruth's financial adviser and business representative. He did not, however, negotiate Ruth's contracts with New York Yankee owner Jacob Ruppert. In football, the only recorded instance of a player being represented by an agent before Grange was the case of Ohio State's three-time all-American halfback Chic Harley. He was signed by George Halas and Ed Sternaman of the Chica-

go Staleys (later the Bears) in a deal arranged by his brother, sportswriter
Bill Harley, in 1921. Apparently Bill Harley represented his brother only
on that one occasion.[17]

Although Grange's account of his meeting and dealings with Charlie Pyle
in the fall of 1925 most likely accurately outlined their agreement with the
Chicago Bears, it also contained inaccuracies and raises a number of questions. In his autobiography, Grange stated that his first meeting with Pyle
was "during the second week of my senior year at Illinois," that is, sometime in September 1925. Pyle's letter to Ed Sternaman, which resulted from
the Grange-Pyle meeting, was dated August 9, 1925, however. Grange also
maintained that Pyle invited him to his office for their first meeting: "I had
heard his name mentioned many times before, but never met him." In a
slight variation of that account, Grange told football historian Richard
Whittingham in 1984 that when the usher asked him to go to Pyle's office,
"I said who is Mr. Pyle? Never heard of him." In fact, Grange had known
and been associated with Pyle since at least May 1925 and probably before. On May 13, 1925, the Milwaukee *Journal* carried a photograph of
Grange posing with Universal Pictures film star Virginia Valli in that city.
The caption explained that Grange was in Milwaukee to negotiate a contract that might lead to a film career. The following day the *Journal* reported, "Grange arrived in Milwaukee Tuesday night with his pal and fellow-
student, Doc Cooley, and Charles C. Pyle and H. E. McNevin, theater men,
with a chain of theaters in Champaign, Ill., and other cities. Pyle and
McNevin believe, and seem to have convinced producers, that the famous
football star is a second Wallace Reid."[18]

Grange took a screen test that afternoon, and the producers offered him
a $25,000 film contract to appear in a motion picture that had an athletic
theme. Grange, possibly on the advice of Pyle and McNevin, declined the
offer on the grounds that he did not wish to risk his amateur standing.
Henry E. McNevin, a Champaign banker and businessman, was vice president of the Illinois Trust and Savings Bank and co-owner with Pyle of the
Virginia and Park theaters. According to McNevin's son, his father and
Pyle later financed Grange's professional football tours and had a stake in
the creation of the American Football League as well as other athletic promotions, including Suzanne Lenglen's U.S. professional tennis tour and
Pyle's transcontinental walking race, the Bunion Derby. They raised money through McNevin's bank. By 1926 McNevin was secretary-treasurer of
the Stoolman-Pyle Corporation, undoubtedly a front organization for the
financing of these and other Pyle ventures.[19]

Although the details are not clear, it seems likely that Pyle, with assistance from McNevin, began representing Grange in the spring of 1925 or before. According to a Champaign newspaper story of December 1925, Grange made his first commercial deal, evidently on his own, around March 1925 with a Champaign clothing store owner, H. I. Gelvin. He apparently signed a contract with Gelvin that allowed the merchant to sell "Red Grange Socks" at Gelvin's Clothes Shop. Gelvin later maintained that the contract "was considered ironclad by attorneys" and the product was registered in the U.S. Patent Office. It may have been soon after this deal that Pyle and Grange met and Pyle suggested that Grange needed a business manager to better protect his interests. It should also be pointed out that Johnny Small, a Wheaton vaudeville performer, alleged in 1926 that Grange signed a contract with him in August 1925 to appear on stage after the college football season ended. Small charged in a lawsuit that Grange subsequently changed his mind and signed with Pyle. After meeting Pyle, Grange apparently took his time before agreeing that the theater owner would be his exclusive agent. At what point Pyle proposed to Grange that he could make $100,000 remains unclear. It seems likely that he suggested the pro football scheme in late July or early August 1925, nearly a month and a half before Grange said they had first met. The facts that Grange worked only six weeks during the summer of his senior year and took a trip to Panama also lend credence to the likelihood that he was involved in commercial ventures, either with or without Pyle's assistance.[20]

Grange's motive for later fabricating the time of his first meeting with Pyle was undoubtedly not sinister. Up until his last college game, no one cared when he first met Pyle. The press, university officials, the Big Ten commissioner, and the public only wanted to know if he had signed a contract to turn professional while he was still a collegiate player. Not until nearly a quarter-century later would the media began to recognize Grange as a "legendary" figure of the golden age of sport and ask probing questions about the details of his career. His 1953 autobiography, written with Ira Morton, was published in the Putnam Sports Series, which targeted young readers and tended to promote athletes as role models. Grange may have falsified the date of his and Pyle's first meeting in that account in order to conceal the commercial ventures of his senior year. It is important to note, however, that such ventures most likely would not have violated Big Ten or NCAA rules in 1925 although they would have been illegal under NCAA standards in 1953 and thereafter. Grange may have seen no point in admitting an earlier association with Pyle and drawing attention to commercial activities that readers in the 1950s or those who heard of his NCAA football broadcasts could misconstrue. He had not signed a contract with Pyle to turn professional before his last college game and thus had violated no existing intercollegiate rules.[21]

While the media attention focused on him intensified and he consulted with Pyle periodically concerning his prospects, Grange continued to play football. On October 24 Illinois faced Michigan in what regional fans considered to be the premier game of the season. Having been humiliated by Illinois and Grange the previous autumn 39-14, Michigan, with veteran coach Fielding Yost back at the helm, was bent on revenge. Yost had built what he would later describe as "the best [team] I ever had" around triple-threat quarterback Benny Friedman and a rawboned sophomore end named Bennie Oosterbaan. Featuring Friedman's daring passing (he often passed on first down, which was rare in 1925), the Wolverines had annihilated their first three opponents by a combined score of 123-0. The drama surrounding the game was heightened by the anticipation of Illini fans that Grange would perform new wonders against Michigan and the fact that it was Homecoming at Illinois. The Illinois Central Railroad ran extra trains from Chicago to Urbana-Champaign at half-fare to accommodate the expected sellout crowd. More than ten thousand out-of-town automobiles were also expected to converge on the twin cities. Wheaton Mayor Marion Pittsford declared October 24 a holiday in honor of Red Grange, and all the major merchants closed their businesses for the day to allow citizens to attend the game. Despite a heavy rain that ended an hour before game time, sixty-seven thousand fans jammed Memorial Stadium to watch the contest. An estimated twenty thousand more were turned away.[22]

With the entire Wolverine defense geared to stop him and the slippery turf impeding his progress, Grange worked no miracles against Michigan that day. He gained 147 yards in sixty minutes of play but failed to break away on long runs. The game was decided in the second period when Michigan intercepted a Britton pass at midfield and drove deep into Illinois territory on a nifty pass and lateral play initiated by Friedman. After a series of short gains, the Michigan quarterback dropped back and booted a twenty-four-yard field goal from a difficult angle—the game's only scoring. Earl Britton missed two long field-goal attempts in the second and third periods in an unsuccessful effort to tie the game. The outcome was a great disappointment for Grange, from whom so much was expected. Despite the defeat, the game marked a turning point for Grange, who was inserted in the quarterback position for the first time. Zuppke had been preparing him for the shift and contemplating doing so for several weeks. He believed that the team would have more confidence if Grange called the signals. Grange liked the new position and later said that as a quarterback he had learned "things about football I had never even thought of before." Although the move did not pay dividends against Michigan, it did start an Illinois resurgence in 1925 that would cause some fans to nickname the Illini the "November team."[23]

Coach Zuppke had scheduled the upcoming intersectional game with the University of Pennsylvania in Philadelphia during the 1924 season. As was the case with the 1924 Michigan game, he used every bit of psychology he knew to prepare his team for the invasion of the East well in advance. Throughout the summer of 1925 he sent personal letters to his players, emphasizing that easterners looked down on midwestern football and that he had discovered a strategy to defeat Penn. That would be no easy task. Penn was ranked the number one team in the East in 1924 and had gotten off to a fast start in 1925. Going into the Illinois game the Quakers had a 5-0 record, with impressive victories over Brown, Yale, and Chicago. By contrast, Illinois had lost its first three important games in 1925 and had a 1-3 record. Experts were making the Quakers a four-or-five touchdown favorite. Grantland Rice forecast that Grange "may have no chance against Penn, for the Penn line will outplay Illinois unless the Brown, Yale and Chicago battles have worn away its zest and impending weariness slows up its charge."[24]

Despite the apparent mismatch, there was great interest in the game in both sections of the country because it was the university's first football game in the East under Zuppke. The event also marked the eastern media's first and perhaps only chance to size up Red Grange on their own turf against one of the region's best teams. Many eastern sportswriters considered Grange just another highly publicized "western" star who was untested against first-rate competition. As Paul Gallico recalled, "For all Red's astonishing record, he was still a midwestern phenomenon. He had not yet convinced the east." Gallico added that "if ever a stage was set for a highly touted, two-time All-American and possibly over-rated football hero to fall on his face, it was that October afternoon in Franklin field, Philadelphia, before a capacity crowd."[25]

Hundreds of Illini fans, including the university's 150-piece marching band, took advantage of an Illinois Central–Pennsylvania Railroad special $31.14 round-trip fare to make the twenty-one-hour trip to Philadelphia. It was late when they arrived, and an all-night rain and snow storm had left the turf at the newly reconstructed Franklin Field, in Grange's words, "like a big mud cake." By morning the rain had stopped, but it was a cold, damp, and gloomy day for a football game. Yet sixty-seven thousand heavily clad fans, a Philadelphia record for a football game, jammed into Franklin Field. The game also attracted no doubt the greatest media coverage of any football game played thus far. All the prominent eastern sportswriters, Rice, Damon Runyon, Ford Frick, and a host of lesser-known journalists, overflowed the Franklin Field press box facilities. They all wanted to find out whether Grange could possibly live up to the fabulous reputation he had established in the Midwest.[26]

Zuppke's game plan was based on a careful study of scouting reports on Penn's defensive tendencies. He had discovered that Penn coach Louis Young heavily over-shifted his defense against teams like Illinois that ran single-wing formations with an unbalanced line. An unbalanced line meant that four linemen, depending on which side the formation was shifted, positioned themselves to the right or left of the center (the strong side) and only two were on the opposite (weak) side. Grange normally ran to the strong side of the Illinois formation to take advantage of the additional blocking. With the Quaker defense so heavily over-shifted to meet the brunt of the Illinois attack, which generally went to the right, Zuppke reasoned, he might spring Grange loose for long gains by running him to the weak side or left, provided that no definite pattern was established. He instructed Grange to run fullback Earl Britton to the strong side of the Illinois line on the first two plays from scrimmage and then on the third play take the ball himself around the Illini weak side. Zuppke's design did not work to perfection, but it did work.[27]

After he ran the opening kickoff back to his own thirty-six-yard line, Grange twice sent Britton toward the strong side of the Illinois offensive formation, where "he got brutally smeared." After he lost ground on consecutive downs, Britton returned to the huddle and inquired, "What have you guys got against me? I pretty near got killed." Because of the loss of yardage and poor field position, Britton punted out of trouble on the next play. When Penn also failed to gain, Illinois regained possession after a Quaker punt that put the ball on the Illinois forty-four-yard line. Grange quickly lined the team up again with the line unbalanced to the right and ran the ball to the left around the weak side for a fifty-six-yard touchdown. "I didn't even see anybody," he remembered with some exaggeration. "There wasn't anybody over there. And it happened all day long." Before the half was over Grange had set up a second Illinois touchdown with a brilliant fifty-six-yard kickoff return and scored a third on a twelve-yard romp around his left end. If the Pennsylvania team thought Grange could only run to his right, as some experts alleged, they soon learned otherwise. By the end of the first half, many fans at Franklin Field were stunned as the "western team" led 18-2, and Grange was sprinting for yardage across the soggy turf seemingly at will.[28]

Perched high in the stands above the field, John O'Hara, who then worked for a Pottsville, Pennsylvania, newspaper and had contrived an excuse from his job to see Grange play, watched the game unfold in amazement. He recalled, "We in the East had been hearing about this Grange until he had become something between a legend and a bore. . . . Everybody had come to see Grange, but not everybody had come in the hope of seeing him triumph. Well, triumph he did." Then, with about a minute left in the first half, Zuppke took Grange out of the game. He went over to the bench and conferred with Zuppke "while thirty-two assistant managers tried to bundle him up." Grange nodded to Zuppke and then began to trot toward the dressing room. O'Hara captured the drama of the moment:

> All alone, the slow trot down the seventy-five yards to the exit, and there wasn't a man or woman not standing in the whole stadium. And if I was any judge, there wasn't a dry eye, either. There he was, the boy who had come through when the chips really were down, dragging his blanket behind him, and it was wonderful. The men on the field could have pulled pistols and shot it out and no one in the stand would have noticed, because we were all looking at Grange, and we couldn't have heard the shots for hearing ourselves cheer him. Somehow or other I felt that the eyes of the whole East were on that solitary figure, and for some reason or other I was proud of him."[29]

At half-time, Coach Young adjusted his defense to contain Grange's runs to the weak side, but it was too late. Illinois had taken the starch out of the Quakers. The Illini added insult to injury by scoring their last touchdown in the third period on Zuppke's famed flea flicker play. From the Penn twenty-yard line, Grange positioned himself on one knee eight yards back as if he was going to hold the ball for a Britton field-goal attempt. Realizing that Grange had called the flea flicker, Zuppke jumped from the bench and sent in a substitute in an effort to call off the play. Grange waved the new player back to the bench and began to call signals. Zuppke turned his back to the field and put his hands over his eyes. The ball was snapped directly to Britton instead of Grange. Britton lobbed a pass to right end Chuck Kassel, who pivoted around and tossed a lateral to Grange, who had gotten off the ground and was sprinting to his right. Grange ran twenty yards unmolested for a touchdown while Penn players stood dumbfounded. Later that evening, Grange heard Zuppke tell a group of admirers how he had planned to use the flea flicker play in that situation against Penn for months. When the final whistle blew, Illinois achieved a stunning 24-2 triumph over Penn. Grange had scored three touchdowns, amassed 363 yards running on thirty-six carries, and completed one pass for thirteen yards in one of his best efforts as a collegiate player.[30]

In the Midwest and the East—and, for that matter, around the rest of the country—the media reaction to Grange's singular performance was one of ecstasy. The Chicago *Tribune* ran a banner headline: "ILLINI 24, PENN 2: GRANGE!" The usually sedate *New York Times* reported that "Red Grange's Eastern debut on Saturday was one of the greatest individual triumphs of football." "This man Red Grange of Illinois is three or four men and a horse rolled into one for football purposes," wrote Damon Runyon. "He is Jack Dempsey, Babe Ruth, Al Jolson, Paavo Nurmi and Man o' War. Put them all together, they spell Grange." Perhaps Grange's greatest tribute came from Laurence Stallings, a veteran of the Western Front in World War I and author of a realistic, hard-boiled play depicting the carnage of that conflict, *What Price Glory?* Assigned to cover the Penn-Illinois game by a New York newspaper, Stallings paced up and down the press box for an hour after the game, pulling his hair and groaning in despair. When a colleague who had completed his story asked what troubled him, Stallings threw up his arms in frustration and blurted, "I can't write it! The story's too big for me!" Given the penchant of many sportswriters of the 1920s to report major athletic events as if they encompassed some epic grandeur, a sounder assessment of Grange's triumph that day at Franklin Field might be Paul Gallico's retrospective view. He wrote in 1964 that "this chips-down performance must rank with the called home run of Babe Ruth, the tipped-off steals of Ty Cobb, Tilden's danger-line tennis and the Jones' pursuit of four major titles in one year. This was delivering the goods."[31]

After the Penn game, the pace of Grange's life and the commotion surrounding him accelerated. Upon his return to Champaign on the team train, more than ten thousand people awaited Grange and the Illini. He tried to avoid the excitement by slipping out of the last coach of the train, but the crowd spotted him and hoisted him onto the shoulders of several students who led a march through the business district to his fraternity house some two miles away. He was then forced to make two curtain calls at a window and a short speech before the howling crowd would disperse. The following day, the university announced that his number seventy-seven jersey would be retired after the season was completed.[32]

The excitement and hoopla seemed to effect Grange's concentration and play on the field. In a deluge that drenched a standing-room-only crowd of seventy thousand at Memorial Stadium on November 7, the Chicago Maroons and the soaked turf, which Grange described as "a slippery mud unlike the kind we played in against Penn," brought him to a standstill. The *New York Times* reported that "the famous redhead carried the ball from scrimmage seventeen times for gains of eighteen yards and was thrown for a total loss of twenty-six yards." He ended with sixty-four yards of total offense amassed on kickoff and punt returns, one of his worst games as a collegiate. Fortunately for Illini fans, Earl Britton had his best game of the season, booming punts that kept Chicago bottled up deep in its own territory and scoring a touchdown in a 13-6 Illinois victory.[33]

As Grange prepared to play his final game at Memorial Stadium against Wabash College on November 14, he continued to be the object of national attention. Chicago admirers began to circulate petitions to nominate him as a Republican candidate for a special at-large congressional seat. They argued that he would be within six months of the legal age to serve when the Congress elected in 1926 was first scheduled to meet in December 1927 and defied politicians to object that he would be underage. The day after the petition campaign began, rumors circulating in Chicago held that Grange had been offered $40,000 to play three games for the New York Giants of the NFL after his last college game. He refused to deny or confirm the report, and Harry March of the Giants dismissed the rumors at the time. Yet it is clear that Tim Mara, the Giant's owner, did travel to Illinois to make some sort of offer to Grange. The Chicago *Tribune* maintained that he had been "besieged with offers of every description" since the 1924 Michigan game and that more had been piling up since the Penn game, including "contracts to appear in motion pictures, play professional football, and also write for a newspaper syndicate." The *Tribune* also stated that it was understood that University of Illinois officials opposed him playing pro football "but would probably not oppose a career in athletic motion pictures or newspaper writing."[34]

Amid the swirl of publicity, Grange made only a token appearance in the Wabash game, which Illinois won easily, 21-0. The following day, Miami newspapers alleged that Grange had signed a contract to play football in that city on Christmas Day for a syndicate headed by C. C. Pyle and had accepted $5,000 as part of a $25,000 guarantee. When asked about the stories, Grange said, "I know nothing about it." Reporters then descended on Wheaton to seek out Lyle Grange's opinions about his famous son's activities. Lyle maintained that he would not object to Red accepting any of the other numerous offers made to him, but he did not approve of commercialized football. "Every time I read in the paper that Harold has accepted a contract from this or that team, it gives me a shock." The senior Grange added, "I think he's entitled to 'cash in' on the long runs his gridiron fame has brought him. It has been expensive for me to send Harold and his brother Garland through the University. We are not rolling in wealth and I think the public would approve of anything Harold does." At the end of its report on the interview, the *New York Times* noted perceptively that "there probably will break out the most intense argument that sports has ever listened to on amateurism and professionalism" when Grange ended his college career.[35]

Early in the week before his final game with Ohio State at Columbus, the Champaign *News-Gazette* summoned Grange for an interview and accused him of having signed a pro football contract. Grange recalled, "I replied that I had not affixed my signature to any contract and defied them to produce evidence to the contrary. At this point I put on my hat and walked out." Throughout the week he repeatedly denied having signed a professional contract. His purported denial also extended to Coach Zuppke, who had reportedly commanded Grange and Earl Britton (also accused of having signed to play for Pyle in Florida), "If you are ineligible, turn in your suits." Grange did confirm, however, that Pyle, with his consent, had taken action against an automobile company that had used Grange's name in advertising. Reached in Tampa, Florida, where he was negotiating a contract for another game in his proposed postseason pro tour, Pyle stated, "If Grange denies having signed a contract, then he must have some reason for doing so."[36]

During the week, University of Illinois president David Kinley met with Grange and urged him not to accept any offers to play professional football. He later told reporters, "I talked to Harold last week and he told me he was not tied up with anybody and I believe him." After the meeting, athletic director George Huff excused Grange from football practice for two days and advised him to go home to Wheaton and talk matters over with his father. Although Lyle had little to say about his discussions with his son, reporters who questioned him surmised that he had given his consent for Red to play pro football after his last college game. When he returned to campus looking haggard from what he might have supposed was a modern version of the Spanish Inquisition, Grange received the first good news he had heard in days. Ohio State athletic director L. W. St. John announced that he would not challenge Grange's eligibility or ask for an investigation of rumors concerning a pro contract. Meanwhile, Big Ten commissioner John L. Griffith, who had been waffling on the question of whether signing a professional football contract violated any conference regulation, proclaimed that any athlete signing such a contract forfeited amateur standing. He added, however, that he had investigated reports to this effect concerning Grange and "was positive that Grange had signed no contract."[37]

If he thought his week of torment was almost over, Grange was mistaken. He remained in seclusion on the Wednesday evening before the team's last practice for the Ohio State game, admonishing his fraternity brothers not to answer either questions or the telephone. After evading reporters and hurrying to the practice field on Thursday, Grange was confronted outside the locker room by an Associated Press correspondent who held an affidavit sworn by E. P. Albertson of Kokomo, Indiana. Albertson attested that he had seen Grange's signature on a contract with C. C. Pyle making Pyle Grange's agent. The contract with Pyle stipulated that Grange was to receive 45 percent of all income in connection with the use of his name. Albertson further claimed that four other businessmen he named knew of the existence of the contract. In desperation, Grange blurted out his final public denial of professionalism: "They have nothing on me. I have not received a penny. I have not signed a contract. If Pyle were asked the same question he would give the same answer." After Grange abruptly broke off the interview he participated in a short practice with his teammates before preparing to depart with the team for Columbus that evening. On the train, Zuppke asked him for the first time about his future plans. Grange remembered "hedg[ing] by saying I would tell him anything he wanted to know after the game."[38]

As the train carrying the University of Illinois team pulled into Union Station in Columbus just after noon on Friday, it became apparent that the impending game was the sideshow and that Grange and his future plans were the main attraction. The *New York Times* reported that if the train from Champaign "had been bearing the President, Jack Dempsey and Douglas Fairbanks, it is doubtful if the awaiting crowd would have been any larger." Grange had to squirm and dodge through the crowd to a taxi that passed thousands of spectators lined up along the route to the Great Southern Hotel to catch a glimpse of him. Earl Britton led the interference,

which allowed Grange to make the fifteen-yard dash into the lobby.
Throughout the day Grange remained in seclusion. That evening Zuppke
sent a substitute player to impersonate Grange at a large parade he was
scheduled to lead through the city streets and spared his star player the
excitement and aggravation of doing so. Grange remained locked in his
room, refusing to be photographed or to issue a statement concerning his
future plans.[39]

More than a hundred newspapers, press associations, and other news-
gathering agencies sent correspondents to cover the Saturday game. A
record college football crowd of 85,500 jammed Ohio State's massive stadium to watch Red Grange play his final collegiate game; an estimated
twenty thousand were turned away. The game itself was unremarkable,
with the Illini overpowering an injury-plagued Buckeye team in the first
half and hanging on for a 14-9 victory. Grange carried the ball twenty-one
times from scrimmage for a respectable 113 yards and threw nine passes
for forty-two yards, including a seventeen-yard touchdown completion in
the second period that provided the eventual margin of victory. Despite
failing to make a touchdown, Grange played a solid game, especially on
defense where he intercepted two passes, one of which halted a Buckeye
comeback bid near the end of the game.[40]

Five minutes after the final whistle blew and he had reached the safety
of the Illinois locker room, Grange announced to a hoard of reporters that
he would drop out of college and play professional football. In a muddled
statement apparently designed to divert the media from his intention to
travel to Chicago and sign contracts with Pyle and the Chicago Bears, he
declared that he was leaving that evening for his home in Wheaton and
planned to organize and manage his own pro team, which would play its
first game on Thanksgiving Day probably in Chicago. After Grange show-
ered and dressed, Zuppke, visibly shaken by the announcement, accompanied his star player back to the hotel in a taxi. The trip lasted more than
an hour because Zuppke ordered the cab driver to keep circling as he attempted to change Red's mind. At one point, according to Grange, Zuppke said, "Keep away from professionalism and you'll be another Walter
Camp. Football isn't a game to play for money." Grange replied that Zuppke made a living out of teaching and coaching football, "so what's the
difference if I make a living playing football?" When the taxi finally reached
the hotel the two men had made their cases but parted in disagreement.[41]

Reflecting on the incident many years later, Grange pointed out that "all
the college coaches and athletic directors, they were 100 per cent against

professional football. They thought anybody connected with it was going to hell, you might say. When I joined the Chicago Bears, as far as the University of Illinois was concerned, I would have been more popular if I had joined the Capone mob." After the encounter with Zuppke, Grange packed his bags, climbed down a hotel fire escape to avoid detection, and took the next train for Chicago, where he checked into the Belmont Hotel under an assumed name. The next day he signed a contract with Pyle, making him his manager; they then both signed a contract with Halas and Sternaman of the Bears. Grange was now officially a professional, but it is unclear whether he fully comprehended the firestorm of controversy his signing those contracts would evoke or the rigors that Pyle's deal with the Bears would entail.[42]

6

The Great Debate

THE SAME DAY THAT GRANGE SIGNED the contracts with Pyle and with Halas and Sternaman in Chicago that made him a professional, he attended the Bears game against Green Bay at Cubs Park. Accompanied by Pyle and attired in a sumptuous raccoon coat, Grange entered the field through the baseball dugout and took a seat on the Bears' bench. When the fans saw him, they stood and roared a deafening tribute. Police had to be summoned to prevent a boisterous crowd from mobbing their idol. After the half-time interval, Red remained in the Bears' locker room a full five minutes after the kickoff to prevent further disturbances, but a throng of three thousand fans refused to return to their seats and blocked the runway from the clubhouse to the field until he emerged. When he did appear, it required a squad of police to get him through the frenzied mob and safely back to the bench. The Milwaukee *Sentinel* remarked that "Babe Ruth or Jack Dempsey, in their palmiest days, never were accorded a nosier or more enthusiastic tribute than that which Grange achieved in his first appearance as a professional, even though it was strictly an appearance."[1]

Given the massive and intrusive publicity he had endured during his senior year and the near certainty that it would continue after signing contracts with Pyle and the Bears' owners, why did Grange decide to play professional football? After all, he was a shy, humble, self-effacing small-town midwesterner who disliked publicity and on occasion hinted that he did not like football all that much.[2] The most obvious reason for launching a career in pro football was the money: $100,000 in hard cash. That amount was the equivalent of several million dollars in terms of the 1990s. But Grange could have made substantial sums of money, although possibly not $100,000, in any number of business ventures offered him without subjecting himself to the intense public scrutiny he knew pro football would bring. In addition to the lure of $100,000, Grange's decision to turn professional was based on several factors: his desire for long-term security, his hard-nosed midwestern practicality, his innate honesty, and the influence of Charlie Pyle.

As a boy, Grange had been shunted around from one household to another and later struggled with domestic chores and responsibilities in order to help provide a decent home life for Gardie, his father, and himself. He wanted what he had not had as a youth except on those occasions when the Dollinger family helped provide it—security. The money he could amass, presumably quickly, in pro football would allow him to have the material things denied him as a youth as well as, and more important, the security he craved.

Grange also chose pro football over other business options for a very practical reason. He believed Charlie Pyle's projection that he could make a small fortune in a relatively short time by casting his fate with Pyle and the pro game. For Grange, that meant being able to pay back his father for funding his education, providing for his and his family's future security, being free from the intrusive media and hysterical public in short order, and returning to a normal life. In New Orleans during Pyle's 1926 winter football tour, Grange estimated that his drawing power in professional football and the movies would be over in two years, "but by then" he added, "I'll have enough so I can say when I'll work and where I'll work, and work at what I want." He pointed out confidently that officers of a Champaign bank were investing his earnings in Liberty Bonds and first mortgages on real estate. Already the return on the investments "was several hundred dollars a month."[3]

Grange further believed that when the time came to cash in on his fame, which he never denied doing or regretted, integrity required that he do so by continuing to play football. After signing the professional contracts, he explained one reason for deciding to play pro football: "I have received many alluring offers to enter fields of enterprise in which I have had no training or experience. I believe the public will be better satisfied with my honesty and good motives if I turn my efforts to that field in which I have been most useful in order to reap a reward which will keep the home fires burning."[4]

Although he appreciated the opportunities afforded him at Illinois, Grange was unimpressed by allegations that were already abroad and that would escalate in the coming months: He was said to be betraying his coach, college, and the public by entering the "corrupt world" of pro football. Critics charged that he was making a mockery of higher education and "amateur" college football by dropping out of school and cashing in on the fame he had achieved by attending the University of Illinois. In a statement to reporters shortly after he turned pro, Grange duly thanked his coach and athletic director, the university, the public, and even the press, but he had few illusions about the purity of college sport. The University of Illinois and its athletic officials had provided an education, coaching, and an arena in which to display his enormous talents—but nothing more. Grange was keenly aware of the vast commercial enterprise that college football had become. He pointed out on several occasions that few people would have complained had he signed a contract to play professional baseball. He was, he realized, the victim of a class bias against pro football shared by many associated with the collegiate game. Accusations that he was betraying the college game did not ring true and sometimes angered him. A short time after signing with the Bears, Grange returned to Champaign for a football banquet honoring the Illini team. During the evening, Coach Zuppke gave a speech berating Grange for turning pro and at one point proclaimed that he did not want any more $100,000 football players at Illinois. "I'm somewhat of a bullheaded guy, I guess," Grange recalled, "and that kind of talk riled me up, and I walked out of the banquet (while Zuppke was speaking), and Zuppke and I didn't talk to each other for a couple of years."[5]

Despite his determination to cash in on his fame, Grange might not have summoned the courage to become a pro football player had it not been for Charlie Pyle. The Champaign theater owner had a profound effect on him. Grange had never met a man more articulate, suave, or persuasive. At the time they met, Pyle was everything Grange was not. When asked why Grange, a shy, small-town youth who detested the spotlight, might opt for a career in pro football, his friend Richard Crabb replied that Pyle had "put it in his head. He kicked him in his head. He changed Grange. There isn't any question about that."[6]

Pyle's influence appears to have been an important factor in prompting the retiring young man to challenge the advice of university officials and also conventional wisdom and play professional football. How he accomplished that is not altogether clear. Perhaps Grange saw in him the stylish sophistication and adroitness that was so lacking in his boyhood Wheaton and subconsciously aspired to be part of that world. In later years, when Pyle came to be regarded more and more as a shill and a huckster, Grange went out of his way to defend his former manager and agent. Although he seldom spoke critically about anyone, Grange was particularly protective of Pyle. When sportswriter Myron Cope good-naturedly poked fun at the Bunion Derby, for example, Grange became testy and defensive, describing the transcontinental foot race as "the greatest feat ever put on in this country, from an athletic stand point."[7]

A firestorm of controversy erupted over Grange's decision to quit college before graduating to play professional football. The "great debate" on the merits of his decision and its impact on public perception of higher education in general—and intercollegiate and professional football in particular—would be far-reaching. The controversy concerning the "amateur ethic" associated with college football and the corrupting influences of commercialism and professionalism on the sport was as old as intercollegiate football itself. As a result of the nation's participation in World War I and the role athletics apparently played in training and motivating American soldiers, however, the controversy had been muted for a number of years. During the early fall of 1925, at least in part because of the attention Grange's notoriety was focusing on intercollegiate football, the presidents of some small colleges leveled a blistering attack on the game and emphasized the familiar charges of commercialism and professionalism. A number of sportswriters, notably Grantland Rice, deflected the assault by claiming that the intercollegiate game had largely reformed itself since the turn of the century's lack of regulation. Grange's defection to the professional ranks ignited a new, more intense dispute.[8]

Newspaper opinion to Grange's signing was mixed. The *New York Times,* like many urban eastern newspapers, generally supported his decision, but with a note of sarcasm. In an editorial on November 24, the *Times* expressed "a note of regret" that Red had turned professional but added that when "Grange accepts $10,000 for participating in a single game of football, he is doing well not only for himself but for the community at large. It would have been a distinct social waste if the greatest football genius of the year had set out to make himself a doctor or a lawyer or a real estate agent." The editorial concluded that "there is no reason in morals or esthetics why the rewards should be withheld from the most famous name in the American ice industry since Eliza crossed the Ohio in front of the bloodhounds" in Harriet Beecher Stowe's *Uncle Tom's Cabin.*[9]

The Peoria *Journal,* like many midwestern newspapers, assumed a more serious tone in likening Grange to U.S. Army colonel Billy Mitchell, who had testified in his presidential court-martial that he was "ashamed of the cloth" he wore as an aviator. Referring to the opportunity the University of Illinois provided Grange, the *Journal* maintained that his turning professional before graduation "must be distinctly harmful to any institution in that it confirms critics who contend colleges have gone daft on interscholastic athletic contests and that education has been lost in the shuffle." The editorial pointed out that "without the 'cloth,' we probably never should have heard of 'Red' Grange or Colonel Mitchell." Along a similar line, a Cleveland *Plain Dealer* editorial chastised Grange for quitting school because he had "undoubtedly harmed college football, and has done a disservice to the institution which he has represented on the athletic field."[10]

During the weeks after Grange joined the Bears, college administrators, athletic directors, football coaches, and their allies lashed out at Grange, professional football, and promoters like Pyle, who, they claimed, sullied the good names of higher education and intercollegiate football. Many college presidents, such as Kinley of Illinois, chose to remain publicly silent, confident that the storm would pass and the prestige of American universities would endure. Kinley and his colleagues must have been vexed, however, if they read a *Christian Science Monitor* editorial on November 23 that concluded with the mocking words, "James Russell Lowell once wrote that a university was a place where nothing useful was taught. How admirably Illinois has answered this slur by so instructing an undergraduate that he could earn a million dollars without even the formality of graduating!"[11] College football officials and their confederates were neither as secure about their institution nor restrained in their responses to the controversy as were most college presidents.

Intercollegiate football was the only major American team sport that was developed on college campuses and remained primarily associated with the universities. Although the game was played elsewhere, even professionally, intercollegiate football epitomized football for most Americans. Only college teams could draw thirty to sixty thousand fans to their games on a consistent basis. College football officials, in effect, controlled the game and were intent on maintaining that role. Because football was developed under the aegis of the English amateur ethic, college officials encouraged high school football and other forms of amateur play, but professional football was regarded, in the words of sportswriter John Underwood, "as a dirty little business run by rogues and bargain-basement entrepreneurs." To understand the intensity of college coaches' and athletic directors' feelings against pro football and what it represented, one must remember that intercollegiate football was heavily influenced by the British-exported doctrine of Muscular Christianity. From its inception on eastern college campuses, the experience of college football was seen to instill good Christian character, "manly achievement, generous rivalry, good sportsmanship, fidelity to amateurism, and loyalty to the university."[12]

One of the nation's foremost defenders of the ideals of intercollegiate football and an opponent of pro football was Amos Alonzo Stagg. A former Yale divinity student and star athlete, Stagg, who followed the precepts of Muscular Christianity, viewed intercollegiate football as a missionary sport that built character and uplifted participants to become model citizens and future leaders of the nation. During the 1880s he turned down offers to play professional baseball out of loyalty to Yale and because "the whole tone of the game was smelly." Stagg remained opposed to pro baseball throughout his life and harbored even stronger feelings against pro football. Referring to "cases of the debauching of high school boys" by professional football promoters, in a 1923 press statement he warned that "to cooperate with Sunday professional football games is to cooperate with forces which are destructive to the finest elements of interscholastic and intercollegiate football and add to the heavy burden of the schools and colleges in preserving it in its ennobling worth." Stagg believed that any boy who earned a college degree and a football letter ought to have the "equipment of character" to do a "man's size job, instead of snatching at the first roll of soft money in sight." Of course, Stagg and Zuppke both earned handsome livings as professional coaches, a fact neither found paradoxical or hypocritical.[13]

Stagg and his fellow coaches and athletic directors were not all wrong in their criticisms of pro football. Like post–Civil War professional baseball, early professional football was chaotic. In his autobiography, George Halas remarked that "paid football was pretty much of a catch-as-catch-can affair. Teams appeared one week and disappeared the next." He might have added that betting on games was frequent, as were allegations of thrown games, dirty play, poor officiating, rowdyism by both players and spectators, and players who jumped contract from one team to another. The practice that most incensed college officials was the custom of hiring intercollegiate players—occasionally entire college teams—to play in Sunday games. In a celebrated incident in 1921, two Illinois semipro teams hired most of the University of Illinois and Notre Dame starting teams respectively to engage in a grudge game that attracted heavy betting. College athletic officials also complained about the unsavory characters who were attracted to pro football, and often they were right. In a 1922 NFL game, Ed Healy, a Chicago Bear lineman, remembered moving in for a crushing tackle on Chicago Cardinal star tailback Paddy Driscoll near the Cardinal bench. "And then, holy cow!" Healy remembered. "Out from the Cardinal bench poured a group of men with rods [guns] on! They were going out there to protect their idol, Paddy Driscoll."[14]

During the late fall and winter of 1925, coaches and athletic directors who attempted to strike a blow against professional football found themselves in a war that had two fronts: one against Grange's decision to turn pro and another to defend the integrity of college football. Grange signing with the Bears also set off a storm of criticism from some college students, professors, and university presidents against intercollegiate football itself. The critics proposed a variety of reforms, ranging from replacing football on campuses with some other sport to limiting intercollegiate football games to three or four a season per team. Other proposals included replacing professional coaches by a graduate coaching system based on a professor's salary, no public sale of tickets, and barring coaches from directing players during games. College athletic officials leaped to the defense of their game with familiar arguments, but their counteroffensive distracted them temporarily from their main purpose: the condemnation of pro football.[15]

In early December the Big Ten Conference struck a small blow against the professional game by adopting a rule that made any person who played football for pay ineligible for any coaching positions at member schools. At a meeting of the American Football Coaches Association later in the month, the coaches voted to ban from membership any person actively engaged in any capacity with professional football and prohibited members from selecting all-star or all-American teams. The reasoning behind the latter resolution was that being named an all-American could lead to a career in pro football. As a sop to the critics of the college game, the coaches recommended that football practices be limited to two hours and not begin before September 15. In general, they demonstrated that they could do little about undermining professional football and had little interest in seriously reforming their own game.[16]

Nonetheless, the attack against Grange and pro football continued. In a scathing article in *The Outlook* magazine in January 1926, "'De-Granging' Football," Herbert Reed maintained that to "grange" a game was to exploit it. The "now rather pathetic 'Red' Grange" had "raised the issue." Reed expanded on the American Football Coaches Association's denial of membership to anyone connected with pro football by suggesting a general ostracism of the professional sport. College football referees, he noted approvingly, were now under a similar ban if they associated themselves with the pro game in any way. "This," Reed proclaimed optimistically, "strips the last rag of respectability from the game." Because the football season was of shorter duration than the baseball season, professional football promoters were unable to offer college players a career such as they might have in baseball. Reed maintained that he knew hundreds of employers who had recruited their staffs from colleges and were intent on keeping pro football players out of their companies. "Call it a boycott if you like," he warned, "but the fact remains that this deadly weapon is already beginning to shoot." He further predicted that Dartmouth's E. K. Hall, chair of the Football Rules Committee and an implacable foe of pro football, would cast his weight against "granged" football. Reed was equally confident that the upcoming generation of potential football players were disgusted by Grange's example. They had been "inoculated against professionalism in sport, and it is taking."[17]

In early 1926, NFL owners gathered in Detroit for their annual winter meeting. In addition to the national controversy raging over Grange turning professional, league president Joe Carr and the owners faced another embarrassing situation: amateur athletes. During a late regular-season NFL game against the Chicago Cardinals, the Milwaukee Badgers had used high school players to fill out their lineup. Carr levied heavy fines against the teams involved, banned the NFL player who recruited the schoolboys from the league for life, and ordered that the Milwaukee franchise be sold.[18]

The owners' next issue concerned the controversy surrounding Grange. Because he had drawn the largest crowds in pro football history and promised to continue as a major attraction, there was no sentiment to censure Grange, the Bears' owners, or C. C. Pyle. Instead, the NFL attempted to placate the college football establishment by passing a resolution that became known as the "Grange Rule." Henceforth no college player could be signed to a professional contract before his class graduated. When Pyle and Grange organized a new professional league (the American Football

League) later that month, a similar resolution was ratified by that upstart league. The Grange Rule did not end the criticism of pro football by college officials in 1926 or immediately thereafter, but over time it did pave the way for more amenable coexistence. By the 1930s the Grange Rule facilitated the inauguration of an annual all-star game between collegians and pros and became a cornerstone of the college draft system, both of which aided the growth of the professional game.[19]

The controversy over football's place in American society continued into the spring of 1926 and beyond, in part because of the Carnegie Foundation for the Advancement of Teaching's decision to investigate college athletics. Carnegie Foundation investigators estimated that about one in seven intercollegiate athletes competing in major sports were receiving illegal aid; for first-class football teams, the figure was close to 50 percent. The 1929 report created a stir and resulted in reforms at some schools, but its impact was only temporary. By the early 1930s, subsidization and commercialism in big-time college football were escalating again.[20]

One of the many factors contributing to this trend was Grange's influence on intercollegiate football. During the years after he completed his college career, football coaches nationwide eagerly searched for the next Red Grange who might bring them a championship and fill their stadiums. In 1926 the media projected Forrest "Frosty" Peters as Grange's successor at Illinois; three years later Barry Wood of Harvard and Chris Cagel of West Point were touted as likely to supplant the Galloping Ghost; and in 1931 sportswriters were certain that Ernest Rentner, Northwestern's "Flying Dutchman," would more than fill Grange's shoes. Later in the decade, Chicago high school sensation Bill DeCorrevont and University of Michigan star Tom Harmon were publicized as the next Red Grange, and the process continued. Meanwhile, the stadium-building boom progressed, with a slight interruption during the depression, to ensure that the college fortunate enough to recruit a Grange-like superstar would be in a position to reap financial rewards.[21]

It appears likely that the search for the next Grange contributed to the Carnegie Report's limited impact and helped intensify abuses that the study linked with college football. There was some irony in that turn of events. Illinois was one of the twenty-eight schools that Carnegie investigators gave a clean bill of health. Grange had been not been heavily recruited, nor did he receive significant subsidization during his college days. Paul Gallico best summed up this paradox in 1964: "It is an interesting irony that he

[Grange] should in a way have been responsible for the corruption of so many colleges. Having witnessed the tremendous gates resulting from a unique attraction, they then fractured the amateur codes into so many pieces trying to locate, hire or buy similar stars, that they have not yet been able to put them together again."[22]

7

The Grand Eastern Tour

☆ ☆

AS THE RENEWED AND INTENSIFIED DEBATE over the role of intercollegiate football in American life began in late November 1925 the eyes of much of the nation were focused on Grange and his debut as a professional football player. After only three days of practice Grange was scheduled to play his first NFL game for the Bears on Thanksgiving Day against the league-leading Chicago Cardinals. Interest was so great that the twenty thousand tickets the Bears had printed were sold in three hours on the Monday before the game. George Halas had more tickets printed, and a standing-room-only crowd of thirty-six-thousand fans jammed Cubs Park to witness one of the most publicized football games in history. Outside the park, police battled with an estimated twenty thousand would-be spectators who had been denied admission. Before the game got underway, a number of the outcast fans broke down a gate in the left-field section of the park in an effort to gain entrance, but Chicago police drove them off. The game itself, played in damp and chilling weather on a muddy field, was an anticlimax.[1]

Cardinal tailback and punter Paddy Driscoll, until that time the highest-paid pro football player, made a reported $500 per game and was determined neutralize Grange and achieve victory over the cross-town rival Bears by punting away from him. The strategy, aided by the soggy field, worked well; Grange returned only three of Driscoll's numerous punts. Grange, with "77" sewn on his Bears' jersey, returned those errant punts for fifty-six yards, marking his best offensive performance of the day. From scrimmage, he ran the ball sixteen times for a mere thirty-six yards and failed to complete any of his six forward passes. His most noteworthy feat of the day was intercepting a pass under his own goalposts, which foiled the Cardinal's best scoring opportunity of the game in the third period. For a good part of the afternoon the frigid fans amused themselves by booing and hissing Driscoll for his reluctance to loft punts in Grange's direction. Driscoll later explained, "It was a question of which of us would look bad—Grange or Driscoll. I decided it wouldn't be Paddy." When the game ended in a scoreless tie, thousands of fans swarmed onto the field and tried to reach Grange, but police rescued him and escorted him to safety. George Halas, who reputedly cried while counting the record gate receipts, later remarked on Grange's impact, "There had never been such evidence of public interest since our professional league began in 1920. I knew then and there that pro football was destined to be a big-time sport."[2]

Halas had good reason to weep for joy at the gate receipts, as well as at the knowledge that the Bears' upcoming home game that Sunday with the little-known Columbus Tigers, strictly a road team in the NFL, was already a sell-out. The Bears, like other NFL teams during the early 1920s, had struggled for their very survival. Pro football began as a regional sport that was mainly confined to small cities in the Midwest. When the American Professional Football Association (renamed the NFL at the suggestion of Halas two years later) was organized in 1920, Buffalo and Rochester were the only eastern teams in the fourteen-team league. Franchises were cheap (only $100 when the league was founded, although few owners actually paid), and that led many "tank towns" such as Rock Island, Duluth, and Racine to join the NFL. The pro game was not very profitable, drew crowds that averaged only a few thousand, and was generally not much respected as a sport. John Underwood exaggerated only slightly when he wrote, "People who patronized professional football were thought to be of a caliber you now associate with Roller Derby."[3]

By 1925 pro football had spread into the East, and a team was reestablished in New York City when Tim Mara, a Tammanyite politician and bookmaker, bought the Giant franchise at the behest of NFL president Joe Carr for $2,500, stating that a franchise on anything in New York must be worth at least that much. Even the Bears, one of the best teams in the early 1920s, averaged about five thousand fans for home games and were a shoestring operation. Grange recalled that Halas "would sell tickets and then go to the locker room to tape the players' ankles. After the game, he personally would go around to the Chicago papers to get a little story on the sports pages."[4]

Halas was ecstatic when twenty-eight thousand hardy Chicagoans braved a heavy snowstorm on November 29 to watch the Bears play the winless Columbus team in a game that without Grange might have drawn a few thousand fans at best. Halas had been advertising "see the Chicago Bears with Red Grange," but the ads read "see Red Grange with the Chicago Bears" after the Columbus game. Grange played a much better game than in his pro debut despite an icy field, running for seventy-nine yards from scrimmage and accounting for nearly 140 yards in total offense in the Bears' unimpressive 14-13 victory.[5]

After the game, Halas and Sternaman announced the signing of Earl Britton, Grange's college teammate and premier blocker, to play in the Bears' remaining games. Chicago also added two former Illinois linemen and Johnny Bryan, a former University of Chicago back, to its roster. One of the enduring myths about Grange was that he was the first important college player to play pro football. In fact, dozens of all-American college players had played in the NFL before Grange, and the overwhelming majority of pro players were college men. Grange and Britton, however, were among a lesser number of players who had dropped out of college to join the pro ranks before their class graduated. It was the professionals' practice of raiding intercollegiate or even high school teams for players that particularly infuriated college officials.[6]

After the Columbus game, the Bears embarked on the first of two tours that were to become the highlight of the 1925–26 professional football season, the first from mid-November to approximately December 13, 1925, and the second from approximately December 26, 1925, to January 30, 1926. Chicago had five scheduled games remaining with NFL opponents. To use the term *scheduled games* in the early NFL, however, is misleading. The NFL schedule that team owners determined before the season was often amended as the season progressed. Teams contending for the league championship (decided on the basis of the best winning percentage) routinely added or dropped games toward the end of a season based on their projection of how they might gain the best winning percentage. Halas and Sternaman, most likely with input from Pyle, had road games scheduled with Frankford (Philadelphia), New York, Providence, and Detroit as well as a final game against the Giants at Cubs Park.[7]

Beyond this formidable NFL schedule, Pyle, whom Chicago sportswriter Westbrook Pegler had dubbed "Cash and Carry," added non-league games against makeshift pro teams in St. Louis, Washington, and Pittsburgh. In just twelve days, between December 2 and 13, the Chicago Bears were going to play eight football games. Such a murderous schedule meant that Pyle clearly knew very little about pro football, but Halas and Sternaman should have known better. Early NFL teams generally carried from fifteen to eighteen players, and the starting eleven played all or most of the game, in part from pride and also because of the substitution rules. Grange was only required to play thirty minutes per game under his contract, but he would likely be a special target for opposition tacklers. The tour was suicidal. It had nothing to do with good football or competing for an NFL championship and everything to do with making money by exploiting the Grange phenomenon to its fullest.[8]

The tour began in St. Louis on a bitterly cold day against a hastily assembled team called the Donnelly Stars that was sponsored by a local mortician. With the temperature hovering at twelve degrees, a midweek crowd of only eight thousand braved the elements to watch Grange play one of his best games of the tour. He scored four touchdowns on short rushes, ran for eighty-four yards from scrimmage, accounted for seventy-three yards throwing and receiving passes, and made the longest gain of the day on a thirty-three-yard punt return. The Bears easily defeated the over-matched Stars 39-6. Jimmy Conzelman, on temporary leave from the NFL Detroit Panthers, made the only St. Louis touchdown. When Grange sat out most of the second and third periods the crowd put up several yells for his return. A deputy sheriff briefly interrupted the game when he served garnishment papers on Grange, the result of a lawsuit against the Pyle Motor Service Company, allegedly owned by Charlie Pyle. The game was typical of the tour in that it was played in bad weather, Grange's teammates allowed him to make touchdowns whenever possible, he sat on the bench for long stretches of time, and fans became restless during his absences and demanded his return to action.[9]

After the St. Louis game, Grange and the Bears enjoyed the first tour's longest period of rest between games, two days, although one was spent on a train bound for the East. In Philadelphia, some of the major sportswriters of the day, including Grantland Rice, Damon Runyon, and Ford Frick from New York newspapers and Westbrook Pegler of Chicago, covered the Bears' game with the Frankford Yellow Jackets and remained with the Bears for most of the remaining eastern games. "I knew pretty well after that that pro football had come a long way," Grange remembered, when prominent sportswriters began to follow the tour. The game at Schibe Park, which attracted thirty-five thousand fans, reminded Grange of his first appearance in Philadelphia a few weeks earlier in that it was played on a cold, rainy day that turned the field into a quagmire. He turned in what the *New York Times* described as "a worthy performance under the conditions" by scoring both Chicago touchdowns on short runs after setting up the first score on a twenty-yard pass reception and the second on a twenty-yard pass to halfback Johnny Mohardt. Chicago defeated the stubborn Yellow Jackets 14-7 in a game shortened by darkness. Although Grange only played one full period and part of two others, the fans were satisfied with what they saw. After the game, the Chicago players, still in muddy uniforms, rushed to the train station to catch the last train for New York where they were scheduled to play the Giants the following afternoon. As they changed out of their mud-soaked equipment, the players realized they would have to wear the same soggy gear the next day. The ever-present Pyle turned to Halas, who also played end for the team, and assured him, "This tour will make you so wealthy, Halas, that next year you'll be able to afford two sets of uniforms."[10]

The invasion of New York by Grange and the Bears proved to be both the highlight and the undoing of the first tour. Because the game had been announced two weeks earlier, the New York media had publicized the coming of Red Grange as only they knew how. Allison Danzig of the *New York Times,* emphasizing the rural-urban division that was a prominent issue during the 1920s, described Grange as "the youth who has arisen from the obscurity of a Middle Western village to the position of the most advertised athlete the world probably has ever known." He further tried to account for the mass appeal of athletic celebrities such as Grange by suggesting that his many admirers were "victims in common of that fetish for hero worship which is inspired by the man of might on the baseball diamond, in the boxing ring or on the football gridiron. They were attracted to Red Grange because he is the living symbol of the power and the glory that all aspire to and dream of and which only the chosen few attain."[11]

Because of the intense publicity and extraordinary interest in Grange, the city, under its new mayor James J. Walker, assigned a special detail of fifty police to escort the famous redhead to his dressing room. Two hundred and fifty other patrolmen were disbursed to handle the expected record crowd at the Polo Grounds. To further heighten interest, Pyle issued a statement assuring fans that Grange, barring injury, would play the entire game. Although estimates of the official attendance vary, based on the net gate receipts of $142,000 it seems likely that between seventy and seventy-two thousand fans jammed every nook and cranny of the Polo Grounds, which seated sixty-five thousand, to watch Grange play. It was the largest gathering ever to see a football game in New York and by far the biggest crowd in pro football history. The game likely saved the NFL franchise in New York. Giant owner Tim Mara, who had rolled up a debt of $35,000 in his first season in the league with no relief in sight, recalled, "When I saw that crowd and knew that half the cash in the house was mine, I said to myself, 'Timothy, how long has this gravy train been running.'"[12]

Grange responded to the massive crowd by playing his best all-around game of the two tours. Despite a muddy field he rushed for fifty-three yards from scrimmage in eleven attempts, completed two passes for thirty-two yards, caught one pass for twenty-three yards, and ran back two kicks for thirteen yards. Beyond that, he threw the key block that allowed quarterback Joey Sternaman, the star of the game, to score one of his two touchdowns. In the final period Grange secured Chicago's 19-7 victory when he intercepted a Giant pass and sprinted thirty-five yards for a touchdown. He accomplished all this in about thirty-five minutes, a little more than half the time that Pyle had promised New York fans they could expect to see his client on the field.[13]

During that time, the Giants appeared intent on roughing up Grange, who later described the game as "one of the most bruising battles I had ever been in." In the second period after Grange knocked down a Giant pass, Westbrook Pegler described how "Red was slugged with a Firpoesque slam on the back of the headgear by [Joe] Williams of the Giants, who had been sent out to receive the throw." The Chicago *Tribune* sportswriter related that "Red stumbled unsteadily but did nothing about it, and neither did the officials who were about as hostile to fist fighting as Tex Rickard is, all afternoon." When Grange returned to action in the final period, Pegler continued, "Red was kicked on the forearm by [Tommy] Tomlin of the Giants' front line and it wasn't long after that till Joe Alexander, the Giants' center, stopped him in a line play and squatted on the ground with Grange in his lap, trying to twist his head off to see what kind of sawdust he's stuffed with. The officials told Alexander he oughtn't to do that but didn't charge him anything for it."[14]

After the game, Grange, battered and bruised and suffering from a head cold as a result of his afternoon's work, gave a radio address in support of Near East Relief, a talk heard in a dozen cities from Washington, D.C., to St. Paul, Minnesota. Although reporters speculated that he had earned $30,000 for his thirty-five minutes of play against the Giants, Grange assured listeners that football's "rewards are spiritual rather than material, but they are certain." The following morning, while the rest of the Bears enjoyed a rare day off, Pyle, with Grange at his side, set up shop in Grange's suite at the Astor Hotel to welcome all endorsement proposals. According to George Halas, Pyle, who was shaving, pointed his straight-edge razor at Grange and said, "Son, this is the blade that knows no brother. We are going to take a deep cut at the dough on Old Broadway, let the gyps fall where they may." Grange remembered that "the only thing I needed to do was just meet the people. I never had any part in the discussions or anything." To heighten interest in the endorsement auction, Pyle wrote out a check for $300,000 and flashed it around to the press, claiming it was payment for a movie contract Grange had signed. Grange remembered it as "strictly a friendly promotion, and we didn't receive anything near that amount, but he had a lot of people believing it." The *New York Times* reported the next day that Grange would receive the $300,000 from the Arrow Production Company to make one movie in March. His only comment was that "he had refused to be a 'sheik.'" From that point on during the two tours, Grange's teammates called him "Rudy" in reference to Rudolph Valentino, who had played the romantic role of a sheik in a recent film.[15]

Pyle and Grange secured endorsement contracts totaling an estimated $40,000, excluding the bogus movie check. Grange remembered that Pyle "wasn't afraid to talk money. When the average guy would say $5,000, Pyle would say twenty-five or thirty thousand. He got mostly cash. Cash or check. He didn't fool around." In New York, Grange agreed to endorse a sweater ($12,000), a football doll ($10,000), shoes ($5,000), ginger ale ($5,000), a cap ($2,500), and even a meat loaf. He balked at a $10,000 offer to say he smoked a certain brand of cigarettes but accepted $1,000 from the tobacco firm to use his name in advertising with the stipulation that no insinuation would be made that he smoked. During the course of the next year, Grange would add another dozen or more endorsements to those obtained in New York. As he later observed, "I guess I was the first football player to have a manager or business partner like that." In fact, Grange's endorsements and their commercial success would pave the way for future football stars to cash in on their fame, as Honus Wagner, Ty Cobb, Babe Ruth, and others had earlier done in baseball.[16]

Despite his athletic and commercial triumphs in New York, Grange, apparently still tormented by the controversy that surrounded him, departed the city on a defensive note. "I have been criticized for leaving college and turning professional," he told reporters. "If I were a baseball player and joined the Chicago Cubs or the White Sox there would be no criticism, but because I happen to be a football player there seems to be some question of the ethics of my decision."[17] When Grange and his teammates boarded the train en route to their next game in Washington they were exhausted and bruised, the cumulative result of playing five games in the eleven days since Thanksgiving. What was worse, the Bears were scheduled to play three games in the next three days. By the time he reached the nation's capital, Grange's left arm was beginning to swell, most likely as a result of a bruise he had sustained in St. Louis and aggravated by a blow from Tommy Tomlin at the Polo Grounds.

At the American League Park before a disappointing crowd of seven thousand, the Bears played the Washington All-Stars, "a tough bunch of sandlot players who mauled and roughed us up at every opportunity" in Grange's description. Chicago prevailed over Washington 19-0 in a game marred by a fistfight, but Grange did little except appear on the field for his contracted thirty minutes and drop-kick an extra point. He carried the ball eleven times for a net gain of only eight yards. For Grange, the highlight of the day was meeting President Calvin Coolidge at the White House. George Halas may be the source of an anecdote that Grange frequently recalled over the years: After Grange was introduced to the president as "Red Grange, who plays with the Chicago Bears" the tight-lipped Coolidge shook his hand and said, "Nice to meet you, young man, I've always liked animal acts." The *New York Times* reported that after Senator William McKinley of Illinois introduced Grange to Coolidge, "The President shook hands, asked him where he lived and wished him luck."[18]

Before leaving Washington for New England, Grange admitted to a correspondent for the New York *Evening Post,* "Gee, I'm tired. I'm played out, pipped." Sporting two blackened eyes and a bruised nose in addition to his injured arm, he admitted, "It's not all as easy as I thought. And the criticism—whew!" "I went into this thing for all I could get," he stated. "I'm getting it—in the neck." The midweek game against the NFL Providence Steam Roller, which had been shifted to Boston's Braves Field to maximize attendance, could not have been played under worse conditions as far as the battered Bears were concerned. At kickoff time the temperature was six degrees below zero and the field was frozen solid. Whenever possible, runners headed for the sidelines rather than risk being tackled on the hard turf. To boost the gate, Steam Roller general manager Charles Coppen had hired a group of former college stars, including Don Miller and Jim Crowley, who were two of Notre Dame's famed Four Horsemen, and Fritz Pollard, a former Brown all-American halfback who had played the 1925 season with the Akron Pros. This became a common practice for Bears' opponents during their second tour, as former college players tried to cash in on the Grange phenomenon. Despite the promotional efforts, severe weather conditions and high ticket prices for the Wednesday game restricted the crowd to about fifteen thousand.[19]

Boston fans gave Grange an enthusiastic reception. Three thousand mobbed him before the game and forced him to warm up in an area the size of a clothes closet. But their adulation did not last long. Grange played his obligatory two periods but with limited results. He carried the ball five times for eighteen yards, threw three passes with no completions, and had another pass intercepted. "My arm was in such pain I couldn't do anything right," he remembered. The climax of the game came in the third period when Steam Roller punter Red Maloney intentionally booted the ball directly at Grange, who stood dead in his tracks and deliberately allowed the ball to sail over his head and out of bounds. A Providence *Journal* reporter recounted that "the freezing fans, with the fickleness of a mob, rose as one man at the end of the third quarter when a substitute left halfback trotted on to the field and booed and hissed and jeered with cries of 'get the ice tongs'" as Number Seventy-seven left the game. When the final whistle blew, Providence had upset Chicago 9-6, ending the Bears' unbeaten string since Grange had joined the team on Thanksgiving Day. "As Grange went down the hole to his dressing room and the mob pressed in on him, mocking the fellow whose name was something of a national boast a few weeks ago," Pegler reported, "one of the civilian handlers of the Bears, took a smack at the nearest of Red's tormentors and a brawl began that surged over a full acre and needed lots of cops." Grange remembered being booed for the first time in his career in Boston and learned that "a pro must deliver, or else."[20]

After an all-night journey to Pittsburgh, the Bears played the next day on the icy turf at Forbes Field against the local All-Stars. The Bears were so desperate for able-bodied players, Grange recalled, that "we suited up our trainer, Andy Lotshaw, who was a big guy, but he had never played football and we put him in as tackle. He played about half a game before they killed him. Not literally, of course." Grange himself lasted for only ten plays into the first period before being struck on his injured arm, forcing him to retire for the afternoon. Many in the crowd of 4,111 booed him as he walked sluggishly to the dressing room. The All-Stars went on to overwhelm the listless Bears by a score of 24-0.[21]

Gustav Berg, team physician for the Pittsburgh Pirates baseball club, diagnosed Grange's injury as a torn ligament and a broken blood vessel in the arm and recommended that he rest for two weeks or more. George Halas, who had earlier predicted that his star player would be able to play in three or four days, promptly ordered a second opinion. Charlie Pyle, who the press and some of the Bears would blame for the foolhardy schedule of games that led to Grange's injury, was on the West Coast making arrangements for a second tour. The following day in Detroit, where Chicago had a game with the NFL Panthers, a second physician confirmed the diagnosis and warned that a blot clot that had formed in Grange's arm could prove fatal if it reached his heart. He put Grange's arm in a sling and ordered an extended rest. Grange watched from the sideline as the Panthers decisively defeated the weary Bears 21-0. Despite his obvious pain, Grange was introduced to the sparse crowd at half-time. After it had been announced that he would not play, nine thousand fans exchanged their tickets for a refund at the gate. Detroit coach Jimmy Conzelman was irate because, he claimed, Chicago had not contracted the games in Washington, Boston, and Pittsburgh when the Detroit game had been arranged. The Panthers folded after the 1926 season, and NFL football did not return to the Motor City until the Lions entered the league in 1934. Conzelman was convinced that the struggling Panther franchise would have survived if only Grange had played that day.[22]

Even before Grange's injury in Pittsburgh, a Champaign newspaper reported that Lyman "Beans" DeWolf, Grange's friend and former Wheaton schoolmate, would join him on the tour in the capacity of personal adviser, confidant, and secretary. The story related that the addition of DeWolf to Grange's retinue "was urged by Grange's father." Red was already receiving personal advice and assistance on the tour from Marion "Doc" Cooley and Dinty Moore, two pals from the University of Illinois. The addition of DeWolf to his entourage indicates that Grange was beginning to feel more like a victim than the feature performer in the Pyle-Halas traveling show. Despite the concerns he and his father had about the effect of the tour on Red's reputation and physical well-being, the younger Grange was determined to see it through so he would be "set for life."[23]

Chicago played its final game of the first tour against the New York Giants at Cubs Park on December 13. Grange, without the sling, was on the bench and wrapped in his raccoon coat. With him out of action, the Bears made refunds at the gate to thousands of ticket-holders, but still fifteen thousand fans attended the game. The Giants subdued the stubborn but sluggish Bears 9-0. James Crusinberry reported in the Chicago *Tribune* that "when the combat was over the weary Bears dragged themselves off the field as if they wished to go to bed for the rest of the season. Undoubtedly they are convinced that one must be a superman to play football five times a week." After the game, a dozen policemen escorted Grange out of the park and into a waiting taxi to protect him from the admiring throng. The following day Halas announced that a game with the NFL Cleveland Bulldogs scheduled for the next Sunday had been canceled. The most arduous tour in football history was over.[24]

A number of commentators have asserted that Grange's debut in pro football was the making of the professional sport. George Halas was closer to the mark when he stated during the eastern tour, "We have been doing well in professional football and making money for several seasons. We were gaining ground steadily but slowly." That was not true for all NFL teams, but the pro game by the mid-1920s had already emerged from the chaotic dark age of the 1910s and early 1920s. Grange's first eight games as a pro, however, did bring pro football to the attention of sports fans as never before. In those games he played before more than 175,000 fans, many of them viewing a professional football game for the first time. Millions of others read extensive newspaper accounts about Grange and the tour. How many spectators or readers became converts to pro football as a result of that experience remains in doubt. Michael Oriard has argued convincingly that fans came out to see Grange rather than professional football and that few became loyal followers of the pro game. He maintains that pro football like other sports of the 1920s was rooted locally and "could not connect with fans outside the relatively few cities where franchises were located."[25] Football fans could identify with Red Grange, but their interest did not carry over to the NFL in this pre-television era. Although Oriard's observations are correct, the game made substantial short-term incremental progress before television exposure made it a national sport. As a result of Grange's tour, major sportswriters watched and wrote about pro football for the first time, and many continued to follow the game after interest in Grange diminished. The expanded coverage was a small but important step forward for professional football.

The fact that Grange turned pro also helped the NFL evolve from a distinctly small-time operation in 1925 to a more firmly established league by the early 1930s. Given the history of major league baseball, it seems clear that the NFL of the mid-1920s was changing from a league burdened with too many marginal franchises in small cities to one that was beginning to recognize that success and prosperity were linked to promoting teams in larger cities. When Grange arrived on the scene, Joe Carr was already moving cautiously in that direction. In terms of weeding out some of the tank town franchises that made up the NFL, however, he was impeded by the facts that they had been the core of the league when it was founded in 1920 and their owners remained a considerable force in NFL affairs. After Grange demonstrated that pro football could potentially attract crowds of thirty, forty, and even seventy thousand to a single game, it was difficult to resist the process of transforming the NFL from an organization based on small franchises primarily surrounding the Ohio Valley to one grounded in larger cities. Such a transformation was inevitable if the league were to prosper, but Grange's impact on pro football speeded the transition.[26]

Grange did not play up to his college standard in his first eight pro games. He scored seven touchdowns (four against the makeshift team in St. Louis), kicked one extra point, and gained about 655 yards. After his superb performance and injury in New York he could do little more than go through the motions on the field. A few observers both then and later claimed that the public became disillusioned with Grange and pro football as a result of the tour. Frankford Yelllow Jacket player-coach Guy Chamberlin maintained that "Grange broke down mentally and physically, because more was asked of him than any human being could perform. The pro players on other teams were affected by the Grange splurge, and the public is disillusioned." That might be partially true. The problem, however, was not Grange but the tour itself. It was an ill-conceived and murderous series of games played at the end of a hard season that eventually maimed not only Grange but also most of the Chicago team. Playing ten games in seventeen days and mainly sleeping on trains on off-days was, Grange remembered, "a killing pace under any circumstances, but especially so when considering the team carried only eighteen men." Most of the games, moreover, were played in abysmal weather. Grange maintained in 1953 that "no other team before or since has ever attempted such a grueling schedule as the 1925 Bears—and I'm sure never will." As disenchanted as he was with the tour and pro football by mid-December 1925, however, Grange was determined to make his fortune while the opportunity existed and prepared himself for the second installment of the Pyle-Halas traveling football show.[27]

8

Barnstorming, Hollywood, and the AFL

☆ ☆

AFTER THE BEARS' FINAL GAME in Chicago, Grange left for Danville, Illinois, to be examined by Dr. E. B. Cooley, the father of one of his personal advisers. The elder Cooley made an X-ray examination of the injured left arm and pronounced that with rest Grange would be able to resume play by Christmas. Three days later he felt fit enough to appear in a benefit show at the Studebaker Theater in Chicago along with numerous vaudeville stars. Meanwhile in New York, the Motion Picture Theater Owners of America threatened to boycott any film in which Grange might appear because his alleged $300,000 deal with the Arrow Picture Corporation was "bunk publicity." Grange refused to discuss the $300,000 film contract at the time, but a few weeks later admitted that it was phony. Pro football received another black eye as the Bears, reinforced with four additional players, prepared to embark for Florida the week before Christmas on the first leg of their second tour. A Chicago newspaper reported that the Milwaukee Badgers had used four high school players in a December 10 game against the Chicago Cardinals.[1]

Unlike the hastily arranged first tour, the Bears traveled in style to Florida and on to the West Coast. Pyle arranged for the players to ride in their own Pullman car ("Bethulla") and have a personal porter to handle their baggage. He also had them outfitted in sweaters imprinted with the word

Bears, matching knickers, and knee socks. Earl Britton remembered that the players called the Pullman car the "Dog House" and "everybody learned to bark like a dog." Barnstorming—teams traveling from town to town during the off-season to play exhibition games for profit—was an established practice in professional baseball but relatively new to pro football. Fritz Pollard and the American Professional Football Association champion Akron Pros had conducted one of the first pro football barnstorming tours in California after the 1920 season but without much success. Pyle and the Bears had scheduled a much more extensive trip that would begin in South Florida, end in Seattle, and eventually cover more than seven thousand miles.[2]

When the team arrived in Miami for a game against the Coral Gables Collegians, scheduled for Christmas Day in that Miami suburb, Florida was in the midst of a building boom. Advertised as "America's Most Beautiful Suburb," Coral Gables had more than a thousand houses and other structures under construction. William Jennings Bryan had once been engaged by the community's principal landowner to sit under an umbrella on a raft in a lagoon to help sell lots to a crowd assembled on the shore. Three days before the game, however, there was no place to play a football game except for an open field where the Bears had been directed to practice. The following day, two hundred carpenters went to work and built a wooden stadium seating twenty-five thousand. "They sold tickets ranging up to $20 apiece," Grange recollected, "and the next day they tore down the stadium. You'd never know a ball game had taken place there."[3]

George Halas was shocked by the miserable condition of the playing field. He immediately telephoned New York and ordered new shoes with long spikes that would improve footing, including a pair with a hard toe for his kicker, Earl Britton. Britton protested that the hard toe wouldn't be "worth a damn for punting," but Halas ordered him to wear the shoes in the game anyway. After Britton booted two mammoth punts, nearly fifty yards up and fifty yards straight down, Halas relented and allowed his punter to change shoes. Britton would later redeem himself as the Bears defeated the Collegians, most of them pro players who had attended Pennsylvania colleges, 7-0. Sporting a black eye he had received in a practice scrimmage, Grange was the outstanding player of the game, making two long runs and scoring the winning touchdown on a short plunge. Financially the game was a disappointment. Fewer than eight thousand attended, primarily because of ticket prices more than five times higher than normal NFL rates. As was the case with a number of games on the second tour, Pyle's contract called for a sizable guarantee and allowed local promoters to set ticket prices. The promoters set the prices too high, which helped account for smaller crowds than anticipated.[4]

At the Bears' next stop in Tampa, Grange would face football legend Jim Thorpe and a team composed primarily of his teammates from the Rock Island Independents. Grange recalled that Thorpe, thirty-seven, was pathetically out of shape, fumbled several times, and had lost his former speed. "I never saw him in his prime," Grange declared, "but Halas did and he said he lived up to his clippings." Pyle had arranged a more reasonable schedule for the second tour, and the players had a week to bask in the Florida sunshine before the New Year's Day game against Thorpe's team, which local promoters had named the Tampa Cardinals. Although he had good friends on the Bears' team, half of whom were University of Illinois alumni, Grange also fraternized with the rich and famous. When he was arrested for driving sixty-five miles an hour in Tampa on the eve of the game, Grange was accompanied by Jim Barnes, the British golf champion; Helen Wainwright, an Olympic swimming champion; and Johnny Farrell, a golf professional from New York. With a game scheduled the following day in Jacksonville and the temperature around 80 degrees, Grange played only thirty minutes against the Cardinals. He was ineffective until the final period, when he broke away on a seventy-yard touchdown run that elated the crowd. The touchdown broke a 3-3 tie, and the Bears went on to win 17-3. Despite another small crowd of eight thousand, Pyle collected a $10,000 guarantee from local promoters. Before leaving Tampa, Grange and Pyle each invested $17,000 in local real estate, an unfortunate decision because a devastating hurricane later that year ended the Florida land boom of the 1920s.[5]

The Bears' game against the Jacksonville All-Stars was the most highly publicized of the Florida exhibitions because of the presence of Stanford's triple-threat all-American Ernie Nevers in the local team's lineup. Next to Grange, Nevers was the most publicized football player of the mid-1920s. Stanford coach Glenn "Pop" Warner, who had also coached Thorpe in college, considered Nevers a better all-around player than his former Carlisle star. Shortly before Christmas, promoter John O'Brien had signed Nevers for a reported $50,000 to play five exhibition games in Florida, of which the Bears' game was the first. Nevers would play in a second game against the New York Giants before an injury forced him to abandon the exhibition tour. O'Brien was so excited about the impending game with the Bears that he announced to Pyle, "I aim to cover the South with announcements that no red-blooded man should miss the titanic struggle between the Galloping Ghost and the Lion of the Sierras—Red and Ernie. It will be a sell-out with lamentable numbers turned away at the gate." With ticket prices ranging from $5.50 to $8.50 (four times the normal NFL rate), however, only 6,700 turned out for the heralded contest. Pyle was not overly disturbed by the sparse crowd because he had already collected a $20,000 guarantee and shared in 65 percent of the net receipts.[6]

The game did not live up to advance publicity because neither of the highly touted stars performed any spectacular feats. Grange threw a twenty-six-yard touchdown pass to end Vern Mullen for the Bears' first score but gained little yardage in only five carries. Nevers showed some of his triple-threat potential by completing eight passes, doing some excellent punting, and scoring a late touchdown on a five-yard plunge, but his repeated fumbles helped Chicago register a 19-6 victory. Halas remembered the contest as "a dirty game" that at one point resulted in some of the Bears chasing an offending All-Star player into the stands. O'Brien and the Jacksonville promoters reportedly lost nearly $12,500 on the game. With their game with the New Orleans All-Southerners not scheduled for more than a week, the Chicago contingent enjoyed a leisurely junket along the Gulf Coast to the Crescent City.[7]

In New Orleans, Halas had the Pullman parked in a remote part of the railroad yard and put lineman Ed Healy in charge of the players while he, Ed "Dutch" Sternaman, Pyle, and Grange moved into the Roosevelt Hotel. Before he had much time to enjoy the easy pace of life in New Orleans, however, Grange was engulfed in another controversy. In Chicago, Archie Schatz, known in the theatrical world as Johnny Small, sued him for $50,000 damages for breach of contract. Schatz, who was from Wheaton, claimed that Grange had entered into a thirty-two-week vaudeville contract with him the previous August. Grange was to receive $2,000 a week to perform on stage. He immediately denied the charges but made a $750 out-of-court settlement with Schatz in April. The settlement further indicated that Grange had not been forthright in revealing the extent of his commercial interests while still a college player.[8]

Before the game, the Bears were guests at Fair Grounds Racetrack to watch the feature race, the Red Grange Handicap. Prickly Heat was the winner, and Grange appeared in the winner's circle to present the jockey with a massive pink floral football. The publicity stunt did not do much to generate interest in the football game, however, because only six thousand fans attended the contest at Heinemann Park. Chicago easily subdued the local team led by Tulane star Lester Lautenschlager 14-0, its fourth straight victory on the tour. The team's success was not unexpected. The Bears' opponents, despite some exceptional individual stars, were of dubious quality and did not enjoy the advantage of having played together before. Grange scored one of the Bears' touchdowns in New Orleans on a short plunge and electrified the crowd with a fifty-one-yard punt return that was reduced by thirty yards because of a holding penalty.[9]

After the game and before leaving for the Bears' next stop on the West Coast, Grange gave an interview to local reporters and attempted to counter some of the criticism leveled against him. He might have been motivated by the Schatz affair or by the steady stream of what he considered to be misleading stories written about him. According to one version of the interview, Grange began by saying, "I'm tired of being a target. I want to do a little shooting myself. I've got a few things I want to get off my chest." He commented on a number of subjects, ranging from the number of his alleged girl friends (none, although he reportedly received two hundred thousand fan letters from women in 1925) to his now familiar justification for joining the Bears. Newspaper reports of the interview, however, focused on what he had to say about his former coach Bob Zuppke. Grange criticized Zuppke for saying that Red owed it to Illinois not to become a professional player. "What's Zuppke but a professional?" Red asked. "Does he feel that he owes so much to the University of Illinois that he wouldn't leave them at the end of his contract if some other university offered him $5,000 a year more to coach for them?" After the interview was published, Grange wrote to Jimmy Corcoran of the Chicago *American* and denied having said anything derogatory about Zuppke or the University of Illinois.[10]

While the Bears were en route to Los Angeles for their next game, John B. Kennedy published an article in *Collier's* that called Grange "the saddest young man in America." The author, who had earlier interviewed Grange, compared him to Rudolph Valentino, whom he described as the last word in unhappiness. Whatever his mental outlook, Los Angeles could not wait to welcome Grange. Damon Runyon reported that the commotion surrounding Grange's arrival was astonishing. He noted that the Bears would face a worthy opponent in the Los Angeles Tigers, led by George "Wildcat" Wilson, a former University of Washington all-American halfback and recent Rose Bowl star, but drolly remarked, "I doubt that many persons understand this. The popular impression seems to be that only Mr. Red Harold Grange will play for his side against the Los Angeles Tigers.

The game is referred to as 'the Grange game.'" Pyle was in his element in the motion picture capital and had Grange and his teammates posing for photographs with everyone from Harold Lloyd and Mary Pickford to Luther Burbank. He even concocted a stunt in which some Chicago players threw footballs from the roof of the Biltmore Hotel to an awaiting crowd of five thousand who hoped to catch a ball and reap the $25 in prize money Pyle offered. Considering that the building was thirteen stories high, it was a wonder no one was seriously hurt.[11]

The publicity and hoopla paid off, and an estimated seventy-five thousand fans, the largest number ever to attend a pro football game, turned out at the Los Angeles Coliseum to watch Grange. Total gate receipts were nearly $135,000, and Grange later estimated that he and Pyle shared nearly $50,000 after paying players on both teams from $100 to $200 a man and covering other incidentals, including a substantial share for the promoter. Wildcat Wilson lived up to advance billing by rushing for 118 yards to Grange's 33, but Red, playing almost the entire game, set up two Chicago touchdowns on pass plays and scored two himself on short runs. The Bears easily defeated the Tigers, who had future movie star Andy Devine in their lineup, 17-7. Bob Zuppke attended the game, the first time he had seen a pro football event, and pronounced Grange still brilliant but his skills dimmed by the nature of the pro game, which, Zuppke maintained, had no real blocking and little team play. The University of Illinois student newspaper had reported that Zuppke and Grange were scheduled to dine together in Los Angeles and speculated that if they did "they must be going to eat swordfish." When they did attend a dinner sponsored by Illinois alumni, the Los Angeles *Times* reported that the tenseness of the situation was defused when Grange walked across the room and shook Zuppke's hand. Grange invited his former coach to sit on the Bears' bench, but Zuppke declined, saying, "I've sat on enough benches for some time to come."[12]

After the exciting spectacle at the Coliseum, the following day's game at a San Diego high school stadium against a group of local players called the California All-Stars generated little excitement. Only ten thousand watched Grange perform listlessly during his thirty minutes of play. He scored one touchdown late in the final period but otherwise, a newspaper reported, "his notable effort was the run he made from the field to the dressing room, [Larry] Walquist running interference for him." Fatigued by the back-to-back games, the Bears went through the motions in defeating the All-Stars 14-0 in a shortened game. After a week's rest, the Bears again faced Wildcat Wilson's Tigers at Kezar Stadium in San Francisco before twenty-three thousand fans who witnessed Chicago's only loss on the second tour by a score of 14-9. Before he left the game because of an injury in the fourth period, Wilson decisively outplayed Grange, who gained only forty-one yards in seven carries. In recalling the San Francisco game, Grange noted that although Chicago players generally got along well together they could occasionally become volatile. "I've seen more doggone fights by football players," he said. "They didn't have anything else to do, so they'd fight." At the hotel in San Francisco before the game, Dutch Sternaman informed the Bears' massive center George Trafton that he wasn't starting. In that era, it was an insult for regular players not to be in the starting lineup or to be taken out of the game. Trafton promptly slugged Sternaman, knocking him through a window and out onto the lawn. The next winter in Chicago, Grange remembered, the diminutive Sternaman and Trafton decided to finish the fight. "Sternaman told Trafton to take his overcoat off and when Trafton had his overcoat about half way off, Sternaman started in on him and gave Trafton a good wailing."[13]

Chicago played its last two games of the tour and the season in late January in Portland and Seattle. Most of the Bears' opponents, the Portland Longshoremen and the Washington All-Stars, were semipro players who were badly outclassed. Wildcat Wilson, who played in both games, could do little to spark either team. With only six thousand fans attending at the minor league baseball park in Portland, Grange scored two touchdowns and gained more than a hundred yards from scrimmage before sitting out the second half with a minor injury. "The Bears loafed through most of the game," the Associated Press reported, while piling up a 60-3 final score against the local team. The following day in Seattle before another sparse crowd (five thousand), Grange ended the tour on a high note by running for two thirty-yard touchdowns and throwing a sixty-yard touchdown pass before sitting out the second half. Chicago won easily, 34-0.[14]

The Bears finished the second tour with an 8-1 record and played before approximately 150,000 fans. It is estimated that Grange and Pyle cleared about $150,000 from gate receipts on the second tour, which, in addition to their $100,000 (including endorsements) from the pre-Christmas tour, totaled an impressive $250,000. The newspapers and promoters of the two tours tended to overstate attendance, however, as well as Grange's share of gate receipts; the actual amount he collected is unknown. The Bears' organization netted about $100,000 from both tours, which George Halas described as "the first financial cushion we'd managed to accumulate." Chicago players who participated in both tours earned on average a little over $3,000 for playing in seventeen football games. Red Grange did not save pro football—or, for that matter, make it a respectable game as some commentators have claimed. Other pioneers of the game had already accomplished that. He did, however, provide the pro game with much-needed publicity. Many years later, Halas summarized Grange's initial impact on what some NFL officials euphemistically called postgraduate football: "I believe that as a result of our Grange tour, pro football for the first time took on true national stature." Michael Oriard has pointed out, however, that Grange and the much-publicized tours could not transform pro football into a sport that had a large national following during the 1920s.[15]

During the long trip home from Seattle to Chicago, Pyle huddled with Halas and Dutch Sternaman to discuss the financial arrangements it would take to keep Grange in a Chicago uniform for the 1926 NFL season. The Bears' owners believed that the 1925 deal had heavily favored Grange and Pyle but were willing to accept the same arrangement for another year in order to retain the services of Grange, later described by Halas as "the golden lad." Pyle was amenable to the fifty-fifty split of gate receipts, but only if he and Grange also received a one-third ownership in the Bears. Halas and Sternaman rejected the proposal unequivocally. Several more days of discussions among the three men failed to produce an agreement. Finally, Pyle boldly announced that without the one-third ownership he would be forced to organize his own team built around Grange. Halas and Sternaman refused to budge, and Grange and Pyle parted company with the Bears' owners.[16]

Pyle had to act quickly if he hoped to secure an NFL franchise for the 1926 season; league owners were scheduled to conduct their winter business meeting in Detroit in early February. He and Grange hurried to the Motor City to make an application for an NFL franchise in New York City, which they would jointly own. By telephone, Pyle was able to obtain from New York Yankee business manager Edward Barrow a five-year lease of Yankee Stadium. The men had less success in Detroit. After being put off for a day while the owners discussed a resolution that eventually became the Grange Rule, they received word that New York Giants owner Tim Mara would not grant permission for a rival NFL team to operate in New York City. Mara disliked Pyle personally, but his objection to another New York team was more practical. His franchise might be devastated if Grange played for another NFL team across the Harlem River. League president

Joe Carr, who had recently suspended the Pottsville franchise for playing an unauthorized game in Frankford Yellow Jacket territory (Philadelphia) during the 1925 season, upheld Mara's veto. Pyle was infuriated by the Giants' veto and, according to Halas, told Grange, "No blasted Irishman is going to keep me out of New York!" He promptly announced that he would organize a new league at a February 17 meeting in Chicago that would compete with the NFL. In other business related to the Chicago Bears' recent tours, NFL owners voted to raise the team roster limit from sixteen to eighteen players and restrict teams from playing more than two league games per week.[17]

The American League of Professional Football Clubs (AFL) was formally organized in mid-February in Chicago. In a meeting at the Morrison Hotel, Pyle announced the formation of the league's flagship team, the New York Yankees, who would play at Yankee Stadium and feature Red Grange. He and Pyle were co-owners of the team. The ownership and location of the other proposed eight or nine teams were less certain as Pyle and other organizers frantically entertained and evaluated propositions from potential owners at the meeting and via long-distance telephone.[18]

Eventually, the AFL would be composed of nine teams ranging from the Boston Bulldogs in the East to the Los Angeles Wildcats in the West, the Wildcats playing strictly as a road team. In five cities there would be head-to-head competition with NFL franchises. After Walter Eckersall declined the position as league president, William "Big Bill" Edwards, a former Princeton football captain and well-known football referee, accepted the job at an annual salary of $25,000. It was reported that he would have broad powers akin to those of Kenesaw Mountain Landis, the major league baseball commissioner, but few doubted that Pyle actually would be in control. Edwards's first action was to uphold the integrity of the AFL by adopting the recently established NFL rule that no college player would be eligible to play until his class graduated. He pronounced that "the good qualities of the game and the tremendous public interest in it combine to make it now the property of the public, and it must be played by others than college men and schoolboys."[19]

After assisting Pyle in establishing the framework for the AFL, which the press referred to as the "Grange League," Red returned to Wheaton, where he bought his father a new home. The large, three-story house on the outskirts of town, complete with an automobile repair shop, cost Grange the then-substantial sum of $25,000. With his pockets bulging from the recently completed tours, Grange developed a fondness for the good life and enjoyed spending his money. He particularly liked fast, expensive cars and usually owned two or three at a time that he tinkered with at the repair shop. "I spent money like it was going out of circulation, until I learned better," he explained to sportswriter John Underwood in the mid-1980s. "I was a big shot. I drank Dom Perignon champagne. I wore a raccoon coat. I'd go to a restaurant and order from the right side of the menu. After I became a pro, if something I ordered didn't cost $20, I didn't want it." Richard Crabb maintains that the normally shy and modest Grange responded to his new-found wealth like any young man in his position would have. "Here is a person who never had anything and suddenly I'm rich. And there was really no income tax to speak of at that time," Crabb commented. "So he was responding to peer pressure, really. He was in business by this time himself and he was dealing with people like Halas and these other owners." Crabb concluded that Grange's big spending and flashy life-style were "completely uncharacteristic." Although his extravagant habits may have been normal for someone who came into wealth suddenly—and uncharacteristic of his later behavior—Grange continued his free-spending ways until he was married in the early 1940s.[20]

Grange also devoted some free time supporting worthy causes. During February and March he played in two all-star basketball games in Wheaton, all proceeds going to the improvement of the new high school football field that had been named after him. Even during the off-season Grange could not escape from controversy over the alleged "professionalization" of football he had helped generate. When he went to Newark, New Jersey, in March to deliver a speech entitled "Clean Living" at a local department store as part of a publicity campaign for the new AFL team in that city, Newark's director of physical education ordered employees to boycott the affair. He reasoned that allowing physical educators to attend the function would send a message that Grange had "acted ethically in giving up his diploma for the sake of the paltry dollars he got for playing professional football." Pyle countered the adverse publicity by assuring the audience that Grange would return to the University of Illinois the following February and finish his coursework. He never did return to the university as a student or earn his degree.[21]

When he returned to Wheaton, the town and the entire state were in an uproar over an article that University of Illinois alumnus Frazier Hunt had written for *Cosmopolitan Magazine*. Hunt interviewed six students at his alma mater and discovered that they all were in school to learn how to make money like Red Grange. Despite Hunt's allegation that Grange had lied to university officials about having a contract with Pyle, Grange remained the students' hero. Hunt was sad when he left campus and bitter that the ideals of his university had been corrupted. The fallout from the article continued for weeks. Grange no doubt was relieved to be leaving for Hollywood, where few people frowned on anyone making large sums of money.[22]

On the eve of his departure for California, the Arrow Picture Corporation, which reportedly paid Grange $300,000 to make a film, went into receivership. Pyle immediately announced that Grange's film contract had been made directly with the firm's president W. E. Shallenberger and the movie would be made. In fact, Pyle and Shallenberger had not been able to find a film studio willing to make a movie featuring Grange until Joseph P. Kennedy, who had recently bought Film Booking Office (FBO), a production and distribution company, decided to take a chance on him. Kennedy was not concerned about Grange's acting ability. He merely asked his two young sons, Joe Junior and Jack, whether they would like to see Grange in the movies. When they responded enthusiastically, he signed the football idol to a contract. Grange would star in a football film hastily written by Byron Morgan and tentatively entitled *The Halfback*. Sam Wood directed the film, which featured Mary McAllister as Grange's romantic interest, and retitled it *One Minute to Play*.[23]

Accompanied by Beans DeWolf as his traveling secretary, Grange met Pyle in Hollywood in late May to begin work on the film. Never one to scrimp on amenities, Pyle rented two luxurious suites at the Ambassador Hotel for the three of them. The film, which Grange described as a "rah-rah college story," was shot primarily at the Pomona College campus. The plot of the comedy revolved around Grange (Red Wade), sent off to college by his father with the proviso that he not play football. After Red mistakenly enrolls at the wrong school he plays for Parmalee College until the pivotal game with Caxton at which his father discovers his deception. Wade sits out the pivotal game until his father relents in the waning moments of the contest and Red scores the winning touchdown in dramatic fashion.[24]

Inducing a large crowd to be costumed in hats, coats, and scarfs (the game was scripted to be played in the Midwest during late autumn) was a problem, given California's scorching July temperatures and the fact that the film's low budget ruled out hiring thousands of extras. Charlie Pyle came up with a solution, however. He scheduled a regulation football game between a team led by Grange and one captained by George Wilson to be played at the Pomona College stadium. The studio ran an advertisement in a Los Angeles newspaper stipulating that admission was free to anyone who came to the game dressed in autumnal apparel. "Twelve thousand people dressed like that showed up in the middle of July," Grange recalled, "and we were able to shoot all the crowd reactions we needed." Grange marveled at Pyle's sagacity. "He always figured the angles. He wasn't anybody's chump that way."[25]

Grange was escorted around Hollywood by Bill Pickens, a local resident and sports promoter who assisted Pyle. He had just returned from Europe, where he had signed French tennis sensation Suzanne Lenglen to a professional contract for a forty-city, four-month American tour organized by Pyle. Pickens and Grange attended some Hollywood parties and functions together, and Grange had the opportunity to rub elbows with the filmland elite. He remembered fondly picking out a tweed suit at a haberdashery owned by Douglas Fairbanks, Jr., and flipping a coin with the film star double or nothing for the price of the purchase. Grange won the toss and proudly kept the suit for the next fifteen years. Above all, Grange remembered that being a movie actor was "the worst drudgery I'd ever experienced." He spent day after day before the cameras, wearing full football regalia from dawn to sunset in abnormally hot temperatures. "By the time I got back to the hotel at night, I cared about nothing except falling into bed. I was so tired and bored that I counted the days until the film was completed so I could get back to Wheaton."[26]

In mid-July, with the shooting of *One Minute to Play* completed, Grange started for home and his familiar job on the ice wagon. "There's nothing like carrying ice up three flights to develop a football constitution," he remarked. When he did return to his job with Luke Thompson in early August he had a good-natured dispute with his boss. Grange routinely parked his new Packard Cabriolet with white velvet upholstery in front of Thompson's store before going to work. Thompson delighted in appearing at the doorway and shouting in his foghorn voice, "Grange, see here, you better drive that car around back. I can't tell who's hiring whom."[27]

Grange spent a good part of the summer denying various rumors and allegations about his activities in Hollywood. Through Pyle, who was on his way to Paris to escort Lenglen to America, Grange disavowed a story that he had proposed marriage to movie actress Vivian Segal. Three weeks later he was named in a Hollywood divorce suit brought by Charles E. Taylor, a wealthy oil supply dealer, against his wife. Taylor charged that his wife was infatuated with the football star and that, among other things, "She refused an empty seat in an automobile next to him [Grange] and proceeded to sit on his lap, clasp his face in her hands, and kiss him." Grange denied the charges by purportedly saying, "Not me, I'm no love pirate. I'm in the ice business myself." Even when Grange and his father tried to enjoy some relaxation by attending a family reunion in Forksville, Pennsylvania, they could not escape the glare of publicity. Red was stopped for speeding in a village near Chicago, much to the delight of the press, which made illusions to his lack of swiftness in trying to outdistance the county patrolman. Lyle Grange, now retired from his job as a deputy sheriff, was incensed by the arrest and the $25 fine.[28]

In mid-August, when executives at FBO viewed the final version of *One Minute to Play* for the first time, they were elated by the film and Grange's performance. They even considered holding the premier at Madison Square Garden, where they would be able to show the film on four screens simultaneously in the center of the arena to accommodate an audience of up to twenty thousand. The idea was abandoned in favor of an initial showing at the Colony Theater on Broadway in early September, complete with pennants, a collegiate band, and ushers wearing football sweaters. The opening was a great success. When Red Wade enters the game in the final minute, the audience exploded with "a genuine outburst of applause" followed by cries of "attaboy, Red" after he scores the winning touchdown and conversion. After the presentation, Grange gave a brief talk and described how uncomfortable he was the first time he used paint on his lips. He also attended premiers in other cities.[29]

One Minute to Play was both a critical and financial success. Mordaunt Hall of the *New York Times* praised the comedy as "skillfully handled" and added that "the grand-stand scenes and those of the football field, with the panting players, are set forth so well that they seem like the real thing." He judged Grange's acting as "pleasingly natural" and reported that he "demonstrated his ability to tackle the role of a college hero and portray it far more convincingly than most of those handsome young men who are thoroughly accustomed to greasepaint and facing the camera." Film critic Rose Pelswick agreed that Grange had "an attractive screen personality" and criticized director Sam Wood for not letting him play more football. The movie did so well at the box office that Joe Kennedy tried to convince Grange to give up football and make movies full-time for FBO. Grange declined the offer; as he told Kennedy, his profession was playing football and not acting.[30]

Whereas other sports celebrities such as Babe Ruth and Jack Dempsey were poor actors and their films only marginally successful at the box office,

Grange's debut in *One Minute to Play* helped pave the way for a new type of Hollywood actor, the football idol. Grange would appear in two more films that did not have football themes and were not as successful as his first. By the late 1920s, however, Johnny Mack Brown, the 1926 Rose Bowl star from the University of Alabama, would become a Hollywood leading man and later have a long career in B-grade westerns. The Four Horsemen of Notre Dame and Ernie Nevers would also appear in films during the early 1930s. It is also conceivable that Ward Bond and Marion Morrison (John Wayne), two little-known University of Southern California football players, might have been encouraged by Grange's film success.[31]

While Grange worked himself into shape toting ice in Wheaton, Pyle and his colleagues completed arrangements for the nine-team AFL to begin play in late September. In addition to the Los Angeles road team, the Boston Bulldogs, and the showcase franchise in New York, the new league included teams in Philadelphia, Cleveland, Chicago, Brooklyn, Newark, and Rock Island. The latter franchise had been part of the NFL in 1925 and transferred allegiance to the new league. Pyle and Grange each had a half-interest in the Los Angeles Wildcats as well as the Yankees, and Pyle had a controlling interest in the league. Both men poured additional money into the AFL to support weaker clubs as the year progressed. At the onset of its first campaign, however, the league appeared to offer strong competition for the NFL because its owners had signed a formidable group of young stars, most of them recently graduated all-American backs who were well known to fans. Among them were Eddie Tryon of Colgate, Harry Stuhldreher of Notre Dame, Wildcat Wilson of Washington, and Al Kreuz of Pennsylvania. Joey Sternaman, Grange's teammate with the Bears during the 1925–26 tours, jumped to the AFL as owner, coach, and quarterback of the Chicago Bulls, and other NFL veterans signed to play in the new league. The Bulls outbid the Chicago Cardinals for the right to play at spacious Comiskey Park and promised to provide serious competition for both NFL franchises in that city. The Brooklyn Horsemen, with only one of the famed Notre Dame foursome (Stuhldreher), posed an immediate problem for the league when the rival NFL Brooklyn franchise gained the lease to Ebbets Field.[32]

Pyle and Grange spared little expense in stocking the Yankees, and, to a lesser extent, the Los Angeles team, with top-flight talent. They offered Chicago Bears' all-NFL tackle Ed Healy $10,000 to coach and play for the New York franchise. Healy recalled that he was stunned by the fabulous proposal (he made $150 a game for the Bears at the time) that Pyle made at the Morrison Hotel. Also present were Grange, Suzanne Lenglen, and a woman in an adjoining room, who, as Healy put it, "did not answer to the name of Mrs. Pyle." He rejected the offer because, among other things, "I figured that any man that could be married and divorced three times and come up with a woman in another room, I didn't have any business working for him." Pyle eventually hired Bears' tackle Ralph Scott to coach the Yankees for an undisclosed sum. The Yankees had a talented and expensive backfield that included all-American–caliber players Pooley Hubert of Alabama and Harry Fry of Iowa as well as Tryon. Grange and Pyle also paid a substantial sum to secure the services of Wildcat Wilson for the Los Angeles team, which was managed by Beans DeWolf.[33]

To counter the threat the new league posed, the NFL expanded to twenty-two teams, an all-time high that stood until 1970. Three teams, including Rock Island, were dropped from the 1925 roster, but new teams were established in Hartford, Brooklyn, and Racine, Wisconsin, while the Louisville Colonels and Los Angeles Buccaneers were organized as road teams playing out of Chicago. The established league's strategy appeared to be to use as many players as possible and deprive the AFL of their services, but the franchises proved to be deadweight. On the positive side, the Chicago Bears managed to obtain Paddy Driscoll, who many considered the premier pro player of the era, from the Cardinals when that team could no longer afford his services after being evicted from Comiskey Park. The AFL also failed to sign Ernie Nevers. Ole Haugsrud, who had recently purchased the shaky NFL franchise in Duluth for a dollar and renamed it the Eskimos, matched Pyle's offer to Nevers and agreed to pay him $15,000 for the season and a percentage of the larger gate receipts. Nevers and the Eskimos, who Grantland Rice dubbed "the Iron Men from the North," became a major attraction, played twenty-nine league and exhibition games from mid-September until early February, and posted a respectable record of 6-5-3 against NFL competition. Pro football may have gained in popularity, but the question of whether it had a strong enough following to support two leagues and thirty-one franchises remained.[34]

The AFL got off to a good start on September 26, when the New York Yankees, attired in bright red jerseys, drew twenty-two thousand fans to Cleveland's Luna Bowl for a game against the hometown Panthers. It was the largest crowd ever to watch a football game in Cleveland. The Yankees had only practiced together a few times and had competed in one preseason game in Aurora, Illinois, and the team played sluggishly in a disappointing 10-0 defeat. Cleveland completely stopped Grange except for a twenty-one-yard punt return. The Yankee line, the team's greatest liability throughout the season, appeared unusually weak. Pyle had encouraged Coach Scott to sign big-name backfield stars to help boost attendance but had overlooked the importance of a strong forward wall. Although he would eventually add new linemen, Pyle was preoccupied with Suzanne Lenglen's tour debut, set for Madison Square Garden in early October. Grange made a number of personal appearances with Lenglen but denied having any financial stake in Pyle's tennis venture. The following Sunday, the Yankees (the "Grangers" as New York newspapers referred to them) rebounded with a convincing 26-0 road victory over Rock Island. Grange scored his first two AFL touchdowns, one on a pass reception and the other on a twenty-five-yard end run. Heavy rains helped account for the crowd of only five thousand.[35]

The fate of the AFL was determined to a significant extent by the weather. In later years, Grange often could not recall much about the new league, but he did remember the abysmal weather. "I'll never forget that it rained every Sunday all fall. I don't think we had one sunny Sunday. And of course in those days people did not buy season tickets." A cold, damp day in Boston resulted in a small turnout for the Bulldogs' home-opener against the Yankees as Grange made good gains from scrimmage in a 13-0 New York triumph. After an exhibition game against the New Britain All-Stars in Hartford, the Yankees headed west to play Joey Sternaman's Chicago Bulls. The sixteen thousand who watched the former Chicago Bears' teammates clash turned out to be the largest crowd of the season for the Bulls. Sternaman was delighted that his Bulls outdrew the Bears, who hosted the Giants across town that same day, but he remembered, "We didn't get the crowds. We played out at Comiskey Park on the South Side, not the best of neighborhoods in those days, and we just couldn't make it go." Johnny Mohardt, a former Notre Dame star, stole the show from Grange and Sternaman at Comiskey Park, scoring both touchdowns in a 14-0 Bulls' victory. After four league games the Yankees had a disappointing 2-2 record and trailed the league-leading Cleveland Panthers and Philadelphia Quakers, both with 3-0 records, in the standings. Grange and his teammates eagerly awaited their home-opener against the Los Angeles Wildcats at Yankee Stadium.[36]

With the completion of the memorable 1926 World Series between the baseball Yankees and the St. Louis Cardinals in which forty-year-old Grover

Alexander's masterful late-inning relief performance in the seventh game secured a St. Louis championship at Yankee Stadium, the football Yankees were set for their New York debut. Preparations were made for a large crowd of forty to sixty thousand, but a heavy rain held attendance to about twenty thousand. A collegiate band in brightly colored uniforms was drenched as the afternoon wore on, and two cheerleaders in sweaters with a Y on their fronts stayed in the Yankee dugout after a few ineffectual cheers. For more than two hours the lethargic crowd sat in a steady downpour as players on both teams slipped and slid in the mud, futilely trying to advance the ball. More than once Grange threatened to sweep past the defense and into the open field, but each time he fell on the slippery turf. Finally, in the fourth period, with the Yankees backed up in front of their goalposts, Eddie Tryon broke loose and sloshed his way eighty yards for a touchdown and a 6-0 Yankee victory. Despite the disappointing turnout, Grange and Pyle could take some consolation in the fact that the NFL Giants playing across the river in the Polo Grounds had drawn fewer than ten thousand.[37]

The narrow victory over Los Angeles began a surge that would propel the Yankees to the top of the AFL standings. The Grangers confronted the Philadelphia Quakers in a highly publicized game at Sesquicentennial Stadium the following Saturday. Grange would face Al Kreuz, a former University of Pennsylvania fullback and now the Quaker field-goal and defensive specialist, who had missed the famous 1925 Illinois-Penn collegiate game due to an injury. Built around Kreuz and interior linemen Century Milstead, George Tully, and Karl Robinson, the undefeated Quakers had the best defensive team in the league. They had not allowed an opponent to cross their goal line in four AFL games. Thirty thousand fans watched Grange outplay Kreuz while amassing eighty-five yards in total offense against the vaunted Quaker defense. Kreuz not only failed to contain Grange but also missed two field-goal attempts on the wet field. Yankee quarterback George Pease led a furious final-period assault that resulted in a resounding 27-0 New York victory. Grange and the Yankees left immediately for New York and a game the following day with the Newark Bears, but that game was canceled because of a torrential rain that flooded the playing field at Yankee Stadium and paralyzed New York's transportation system. The cancellation of the potentially lucrative Yankee game and the effect of the persistent inclement weekend weather on attendance prompted the Newark owners to disband operations. Within the week the Cleveland franchise also folded. The New York Yankees were on the upswing, but the AFL was facing a crisis.[38]

Pyle, on the road with Suzanne Lenglen's tour, hurried back to New York in hopes of reestablishing confidence in the league. He was under fire from the media for allegedly defiling the amateur game of tennis and now faced further criticism as the AFL appeared to be unraveling. Grange remembered, however, that most reporters genuinely liked Pyle. When Pyle was at his office at the Astor Hotel during the 1926 season, "Westbrook Pegler would be down there every morning. This was during Prohibition, and each morning when Westbrook left he would take a couple of bottles of Pyle's scotch with him, and then he would turn around and write a column and call Pyle everything he could lay his tongue to that could go in the paper. Charlie sometimes would complain, but Westbrook would say, 'Just as long as I keep your name singular, don't holler. I'm writing about you.'"[39]

Amid rumors that the two pro leagues would amalgamate to cut down on expenses, Pyle reassured fans that the AFL was "intrinsically strong. We have had bad luck on the weather but that kind of thing can't go on forever." In rare clear weather on Election Day thirty thousand watched the Yankees smother Rock Island, now playing strictly as a road team, 35-0. Grange made steady gains against the hapless Independents and scored on a twenty-one-yard touchdown run. After two more games Rock Island withdrew from the crumbling AFL. Grange took time out from the rigors of the AFL schedule to attended the Tuskegee-Lincoln college football game in Philadelphia in the company of Fred "Duke" Slater, an African American star who was a Rock Island lineman, and Bob Folwell, coach of the Philadelphia Quakers. Having honed some of his football skills while playing with African American children in Wheaton, Grange admired black athletes, pronounced the play of the two black college teams excellent, and praised the players' fine spirit of sportsmanship.[40]

The following Sunday the Yankees continued their winning streak before another sizable crowd of thirty thousand at Yankee Stadium by defeating the Brooklyn Horsemen 21-13. Although the Horsemen had added Elmer Layden of Notre Dame's famous foursome to their stable of backs that included Stuhldreher and Earl Britton, they could not match Grange's superb play. He scored one touchdown, reeled off numerous long gains, and caught every pass he could reach in one of his best games as a pro. Several days after the game the Brooklyn franchise also withdrew from the AFL and merged with the Brooklyn Lions of the NFL. Meanwhile, the Yankees extended their winning streak to five in a row with a convincing 28-0 victory over the Los Angeles Wildcats in a game in Toronto, Canada, with Grange scoring a touchdown on a sixty-yard run. Grange was in peak form when the Yankees routed the Boston Bulldogs 24-0 at Yankee Stadium on November 14. He scored three touchdowns, including one on a fifty-yard pass interception in which he weaved across the field in a spectacular open field run. To the delight of twenty thousand admiring spectators, he was sent back into the game and successfully kicked the extra point. The Yankees were a success in New York, but with the withdrawal of the Boston Bulldogs from the league soon after their crushing defeat at Yankee Stadium the AFL was reduced to only four functioning teams.[41]

With his choice of opponents limited, Coach Ralph Scott scheduled another game with Los Angeles at Yankee Stadium on November 21. During the first half, Eddie Tryon was forced to leave the game because of a charley horse; Grange soon followed him to the sideline with a bruised left side sustained from a hard tackle. Neither player returned to the game in the second half. Twenty thousand fans sat silently as Wildcat Wilson led his team to a 16-6 victory over the Yankees. With the defeat, the Yankees surrendered the AFL lead to Philadelphia, whom they met four days later on Thanksgiving Day at Yankee Stadium. Noticeably slowed by his injury, Grange struggled through the first half as the Quakers maintained a slim 6-3 lead as a result of two field goals by Al Kreuz. Early in the third period, Grange broke away on a twenty-yard run, but the tackle that brought him down aggravated his hip injury. He limped off the field and did not return to the game. At the beginning of the final period, Eddie Tryon renewed the hopes of the twenty-two thousand holiday fans for a Yankee victory when he sprinted for a touchdown that gave the home team a 10-6 lead. A short time later, however, Quaker tailback Johnny Scott connected on a forty-yard touchdown pass to Charlie Way to put Philadelphia ahead 13-10. George Pease, the Yankee quarterback, launched a furious passing assault in the final minutes but to no avail. The defeat left the Yankees with a .666 winning percentage against .777 for Philadelphia. New York needed a victory against the Quakers and an additional win over Chicago for the team to win the AFL championship.[42]

Two days later the Yanks and Quakers met again before twenty-two thousand fans at Schibe Park in Philadelphia. With a sweater draped over his back concealing his famous number seventy-seven, the injured Grange watched from the Yankee bench. The third and pivotal game between the two teams was extremely rough, and three players, including Kreuz and Tryon, were sent to the sidelines with injuries. In the end, the formidable Quaker defense dominated the weakened Yankee offense in a 13-6 Philadelphia victory. With the win, the Quakers clinched the AFL champion-ship. As an indication of the relative lack of interest in the AFL and pro football in general during the 1920s, the *New York Times* buried a short story on the Quaker-Yankee game on page seven of its Sunday sporting section. The first three pages were devoted exclusively to the Army-Navy college game that drew 110,000 fans at the dedication of Chicago's Sol-dier Field. The championship lost, the Yankees still had to play two previ-ously scheduled games with the Chicago Bulls. The following day was cold, and only 2,500 turned out to watch the Yankees, without Grange, defeat the Bulls 7-0 at Yankee Stadium. Allison Danzig may have understated the situation when he reported that "the absence of Grange detracted from the interest" in the game.[43]

After the game, Tim Mara, who would lose $40,000 that season trying to compete with Grange and the Yankees, challenged his AFL rivals to a game at either the Polo Grounds or Yankee Stadium on December 12. Pyle was forced to turn down the attractive offer because his team was sched-uled to play its final game in Chicago that day. Grange was convinced that the proposed Yankee-Giant game "would have attracted a huge gate." He and the Yankees completed the season on an ice-coated field at Comiskey Park with a 7-3 victory over the Bulls before ten thousand freezing fans. The turn-out was not enough to rescue Joey Sternaman's nearly bankrupt Chicago franchise. On the same day, the AFL received another black eye at the Polo Grounds in New York, where the league champion Quakers had accepted Mara's offer to play his seventh-place NFL Giants. Philadel-phia was mauled by the Giants 31-0 in a snowstorm before only five thou-sand spectators. With this final humiliation, the AFL's future was uncer-tain. Grange remembered that he and Pyle "lost a bundle" trying to keep the league afloat in 1926.[44]

Although Grange and his Yankees had failed to win the AFL champi-onship, the team did well at the gate and attracted nearly 220,000 fans to its fourteen games. The AFL consistently surpassed the NFL in attendance in important games during the season. That the older league felt the ef-fects of AFL competition was reflected by the fact that the NFL fielded only twelve teams for the 1927 season, the fewest since its inaugural year in 1920. Grange, however, was the only AFL player who could consistently draw large numbers of paying customers. The Philadelphia Quakers broke even, but the other clubs had either folded or were on the verge of collapse when the season ended. Grange and many of his teammates left almost immediately after the season for a barnstorming tour of the South and

California, playing games against a team organized by Wildcat Wilson. The tour was a modest success and helped Grange recoup some of the money he had lost by investing in shaky AFL franchises, but it did not recapture the magic of the previous year's trip. While Grange and his teammates made their way from Dallas, where he was arrested for disturbing the peace, to Beaumont, Texas, and on to the West Coast, he left it to Pyle to determine his next move as a professional football player.[45]

9

Down but Not Out

GRANGE'S 1926–27 BARNSTORMING TOUR ended in San Francisco on February 7. The Yankees had played ten games, most of them in Texas and California. Most players received between $100 and $200 a game and $3 a day in meal money. Grange was paid considerably more. With the exception of the winter of 1928–29, he would continue to make postseason football tours until he retired as a player. Looking back, Grange was convinced that the exhibition games helped popularize the pro game in areas where it was all but unknown: "We spread the NFL across the country, taking it to towns that never saw a pro game, doing anything to push the product." He recalled that in an exhibition game in Memphis during the early 1930s his team was driving for an early touchdown when the event's promoter ran on to the field and stopped the game. The game's financial backer had been stuck in traffic and missed the opening kickoff, "so we started over," Grange said. In later years he was somewhat bitter because the NFL never recognized the importance of the early barnstorming tours. "They're benefitting today because of the things we did," he told a sportswriter in 1985. "And isn't it too bad the NFL never took care of those early players? I complained a few times, because we had guys in hospitals, guys who had had amputations because of football injuries. Guys who had problems. I thought the game could have done something for them, but it never did."[1]

After the tour, Grange remained in California for several months along with Pyle and DeWolf. Never one to remain idle, Pyle came up with a scheme to promote professional ice hockey in the state. The *New York Times* reported that he and Grange had formulated plans to form the California Ice Hockey League, which consisted of four teams. They purchased a large rink in Los Angeles and planned to build a $220,000 structure in San Francisco. Pyle intended to import players from the East. Beans DeWolf was put in charge of promoting the league, which did not develop much of a following on the West Coast and quickly folded. Before plans for the hockey league were completed, Pyle had another promotional brainstorm. Inspired by an account of an Arab messenger who had run ninety miles to complete a mission during the recent Riff insurrection in North Africa, Pyle announced that he would sponsor a three thousand–mile, Los Angeles–to–New York foot race set for the following February. Anyone would be welcome to enter, and the winner would receive $25,000 in prize money. Noting that it would be impossible to charge admission for such an event, columnist James Harrison of the *New York Times* wrote sarcastically that "Mr. Pyle's activities in professional football and tennis are well known, but his role as patron saint of an amateur sport is rather puzzling. By the way, what ever became of Red Grange?"[2]

As Grange and Pyle headed back East in early May to formulate plans for another football season for the New York Yankees, either within an attenuated AFL or in the NFL, they discussed the future of pro football. Grange was not entirely convinced that the pro game had much of a future, but Pyle was enthusiastic. He had announced the previous year that he expected to do big things with the AFL, "things that will astonish the National League." Grange, who marveled at Pyle's visionary schemes, was fascinated by his partner's plans for a domed stadium, which he had first shown Grange in 1926. The stadium would seat seventy thousand and have a retractable roof that had some sort of landing pad on top. Grange remembered that Pyle's blueprints called for aisles to turn into escalators after the game so "you would step out of your seat into the aisle and you never took another step. You could empty the stadium in five minutes." The most interesting feature of the proposed stadium was that "behind every seat they had a crank and you could roll up this piece of glass up or down, whatever you want, and it was magnified like looking through binoculars. The further back you were the higher it was magnified." Fans would have a close-up view of the game from the far reaches of the stadium, the playing field would be constructed on trolley tracks, and the arena could be quickly converted into an ice rink. "Everything was electrically run," Grange enthused years later. "They haven't approached anything like this."[3]

With so many bankrupt franchises, Pyle abandoned his initial plan to reform the AFL into a six-team league. His negotiations with the NFL to merge some of the AFL teams into the older league were put on hold, however, after nineteen NFL owners who attended the league's winter meetings indicated their intention to field teams for the 1927 season. With merger talks between the two leagues stalled for the present, Grange and Pyle left for Hollywood to make another film for FBO. Having grossed $750,000 at the box office with *One Minute to Play*, which cost only $100,000 to make, Joe Kennedy was anxious to begin shooting Grange's second film. Sam Wood and Byron Morgan decided to feature him in a racing film called *Racing Romeo*, with Morgan writing the script and Wood directing. The story revolved around Red Walden (Grange), a poor, small-town garage owner who wants to marry Sally (Jobyna Ralston). After he fails miserably in attempts to earn enough prize money as a race car driver to enable him to propose to Sally, her wealthy aunt insists that Red give up racing if he intends to wed her niece. He complies, but when the wedding is put off he returns to the track for the big race. He speeds "through haystacks, across ditches, under low bridges" (Grange did his own driving in the close-up shots) and wins the race and Sally's hand. The low-budget silent film was shot in only five weeks, mainly at the fairground race track in Ventura.[4]

Right from the start, nearly everything, trifles as well as more serious matters, went wrong with the project. A day of shooting was lost when Grange impulsively entered into a tomato-throwing scene in which he was not scheduled to appear and was hit in the chest with a juicy tomato. His specially made shirt needed for close-ups had to be laundered. Another day, the racing vehicle of Grange and Walter "Fat" Hiers, who played his mechanic, ran into a hornets' nest during the filming of stills. Hiers was so large that neither man could escape from the car, and they were both badly stung. In yet another incident, a racing driver was killed while engaged in stunt driving at the race track. While filming was in progress, moreover, Pyle got into a bitter and protracted dispute with FBO executives over the division of profits from *One Minute to Play*. When Grange became distracted and refused to devote full energy to *Racing Romeo* as he had done in his previous movie, the studio heads, still fuming at Pyle, began to lose interest in both him and the film. As a result, *Racing Romeo* was hurried to completion and the studio did not exert itself in publicizing the finished product. Although the film received some favorable reviews it was not a success at the box office.[5]

Unlike his first venture in Hollywood, Grange thoroughly enjoyed himself during the filming of *Racing Romeo*. As an automobile aficionado who enjoyed speeding along the back roads of Illinois in his Stutz Bearcat at a hundred miles per hour, Grange relished being in the company of race car drivers such as Cliff Bergere, Stubby Stubblefield, and Ernie Triplett, who did most of the stunt driving. He wanted to do likewise, but Sam Wood wisely vetoed the idea as too dangerous. Nevertheless, Grange remained at the track for hours after everyone had left so he could take a turn behind the wheels of souped-up racers that had been assembled for the film. In his off-hours, he stayed with Pyle, DeWolf, and Yankee coach Ralph Scott in an elegant ten-room rented house in Hollywood on fashionable Gramercy Place. They had a weekly poker circle that included Andy Devine and Adolphe Menjou among others and attended a gala party given nearly every Sunday evening by future NBC television executive Tom Gallery and his wife, Zazu Pitts. Grange clearly enjoyed the camaraderie with his house-mates, especially the numerous practical jokes that were part of the summer fun. He also recalled having "some interesting dates" but revealed nothing more about the extent or nature of his romantic interests. When the film was completed in mid-July, Grange and Pyle were eager to return East and shape plans for another season of pro football.[6]

At a special meeting in April, NFL owners had weeded out twelve of the weakest franchises by forcing them either to retire from the league or suspend operations. By July, the Dayton Triangles were added to the NFL roster, with the possibility that a club from Detroit or Columbus would also be added to form a twelve-team league. At that point, the NFL began serious negotiations with Pyle, who was not in a strong position to save much of what was left of the AFL. In mid-August Joe Carr announced that the AFL had been merged into the NFL. In reality, the merger allowed Pyle to lease the now-defunct NFL Brooklyn franchise from Tim Mara of the Giants, who had gained ownership of the team from the league in payment of debts. The second New York City franchise would be called the Yankees and was owned by Grange and Pyle but would be restricted to only four home games at Yankee Stadium, including one with the Giants. With twelve of its sixteen league games on the road and no conflicting dates with the Giants in New York, the Yankees and Grange would not compete directly with Mara's team for New York fans and hopefully boost NFL attendance in other cities. The league's other premier gate attraction, Ernie Nevers, would continue to play for Duluth, which would be strictly a road team. Carr and the team owners delighted at the prospect of Grange and Nevers increasing attendance in many NFL cities. As a face-saving gesture to Pyle, Grange, and the AFL, it was announced that the Chicago Bulls would be merged into the two NFL teams in Chicago.[7]

Grange and Pyle could not have been pleased with the deal they had struck with the NFL, but it was likely the best they could have arranged under the circumstances. In his autobiography, Grange put a positive spin on the agreement that brought the Yankees into the NFL: "If I could only continue as a big gate attraction for a few more seasons, until the Yankees as a team developed a loyal band of followers, we were certain to wind up as co-owners of very valuable football property. I didn't think I'd have much to worry about when my playing days were over."[8]

The Yankees had most of their players returning from the 1926 team but added tailback Wild Bill Kelly of Montana, who replaced Pease; Bo Molenda of Michigan at fullback; and two outstanding ends, Ray Flaherty of Gonzaga and Red Badgro of the University of Southern California. After an exhibition game victory in Minneapolis the Yankees were scheduled to play their first seven league games on the road. They played sluggishly in a 6-3 victory over the Dayton Triangles on October 2 before traveling to Detroit for a highly publicized game against the Cleveland Bulldogs featuring Grange's former Michigan rival Benny Friedman. Before twenty thousand fans at Dinan Stadium, Grange and Friedman both were contained in the first half as the Yankees opened a 13-0 lead. In the second half, however, Friedman unleashed a brilliant aerial attack that would become his trademark and soon make him the most feared passer in the league. Grange also came to life with a series of long gains in which he nearly broke loose for touchdowns. The crowd was well satisfied with the furious final period action as the Yankees managed to hang on for a 13-7 victory. After a 19-0 triumph over Buffalo on Columbus Day, the Yankees were off to a fast start in the NFL with a 3-0 record.[9]

The following Sunday's game against the Bears at Wrigley Field (formerly Cubs Park) was the most eagerly awaited pro football game in Chicago since Grange made his debut there in 1925. With both teams undefeated and Grange making his first appearance against his former teammates, a capacity crowd of more than thirty thousand turned out. Immediately before the game, thousands of fans who could not gain admission rioted and broke through the center field gates, climbed the fences, and swarmed along the sidelines and into the bleacher seats that were under construction. "It literally broke Pyle's heart to see all those people get in for free," Grange recalled. After a quiet first quarter, Paddy Driscoll broke away for two long runs in the second period, which led to touchdowns and a 12-0 Chicago lead. When Driscoll missed a drop-kick for the extra point after the first touchdown, a young fan retrieved the football, which had sailed out of the park, and disappeared with the souvenir. The ever-frugal Halas refused to continue play until the Yankees supplied a new ball. Grange nearly prevented the second touchdown when he stopped Driscoll in the open field on the New York eleven-yard line with a spectacular tackle.[10]

The Yankees attempted a comeback late in the second half and made eight straight first downs while advancing the ball to Chicago's two-yard line. Grange played a prominent role in the New York surge by intercepting a pass and making two runs of more than twenty yards. The *New York Times* enthusiastically reported that he played "one of the best games of his pro career." With less than a minute to play, however, the Yankees still had failed to score. At that point, Eddie Tryon launched a desperation pass intended for Grange near the Chicago sideline. As he reached high for the ball, Grange collided with Bears' center George Trafton. "My cleats got caught in the ground as I fell," Grange remembered, "and when Trafton accidentally toppled on me I twisted my knee. I felt an excruciating pain in the knee and was unable to get up." The game was interrupted temporarily while Grange was carried from the field as "the stands cheered and hundreds formed lines between which the Yankee leader was hurried to the dressing room." Because Trafton had a reputation of being one of the league's roughest players, there was speculation then and later that Grange had been the victim of a malicious tackle by the Bear lineman. Trafton, however, was one of the players who helped carry his former teammate off the field. Grange emphatically stated in the dressing room that the injury was a freak accident and added that the game, which the Bears won 12-0, "was one of the cleanest football games I ever played in."[11]

The initial diagnosis was that Grange had torn a tendon in his knee. New York newspapers ran wire service accounts that conjectured that he might be lost for the season, but the Chicago *Tribune* reported that the attending physician did not consider the injury serious. Grange should be able to play the next weekend in Green Bay. Football historians Dan Daly and Bob O'Donnell have speculated that Pyle may have been responsible for the optimistic report that "could only help the gate in Green Bay." Grange, in fact, had a torn knee ligament, a serious injury for a football player and one that now usually requires surgery. During Grange's era, however, surgery was not a common option. In 1984 he vaguely hinted that team officials had covered up the extent of the injury. "The help you would have, the doctors help or your trainers," he said, "they would keep it quiet. It wasn't publicized." Pyle and the Yankees had every reason for wanting Grange back in the lineup as soon as possible. Without him, attendance at Yankee games would plummet. The effect of the knee injury and Grange's early return to play, however, would have a lasting impact on his football career. "No one knew it then, but they had seen the Galloping Ghost gallop for the last time."[12]

Soon after the injury, Grange's knee swelled, and he was unable to stand on his right leg or bend it without severe pain. He was forced to walk on crutches for four weeks. If Pyle had encouraged speculation that Grange would play the following week in Green Bay, the strategy paid off. The largest crowd ever to watch a pro football game in Wisconsin (eleven thousand) attended the Yankee game. They cheered Grange, who appeared at midfield before the game in full uniform and walking with the aid of a cane. He watched from the sideline as the Yankees were soundly defeated 13-0. The following week at massive Soldier Field in Chicago against the Cardinals, who evidently envisioned a large crowd if Grange was able to play, fans were not as cordial and clamored futilely for Grange to enter the game. New York defeated the Cardinals 7-6 before fifteen thousand disappointed fans. The financial impact of Grange's absence from the lineup was more evident in Cleveland the next week, when only 2,500 spectators showed up in bad weather to watch Benny Friedman and the Bulldogs dominate the Yankees 15-0. Having rejected surgery, Grange underwent diathermy treatments, which seemed to help some. Concerned about flagging attendance and contractual obligations with other NFL teams for Red to appear in games, he and Pyle decided that the Yankee star should test his knee in an Election Day game at Yankee Stadium against the Bears.[13]

Grange was not in the starting lineup against Chicago, but, as the *New York Times* reported, "He romped out on the gridiron shortly after the second quarter opened amid tumultuous applause which lasted for fully three minutes." He played the rest of the quarter and after resting his leg during the third period played the final fifteen minutes of the game. Shifting from halfback to quarterback to minimize strain on his knee, Grange carried the ball only a few times and without much result, but the *Times* generously complimented his defensive play. Thanks to some spectacular pass receptions by end Ray Flaherty, who scored three touchdowns, the

Yankees easily defeated the Bears 26-6. Three days later Grange played only six minutes in an Armistice Day game in Pottsville, which New York won 19-12. Pyle's economically motivated but reckless scheduling methods did not aid Grange in making a gradual comeback from his injury. Two days after the Pottsville game, he was back in the lineup at Yankee Stadium against the Chicago Cardinals. "It was no place for ghosts, particularly injured ones," the *Times* reported, "and most of the ten thousand persons in the stands felt nervous for the limping Grange while he was in the game." Although the Yankees won the game 20-6, the Cardinals played with extreme intensity, knocking Eddie Tryon out of the game and ending Yankee tailback Roy "Bullet" Baker's season with several broken ribs. Less noticed amid the general violence, Grange had aggravated his injured knee. The following day doctors put his right leg in a plaster cast. Charlie Pyle, with Grange's consent, reassured fans that after three or four days in bed his star player "would be in condition to play sixty minutes, or a full game, against Benny Friedman's Cleveland Bulldogs on Thanksgiving Day."[14]

As promised, Grange was in the starting lineup for the holiday contest and played most of the game. He was noticeably hobbling in his few attempts to run with the ball but did complete a few short passes. The Yankees, who established an early two-touchdown lead, appeared dismayed by Grange's inability to add much to their already depleted offense and played lethargically after the first period. Friedman directed an impressive Bulldog passing attack that overwhelmed the home team and resulted in a 30-19 Cleveland victory. It was New York's first defeat of the season at Yankee Stadium. "I was in bad shape and I knew it," Grange remembered, "but I couldn't give up. No one in the stands that day knew I left my cane in the dressing room before coming out on the field." Pressured by the economic reality that the Yankees without Grange would draw few paying customers, Grange and Pyle were determined to finish the season with Red in the lineup. It is difficult to discern whether it was Grange or Pyle who was most adamant that the injured Yankee star continue to play, but play he did.[15]

The Yankees had four games scheduled during the last two weeks of the season. With temperatures in the East dropping as December approached, Grange could expect no relief for his injured knee as playing fields froze and the weather worsened. Against the Steam Roller in Providence three days after Thanksgiving, he played the entire first half in a 14-7 Yankee defeat. He accounted for more than a hundred total yards throwing and receiving passes but was in too much pain to carry the ball from scrimmage. Grange made only a token appearance in a rematch against Providence played in Syracuse on December 3. It was just as well because the game, which the Steam Roller won 9-0, was played on a frozen field. The first of two much-anticipated games with the rival Giants turned out to be anticlimactic because Mara's team had already clinched the NFL championship. Only ten thousand braved a blinding sleet storm to watch the New York teams clash at the Polo Grounds on December 4. Grange played the entire game on the windswept field, with mixed results. Although a *New York Times* headline declared "Grange Plays Brilliantly," the reporter conceded that "Red flashed here and there, but his legs refused to stand up, and hence there was a lack of consistency in his many attempts." Another New York newspaper acknowledged that although he did his best with a bad leg, "All Grange got was the Bronx cheer, a prolonged boo, which must have fallen strangely on the ears of one who has known nothing but the approving roars of many a multitude." Hinkey Haines's first-period, seventy-five-yard touchdown run was all the offense the Giants needed on their way to a 14-0 victory. Among the spectators were Babe Ruth and Lou Gehrig, who had mesmerized the city with their duel for the American League home run crown while leading the baseball Yankees to the world's championship. The Babe, clad in a massive raccoon coat, paid Grange a social call at half-time.[16]

The Yankees concluded what turned out to be a very disappointing NFL campaign with back-to-back games against the Frankford Yellow Jackets and the Giants on the last weekend of the season. Grange was mainly ineffective in a 6-6 tie with the Philadelphia team but played the full sixty minutes with flashes of his old form during a 13-0 defeat at the hands of the Giants at Yankee Stadium. With only eight thousand fans in attendance at the Giants game, Grange and Pyle had to be concerned about their less than expected financial return from the Yankee franchise. Grange's injury and a less than stellar 7-8-1 NFL record had contributed to gate receipts far below those of the previous season. In a year that saw more than 102,000 fans attend the second Dempsey-Tunney boxing match and 114,000 witness the Army-Navy football game, the Yankee co-owners had reason to worry about their substantial investment in pro football. Partly for that reason, Grange and the Yankees left immediately after the Giant game for an exhibition tour on the Pacific Coast that would match the team against various all-star teams headed by Wildcat Wilson and Benny Friedman. Grange was confident that during the tour, which would last through January, he could play himself back into shape. During the postseason games, however, he further aggravated his knee injury. By the end of January, Grange recalled, "It became apparent I had done irreparable damage to the knee." At the age of twenty-four he faced the real possibility that his career as a football player was over.[17]

After the barnstorming tour concluded, Grange remained in Los Angeles, where he told a reporter for the *Examiner* that he intended to settle permanently in Southern California and buy a ranch. "I've had so much fun out here, enjoyed every minute of my stay these last two years, and intend to keep on enjoying life here," he said. "I've promised my Dad to move him to California, and I'm making good." Grange added somewhat ruefully, "I don't know about future pictures and I don't care. But I want that ranch and that ranch home, a horse, a sombrero and you and the rest of the world can pass right on by my door." If he was despondent about his knee injury, Grange's outlook improved when Pyle recruited him to help plan and act as advance man for his International Transcontinental Foot Marathon, which Westbrook Pegler promptly nicknamed the "Bunion Derby."[18]

Although he later emphasized that he had no financial interest in the race, Grange not only helped organize the event but also went ahead to make arrangements in various towns for the runners' overnight accommodations and often acted as master of ceremonies at gatherings where customers who paid 25 cents each could enter a tent city and meet the participants. In an era that featured solo flights across the Atlantic Ocean, week-long dance marathons, and flagpole-sitting contests, the Bunion Derby stands out as a bizarre event. The contestants could walk, jog, or run the 3,485-mile route between Los Angeles and New York City. They started each day at sunrise and had to check in at the next destination point by midnight, where their elapsed time was recorded by noted sprinter Arthur Duffy and Steve Owen, a lineman for the New York Giants. The runner with the best time won $25,000, and the next nine who finished shared in the prize money. Among the 275 entrants, who each paid an entry fee of $25, were serious runners such as England's Arthur Newton, who held the European record for the hundred-mile run, and Juri Lossman of Estonia, who had won a medal in the Olympic marathon. The field also included many amateurs and eccentrics, including a bearded actor who played Moses in Hollywood biblical productions, a Hindu philosopher who chanted as he jogged, and a runner from Italy who sang arias on the road.[19]

The race began on March 4, 1928. Pyle selected the date because it rhymed with "march fore." Grange ignited a bomb as the starting signal, and the runners headed east. At the head of the pack, Pyle rode in a specially built bus that greatly impressed Grange. "He had a bus made for $25,000 in Oakland. I've never seen anything like it in my life," he said. The vehicle slept nine or ten and had a shower, a galley, and even a radio. "And that's the way he went back to New York," Grange remembered. "He couldn't go like the average guy." When he wasn't making advance arrangements Grange followed behind Pyle's "land yacht," as a reporter called it, in a snappy red roadster. In addition to the entry fees and the admission charges for the privilege of meeting the runners, Pyle expected to make money by selling programs to spectators along the way (Grange estimated that he sold a half-million at 25 cents each) and charging towns through which the race passed $1,000 and up for the free advertising they received. If town officials refused to pay, as many did, Pyle would alter the route of the race to pass through more friendly communities.[20]

After leaving Los Angeles, the runners ascended icy, snow-covered mountain roads and then plunged into the Mohave Desert. In addition to the extremes in temperature, acute indigestion, cramps, and general breakdowns began to take a toll on contestants. At the thousand-mile mark in Santa Rosa, New Mexico, only ninety-three continued to endure the grueling pace. Mocking reporters predicted that "Corn and Callous" Pyle would have to halt his "Aching Dog Caravan" and recruit new "slaves." Near the halfway point in Chandler, Oklahoma, several runners went on strike and demanded daily prizes in addition to the final payoff. Pyle refused, and the eighty remaining runners set off for Chicago. In Illinois, Pyle ran into further trouble. A deputy sheriff in Joliet seized his land yacht on a writ against Pyle drawn in favor of the receiver of the now-defunct Illinois Trust and Savings Bank. A day later an association of towns along U.S. Highway 66 near Chicago refused to make a $60,000 payment to Pyle, claiming that he had failed to fulfill his contract. Pyle, who had invested between $150,000 and $200,000 in the race, now figured to end $75,000 in the red.[21]

Before the fifty-six surviving runners headed east out of Chicago, Pyle regained possession of his bus by making a $5,000 payment on the note to the Champaign bank. The news story on the bus controversy related that Grange also owed the bank $21,500, and the receiver planned to file a writ of attachment against some of his property. Finally, on May 25, after nearly three months of averaging about forty miles a day, fifty-five ragged runners limped off the Weehawken Ferry in sight of the towers of Manhattan. Pyle assured waiting reporters that the competitors were "in marvelous health, from the ankles up!" A doctor who examined the contestants estimated that the exhausting cross-country race had cost each of them ten years of life. To wring every dollar he could out of the event, Pyle insisted that the runners circle a small track for twenty more miles in front of eight hundred paying customers at Madison Square Garden. Moving at a snail's pace despite Pyle's prodding, the remaining contestants finally finished the race. Twenty-year-old Andy Paine, an Oklahoma farm boy, was declared the winner. A disgusted reporter who witnessed the inglorious conclusion of the Bunion Derby declared, "The spectacle is about as inspiring as wet wash on a sagging clothesline."[22]

Amid rumors that he was broke, the indefatigable Pyle launched a new money-making scheme. He announced that he was going to write a treatise on chiropody and give away one copy with every purchase of C. C. Pyle's Patent Foot Box. The box, he guaranteed, would contain remedies for every one of the three thousand maladies of the human foot. "I will make vast sums out of this because this country is going marathon mad," he declared. "We are just entering the golden age of the foot." On June 1 Pyle enlisted boxing promoter Tex Rickard to join him in awarding the nearly $50,000 in prize money to the top ten finishers of the Bunion Derby at Madison Square Garden before a disappointing crowd of five hundred. Thus ended the first of Pyle's transcontinental marathons. He would launch a second Bunion Derby in 1929, a fiasco that left him temporarily bankrupt. In later years Grange was defensive about Pyle's transcontinental foot race and his role in it. When sportswriter Myron Cope spoke derisively of the event in 1974, Grange became quietly indignant and insisted it was the greatest athletic event ever held. After lecturing Cope on the athletic endurance needed to compete in such an event, Grange concluded that the transcontinental marathon "was a tremendous thing."[23]

Shortly after the awards ceremony, Grange traveled to New York to discuss with Pyle the renewal of their three-year contract, which by then had expired. Grange stated in his autobiography that he did not renew the contract because his football future was in doubt. He also terminated his interest in the New York Yankees because the team was losing money "and I could no longer afford to continue pouring money into the property." After concluding his dealings with Pyle during the first week of June, Grange returned to Illinois and officially announced his split with the man he would later call "the greatest sports impresario the world has ever known." The news story stated that Grange had permanently retired from pro football due to the condition of his knee. In Champaign, Eddie Jacquin, writing for the *News-Gazette,* which had interrogated Grange about his alleged contract with Pyle in 1925, reminded readers that the newspaper had "indicated in Red's senior year that a three-year contract had been signed in May 1925. It would seem perhaps that the Pyle-Grange affiliation just came to a natural rest at the expiration of the contract." Jacquin lamented, "It seems odd to speak of that great star as having slipped in three years but he has slipped, his bankroll must have grown thinner and his position in the esteem of the public is not what it was."[24]

In addition to his concern about his injured knee, which was not responding to either rest or treatment, Grange faced serious financial problems. Pyle had lost heavily on the 1928 Bunion Derby. "We both dropped plenty trying to get that American Professional league going," Grange acknowledged. Although he apparently had not invested in the transcontinental race, it seems likely that a part of his assets were held by the Stoolman-Pyle Corporation, which was associated with the Illinois Trust and Savings Bank. Both men also had unsecured loans from that bank, which had failed in December 1927. The bank was taken over by a receiver in January 1928. Champaign attorney Sam Wood, acting on behalf of the receiver, George McComb, had visited Wheaton in early 1928 to discover if Grange had cash or property to cover his $17,000 loan from the bank. Wood learned that Grange was in California, but a search at the DuPage County abstract office revealed that Red had no property of his own. The house he had bought for his father was valued at $40,000 but was encumbered by a $12,000 mortgage. Failing to receive payment or locate Grange, McComb had a judgment of $20,278 taken against him in Champaign circuit court in late April. When Grange did not respond, McComb filed a judgment by default in the Illinois Supreme Court in mid-June 1928. The case was not resolved until late 1930, when McComb filed a suit to garnish Grange's wages as a player for the Chicago Bears. By then Grange was no longer able to support his father, who had retired as a DuPage County deputy sheriff in 1926. Lyle returned to Wheaton as chief of police in 1931 and retained that post until he retired again in 1937. Records do not reveal the extent of Red Grange's financial losses in Pyle-orchestrated ventures or the magnitude of his indebtedness in 1928.[25]

During the summer of 1928, Grange and his father left for Hollywood, where Red was scheduled to make a film for Universal Pictures. The deal was arranged by Pyle's friend Frank Zambrino, a Chicago motion picture distributor. Rather than making the trip with an entire entourage, Grange recalled, he and his father traveled alone and rented "a modest little bungalow in Los Angeles." The producer for the film project ran into financial difficulties, and the Granges waited for over two months before Red could no longer stand the inactivity. He made a cash settlement for the time he had invested in the project with Carl Laemmle, Jr., head of the studio, and Grange and his father returned to Wheaton. The 1928 football season was beginning, and Grange felt "like a duck out of water" because his injured knee prevented him from playing for the first season since he was a boy in Wheaton. Depressed and short of funds, Grange signed on with Zambrino for a six-month vaudeville tour that was centered in Chicago but played in other cities in the Midwest and East. Grange's act, given top billing, was called "C'mon Red." It was a football skit that included singing, dancing, and gags and sometimes called for Red to answer questions from the audience about football. "I earned a nice piece of change for my efforts," he remembered.[26]

Like many celebrities, Grange was often the target of lawsuits brought against him by unscrupulous citizens. The suits were especially bothersome during this difficult time. In October 1928 he was arrested as a result of a paternity charge brought against him by a Chicago woman. "There is nothing in this case but an attempt at blackmail," he declared after being released on bond. "I will fight it most strenuously in order to vindicate my reputation." After some legal wrangling, the case was dismissed when Grange apparently made a $900 out-of-court settlement. In December he made another out-of-court settlement with a Chicago man who alleged that he had been injured when Grange's car, driven by Garland Grange, smashed into his taxi. Because Grange seldom commented about his private life, it is difficult to assess the validity of such civil suits, particularly those involving women. It seems likely that most or all were spurious. During the mid-1920s he stated, "I'll never marry "unless I meet some girl far more sensible than the flappers who have flocked around since I became a headliner." He added, "I've never been engaged and don't want to be. When you're in the headlines you can't tell a woman the way to the station without being mentioned as a divorce co-respondent. I've learned that anyone who gets money out of the public earns it."[27]

After the vaudeville tour ended in the spring, Frank Zambrino arranged for Grange to sign another film contract, this time with Stateside Pictures, for a movie to be made in Hollywood that summer. The project was assigned to Nate Levine, "king of the serials," who developed an action story called *The Galloping Ghost*. Dorothy Gulliver played Grange's girlfriend and Stepin' Fetchit (Theodore Perry) and Tom Dugan provided the comic relief. The plot of the talking picture revolved around a group of gangsters who become involved in a taxicab war while attempting to fix football games. Grange, the hero, apprehends the villains after a sequence of hair-raising chases, car crashes, explosions, and fistfights designed to keep audiences on the edge of their seats from week to week.[28]

Unlike during the filming of *Racing Romeo* when he balked at overly long workdays, Grange, in need of cash, complied with a torturous work schedule that entailed shooting every day for up to eighteen hours. The nearly four-hour movie, which was shown in twelve episodes, was completed in just five weeks. Grange was delighted that he was allowed to do most of his own stunt work, although he was "black and blue from head to foot by the time the picture was completed." He remembered the making of *The Galloping Ghost* as "without doubt, the most strenuous work I have ever done in my life." At a time when "talkies" were just becoming common, one of the most difficult adjustments for him, as well as for many veteran actors, was learning and delivering spoken lines. One expert on the "serials" has described Grange's performance in *The Galloping Ghost* in one sentence: "When not in action he had the look of someone who suddenly had found himself on the wrong subway train." Although not an artistic success, the film, not released until 1931, did extremely well at the box office. *The Galloping Ghost* was revived during the 1950s and became standard fare on Saturday morning television. Many young Americans of that era first knew of Red Grange as a swashbuckling action hero rather than as a former football star. In later years Grange was convinced that his brief film career had been "one of the most valuable [experiences] in my life. The experience I got in talking to people and appearing in public—without a football suit, I mean—was a tremendous help. No, without my film experience I'd not have been able to do a lot of things I've done."[29]

After Grange returned from Hollywood in the summer of 1929, Zambrino suggested that he give football another try. The film distributor had been in contact with George Halas, who believed that Grange could still play despite his injured knee. According to Grange's account, "Halas practically insisted I come back and give it a try," and Grange agreed. He and Halas had an odd business relationship in that Grange never had a contract with the Bears' owner in 1929 or thereafter. "I would go along, week to week, drawing what money I needed or what I wanted, and at the end of the season I'd go down to the office, and Halas would say, 'Red, how much do I owe you?' Whatever figure I would mention, he never questioned it." Reconsidering the financial arrangement, Grange added, "Maybe it was good psychology, because you never overemphasize the money thing, you know, when you're making the judgment yourself." When questioned about his average salary during his second tenure with the Bears, Grange could not remember the exact amount but thought it was about $1,000 a game. That sum seems high when one considers that the Bears' highest-paid lineman, George Trafton, made only $135 per game. During the 1920s and early 1930s, however, pro football was based on a star system in which highly publicized backfield players generated large crowds and profits. During those years, Chicago players often joked that Halas "tossed around half-dollars as if they were manhole covers," and he certainly did not over-pay Grange. Fit or injured, the mere mention that Grange was in the Bears' lineup could easily draw three or four thousand additional fans to a game and produce $6,000 or $8,000 in extra revenue.[30]

With the Bears becoming less competitive in the NFL since they posted a 12-1-3 record in 1926 and with little immediate help in sight, Halas apparently believed that the addition of Grange might bolster gate receipts and perhaps produce enough revenue to rebuild the team. Although Chicago was a charter member of the league and enjoyed an excellent football market, Halas and Dutch Sternaman often had to scramble to make ends meet. Grange remembered occasional cash-flow problems despite the fact that the entire Bears' payroll (excluding his own salary) was only about $3,000 per game. In some of the early games in 1929 at Wrigley Field, he said, "Our trainer would wait until they had sold a dozen tickets, then he'd take the ticket money across the street to a drugstore and buy the tape for our ankles." With Grange alternating with thirty-four-year-old Paddy Driscoll at halfback, the Chicago owners hoped to lure fans to the stadium even though the two marquee players might not measure up to their former standards. When Grange returned to the NFL in Chicago's first game against the Minneapolis Redjackets in September 1929, he discovered that he could still run fast, but his weak knee prevented him from cutting, weaving, or changing pace very well. He became a straight-ahead runner, which, he noted, were a dime a dozen. Many years later Grange admitted to Jim Muzzy that some of the difficulty he faced in his comeback was psychological. "The knee might be alright," he explained, "but up in your head it never gets well."[31]

Although he remembered the 1929 season as one in which he carried the ball infrequently and spent much playing time on defense, statistics reveal that Grange had a respectable season as an offensive halfback. He played in all but one of the Bears' fifteen NFL games and rushed 130 times from scrimmage for 552 yards and two touchdowns. Although his running performance was far below his 1925–27 professional standard, it compares favorably with the rushing records of Bo Molenda and Johnny Blood, two backfield stars of the 1929 NFL champion Green Bay Packers, and rookie sensation Ken Strong of the Staten Island Stapletons. Fragmentary passing statistics indicate that Grange completed at least four passes for sixty-five yards and two touchdowns and caught a minimum of eight passes for 120 yards. He recalled having a slow start during the 1929 campaign because his timing was off after a year's layoff, but he played his best game of the season on October 27 against Minneapolis at Wrigley Field. Breaking away for "several sensational dashes" and completing a touchdown pass to his brother Gardie, who was in the first of three seasons with the Bears, Grange helped lead Chicago to a 27-0 victory over the admittedly weak Redjackets. The Bears got off to a good start in 1929 with a 4-1-1 record. Two days later, on what became known as Black Tuesday, the New York stock market crashed, signaling the beginning of the Great Depression. It coincided with the collapse of the Bears, who failed to win another game the rest of the season.[32]

For Grange, the crash meant more financial distress; he had lost most of his savings. The receiver of the Illinois Trust and Savings Bank continued to pursue him, and a recent judgment against him won by the Southern Pacific Railroad for $3,121 stemming from unpaid fares for the 1926 barnstorming tour in California further darkened his financial situation. Although there are no records to provide a full accounting of Grange's finances at the onset of the depression, his indebtedness gave every reason to sustain a bid for a comeback in the NFL. Unwilling to accept mediocrity, he recalled that he "began to work harder than ever on perfecting my defensive play." Grange had every opportunity to do just that during the second half of the season as opponents scored 192 points against only fifty for the Bears. Despite Chicago's dismal performance during November and December, which was partly due to a growing rift between Halas and Sternaman, Grange was delighted to be playing football once again. One of the memorable games of the season was on Thanksgiving Day at Comiskey Park, where Grange witnessed one of the most remarkable feats in NFL history. Ernie Nevers, who, like Grange, was returning to the NFL after a year's absence, scored all of the Chicago Cardinals' points (six touchdowns and four conversions) in a convincing 40-6 victory over the Bears. Four days earlier Nevers scored all of his team's nineteen points in a victory over Dayton. No one has ever matched Nevers's achievement.[33]

Midway through the season, Grange suffered a dislocated shoulder that forced him to miss a game and play the remaining games heavily taped. Toward the end of the year his knee began to bother him again, and trainer Andy Lotshaw constructed a special brace out of elastic with two steel hinges along the sides to provide better support. For the rest of his career Grange would require yards of adhesive tape wound around the knee and the brace fitted over it when he played. He also would wear protective tape around his shoulder for two more seasons. He may have looked like a mummy under his uniform, but he continued to play.[34]

From a competitive standpoint, the Bears' 4-9-2 record was the worst in the team's history. At the gate, however, Grange continued to be a prime attraction and drew large numbers of fans to both home and away games. At Wrigley Field on November 3, the combination of Grange and Benny Friedman, then with the Giants, attracted twenty-six thousand fans who witnessed a 26-14 New York victory. In Philadelphia on November 16 the local press and the Frankford Yellow Jackets heavily publicized his return to the city. They were rewarded when "more than ten thousand fans, one of the largest crowds ever to jam the Yellow Jacket Stadium," watched the home team defeat the Bears 20-14. Frankford's largest home attendance up to that point in the season had been a little over six thousand. Despite his diminished ability to thrill spectators with spectacular open-field running, Grange remained one of the most popular players in the league. George Halas was more than satisfied with his solid play and was delighted by his continuing capacity to draw paying customers. Although he realized that his days as a game-breaking halfback were over, Grange still enjoyed the game, worked hard at it, and believed that football provided an honorable way to make a living. With his financial affairs in disarray, he was determined to play another season with the Bears.[35]

10

A Solid Pro Player

★ ★

GRANGE CONCLUDED THE 1929 SEASON by participating in an exhibition football tour during December and January that terminated in Los Angeles. He remained in California during the spring of 1930 and took a job as master of ceremonies at a roadside nightclub near Culver City. "I have what some people think is a funny job for a football player," he admitted, "but I like it. My job is to introduce these 'hot' celebrities when they come into the place, and kid them along. They like it and so do the customers." When his job in Culver City ended, Grange said, he would take a similar position at the Mark Hopkins Hotel in San Francisco, but, he added, "I don't think I will stay with this kind of work very long." After the wire services reported Red's new occupation, the Cleveland *Plain Dealer* carried an editorial that both pitied him and suggested that the worsening economic slump was bringing to an end the era of ballyhooed sports heroes: "In five years, Red Grange skidded from the top of the world to a job as clown in a restaurant. America, accustomed to such tragedies, says, 'He couldn't stand prosperity.'" Placing some of the blame on the public, "which carried the riotous wine of notoriety through the portals of a university to him," the writer claimed that "the world owes damages to Red Grange for having made him a sacrifice to its passion for excitement and hero-worship."[1]

Writing several months earlier on famous sports figures in history, New York *Herald-Tribune* columnist W. O. McGeehan agreed that the depression had closed the curtain on the sports craze of the 1920s. "Intercollegiate football always should be grateful to Red Grange," he wrote, because he and Pyle had "demonstrated that it could not be successfully professionalized and thrown on the open market like baseball and ice hockey." McGeehan predicted that sports in the 1930s would return to normal. "It seems that there will never be the ballyhoo for another football player that there was with Red Grange. The inducements for football stars have become so lean that the game is safe for the colleges." In the face of media pity, which he detested, and the intimation that he was already a relic, Grange remained firm in his commitment to continue playing pro football, his "profession."[2]

When he reported to Chicago for preseason practice, Grange became part of a Bears' team that had been reorganized and revamped. One of the biggest problems the ninth-place team had experienced in 1929 concerned the divergent coaching philosophies and tension between Halas and Dutch Sternaman. "We had two offenses, one devised by George and one by Dutch," one player recalled. "Nobody knew what to expect on any play. People were running into each other on the field." To avoid further contention and another dismal season, both men relinquished the coaching reins and hired Ralph Jones, a former assistant to Bob Zuppke at Illinois and head coach at Lake Forest Academy, to lead the team. An innovative football strategist, Jones would transform the Bears' offense into the modern T formation. Unlike most college and pro teams, which ran a single-wing, double-wing, or Notre Dame box formation, the Bears had lined up in an old-style T. By splitting the ends, widening the halfbacks, and eventually sending a back in motion, Jones developed a quick-hitting, deceptive offense that would come to dominate pro football. The split T benefited Grange because it opened the Bears' offense, allowed him to get into the open field more often, and was less bruising than the older formations.[3]

With the retirement of Paddy Driscoll, Grange became the regular left halfback. He would have ample opportunity to run with the ball in 1930. According to incomplete statistics, he carried the ball from scrimmage more often than any other Chicago player. The Bears also added two new players who would improve the team on both offense and defense. Carl Brumbaugh of the University of Florida was obtained from the Portsmouth Spartans and would take over the quarterback position from Joey Sternaman, who remained with the team as a substitute. A versatile player, Brumbaugh would prove to be a fine field general and excellent passer. The prize recruit was Bronislau "Bronko" Nagurski from the University of Minnesota, a college player of legendary strength and power who was rated as an all-American at both tackle and fullback during his senior season. When he signed him in March 1930 for the substantial depression-era salary of $5,000, Halas remembered that Nagurski was "six feet two inches and he weighed two hundred thirty-four pounds, and it was all—literally all—muscle, skin and bone. He didn't have an ounce of fat on him. A lot of men have passed in front of me, but none with a build like that man." In the mid-1980s Grange remembered Nagurski as Larry Czonka and Dick Butkus rolled into one—and maybe a little better: "Bronk to me is the best football player I ever saw."[4]

The Bears with their new split-T offense got off to a slow start in 1930, managing only a scoreless tie with the Brooklyn Dodgers in their first regular-season game. Brooklyn guard Ernie Cuneo recalled that his team contained Chicago "by playing Grange first and the Bears second." He remembered that "though Grange was the star attraction as a ball carrier, he won the profound respect of his fellow professionals because he played the game for sixty minutes, offense and defense, like the great athlete he was." The Chicago *Tribune* reported that in the Brooklyn game Grange "appeared to better advantage than since 1925, his first year with the pros." Late in the game, Nagurski was inserted at fullback and failed to plunge over from the Brooklyn one-yard line for the winning touchdown. It was one of the few times in his career he was stopped so close to an opponent's end zone. He became the Bears' regular fullback the following week.[5]

In Green Bay that Sunday, Grange and Brumbaugh accidentally developed the man-in-motion feature of the split-T offense. When they realized that Grange was not being covered when he faked wide to the left on plays to the opposite side of the field, the two backs improvised a play that sent Grange in motion a few seconds before the ball was snapped. He made good gains the rest of the game when Brumbaugh lateraled him the ball after he went in motion to the weak side. Although the Bears lost the game 7-0, Coach Jones incorporated the procedure into his offense with positive results. Despite the innovative offense, the Bears struggled through their first nine games with a modest 4-4-1 record. Grange had his best game on October 19 when the Bears avenged their humiliating 1929 loss to the Cardinals by decisively defeating them 32-6. Showing flashes of his previous form, Grange broke loose for two first-period touchdowns.[6]

In their final five games the Bears had a difficult schedule and faced the

Giants, Packers, and Portsmouth Spartans, teams that already had defeated them. The split T began to function smoothly, however, and the defense that featured Grange's improving play as a defensive back and Nagurski's intimidating, bone-crushing tackling held opponents to just twelve points in the remaining games. At the Polo Grounds on November 16, Chicago frustrated Benny Friedman's Giants, who had a 10-1 record, by shutting them out in a 12-0 victory. The following weekend in Philadelphia Grange broke loose for touchdown runs of fifty-one and seventy-eight yards in leading the Bears to a 13-6 win over Frankford. Philadelphia sportswriter Joe Tumelty remarked that "even though it meant defeat to the home team, it was a grand sight to see Grange doing the deeds that made his name so famous as a college gridder in the yesteryear." He noted that Grange "figured just as effectively on the defense as he did on the offense." After a tight 6-0 victory over the Cardinals on Thanksgiving Day, Grange played what he described as his best game of the season against Portsmouth when he scored one touchdown and passed to Luke Johnsos for another in a 14-6 win over the Spartans. The Bears' final game, a 21-0 victory over the eventual 1930 NFL champion Green Bay Packers, not only avenged two previous losses to the Wisconsin team but also boded well for Chicago's future. With a 9-4-1 record, the Bears finished the NFL season in third place and placed three players, including Grange, on the all-NFL team selected by the Green Bay *Press Gazette*. Although some modern commentators have suggested that he made all-pro teams in his comeback years partly because of his fame and reputation, Grange had a very productive season in 1930. He scored eight touchdowns and amassed more than a thousand total yards rushing and passing and through pass receptions. Incomplete statistics reveal that he likely averaged about six yards per carry rushing from scrimmage. Those figures, moreover, give no indication of his exceptional defensive play.[7]

Near the end of the 1930 season, the Bears stirred up an old controversy when George Halas signed fullback Joe Savoldi of Notre Dame to play in their last three games. Savoldi had been expelled recently from the South Bend school because officials discovered he had been secretly married. Although Savoldi's class had not yet graduated, Halas believed that because of the "extraordinary circumstances" in signing him the Bears were not encroaching upon college football or violating the NFL rule that Halas himself had championed back in 1926. Joe Carr, NFL president, thought otherwise and promptly fined Halas and the Bears $1,000 for violating the league's "Constitution and By-Laws." Given the protracted and contentious debate of 1925, when Grange turned pro before his college class had graduated, media reaction to the Bears' transgression was relatively mild. One reason for this was the growing acceptance of pro football by the media, and to some degree the public, which dated back to Grange's barnstorming tours of 1925–26. Sportswriters such as Don Maxwell of the Chicago *Tribune* were partly responsible for the trend because they had focussed more attention on the pro game. As an indication of the increasing respectability of pro football, venerated Notre Dame coach Knute Rockne agreed to assemble a squad of past and present Fighting Irish players to oppose the New York Giants in a postseason exhibition game, the proceeds of which would go to benefit New York's unemployed. Notre Dame, undefeated during the 1929 and 1930 seasons, was heavily favored, and many of the more than fifty thousand spectators who turned out at the Polo Grounds on December 14 were shocked when Benny Friedman and the Giants easily defeated the Four Horsemen and other Notre Dame luminaries 22-0. Although the game was not necessarily a true test of the relative strengths of pro and college football, it helped undermine the still widely held view that the college game was superior.[8]

Increased public awareness of pro football was also partly due to the onset of the depression. There were numerous critics of the college game during the 1920s, but some of the criticism was muted because intercollegiate football was associated with mounting prosperity. When the economic dam burst, many were quick to single out the intercollegiate game as an institution corrupted by the materialistic excesses of an affluent era. By 1930, moreover, they had plenty of ammunition after the Carnegie Report of the previous year detailed a myriad of violations of the amateur ethic committed by college football programs large and small. Sportswriter and social critic John R. Tunis compared the contemporary dissolute state of intercollegiate athletics with the supposedly pristine days of college sports before the Roaring Twenties. "Laugh if you will at the misguided idealism which sent our fathers out to die for dear old Yale," he wrote, but "at least it was idealism. There is precious little idealism of any sort at present when a squad is asked to go out and die for a $15,000-a-year head coach." He further charged that "the governors of the various sports know perfectly well that the athletes are taking money on the side; the recent Carnegie report showed many of the football players in the colleges to be as plainly bought and paid for as players on the New York Giants." A number of newspapers agreed that college football was "declining in popularity with the sporting public in general." One reason was that only "the most skillful teams are adjudged worth the high admission charges." A second factor was professional football. "Numbers of football enthusiasts," the *New York Times* noted, "prefer the economical skill, the mature precision, the finesse, and the art of the professional game to the comparatively bungling college match."[9]

While the news media conferred some belated praise on pro football the NFL was confronting the reality of the depression. The Minneapolis and Newark franchises folded after the 1930 season, and the NFL sponsored a new team in Cleveland that it hoped might attract financial backers during the 1931 campaign. At the end of that season, however, Cleveland, which struggled on the field and at the gate, dropped out of the league, as did the 1928 champions, the Providence Steam Roller. The once powerful Frankford Yellow Jackets also ceased operations before the 1931 season ended. Like many NFL owners, Grange's financial situation remained precarious. With what money he had left after heavy losses resulting from the stock market crash and his settlement with the receiver of the Illinois Trust and Savings Bank, Grange invested heavily in real estate. It was an unfortunate decision because the continuing economic slump depressed prices. After the 1931 season Grange purchased an interest in the 77 Club, a Chicago North Side nightclub where he worked as master of ceremonies.[10]

When Grange reported to the Bears' training camp in September 1931, the team appeared primed to challenge the Green Bay Packers, who had won back-to-back championships, for the NFL title. Quarterback Joey Sternaman had retired, but Chicago acquired Keith Molesworth, a diminutive halfback from Monmouth College, to help propel the running game still centered around Grange and Nagurski. The Bears were one of the few NFL teams to show a profit ($1,695.93) in 1930, and the league accorded them a favorable schedule. Nine of Chicago's thirteen league games would be played at home. Grange scored the Bears' first touchdown of the season in a 21-0 victory over Cleveland in the first regular season NFL night game played in Chicago, but the team struggled through the first half of the season with a disappointing 4-3 record. A number of key injuries contributed to the team's lackluster performance. Grange scored four of his six touchdowns that season in back-to-back victories over the Giants and Chicago Cardinals in early October but in general the Bears had difficulty scoring against the league's tougher teams, which included Green Bay, Portsmouth, and New York. In fact, shutouts and low-scoring games were the norm in the NFL from 1920 through 1932. In almost two-thirds of the league's games during those years one of the teams failed to score.[11]

When he reviewed his years in the NFL, Grange noted a number of differences between college and pro football and also reasons for the relative lack of scoring in the pro game. First, linemen were bigger and stronger, weighing from twenty to thirty pounds per man more than their college counterparts. They were also more skillful. "You could get probably the finest All-American lineman out of college for a hundred dollars a game," he remembered. Second, the size of the ball and forward passing regulations also contributed to the dominance of defensive football. Although the old rugby-style ball had been pared down by 1929 to twenty-two and one-half inches in circumference, it was not until 1934 and thereafter that the NFL adopted slimmer designs that allowed for more accurate passing. "Benny Friedman threw that old balloon," Grange told Myron Cope in 1974. "He was the first player who pulled teams out of a seven man line. Who's to say what Friedman could do today. After that they redesigned the ball three different times."[12]

Grange also noted that until 1933 the ball could only be passed forward from at least five yards behind the line of scrimmage, and the second incomplete pass during a series of downs drew a five-yard penalty. As a result, most teams resorted to passing only on third down or in desperate situations. The restricted substitution rules, a lack of adequate reserve players on pro rosters, and what Ernest Cuneo described as "macho bravado" resulted in most players competing for the entire sixty-minute game. Moreover, the equipment weighed two-thirds more than modern football gear. After about five minutes of play, Grange said, the felt, canvas, and wool uniform "was soaking wet," uncomfortable, and sapped a player's strength. The flimsy leather helmet, like much of the other equipment, provided inadequate protection. Grange could remember playing "many quarters being dazed after receiving a knee to the head." Given that most players remained in the high-impact, grueling contests until the bitter end and under adverse conditions, NFL play was sometimes sluggish. Games were often decided in the last few minutes when exhausted players broke down or made costly mistakes. Joe Horrigan, vice president of the Pro Football Hall of Fame, also has suggested that the defensive game in those years was improving more rapidly than offensive play.[13]

On the positive side, pro football players of Grange's era did not face the intense scrutiny or pressure their modern counterparts endure. "The fate of the nation did not hinge on whether you won or lost," Grange recalled. "The money wasn't that big—$100 to $150 a game." Pro football, moreover, was not a full-time job for most players. Grange recollected that the Bears only practiced for three hours in the mornings and had a short meeting at night three times a week. "The rest of the day was your own." Many players worked during the afternoons as salesmen or in garages or at similar jobs and had enough time and money to enjoy night life in NFL cities. When Myron Cope asked Grange in 1974 who of his era could compare with Joe Namath, then playing for the New York Jets, he replied, "I could name half of every ball club. Shucks, we found places in New York that Namath hasn't discovered yet." Prohibition "didn't make any difference. There was more drinking in Prohibition than there is now." Reconsidering that remark, he added, "I don't mean they were a bunch of drunks because they were not."[14]

The high jinks and camaraderie often continued on the field. Grange remembered that referee Jim Durfee, a frustrated high school quarterback, sometimes called plays in the Bears' huddle. "And you'd better call it the way he said or you'd have a penalty coming up on your hands." On one occasion Durfee threw a flag and penalized Giants' coach Steve Owen five yards for coaching from the sidelines. When Owen protested and pointed out that the penalty indicated was actually fifteen yards, Durfee responded that five yards was sufficient "given what Owen knew about football." In one of Bronko Nagurski's first games as a pro, Grange, who was supposed to be providing protection on a Chicago punt, agreed to Green Bay tackle Cal Hubbard's request to let him through so Hubbard could find out just how tough Nagurski really was. The massive Hubbard slammed into Bronko, who was the last blocker in front of the Chicago punter, "and bounced off like he'd run into a stone wall."[15]

Although pro football may not have been a life or death matter in 1931, the Bears were anxious to improve their mediocre record and challenge for the league championship in the second half of the season. It would be an up-hill struggle because the Packers led the NFL with a perfect 9-0 record. Chicago defeated Portsmouth 9-6 at Wrigley Field before a large ladies' day crowd of twenty-five thousand and departed on a two-game eastern road trip in mid-November. More than thirty thousand fans attended the Bears-Giants game at the Polo Grounds. Benny Friedman, who had retired after the 1930 season to become an assistant football coach at Yale, had returned to the team the previous week and helped extend the Giant's winning streak to four games. The sometimes irascible Friedman was one of the few pro players who publicly expressed resentment about Grange's notoriety and high salary. In 1932, for example, he alleged that Grange's less than sensational debut in pro football had been the result of hard-boiled and underpaid linemen refusing to "consistently clear a path at the expense of jolts and bruises to give Grange—making ten or twenty times as much per game, an easy road to glory." If that had been the case, other players kept it to themselves. The Bears spoiled the Giants' title hopes that day with a 12-6 victory as a result of Gardie Grange's reception of a Brumbaugh pass for a touchdown with twelve seconds to play. Despite his heroics, it was difficult for Gardie to escape his brother's shadow. "Red Grange's Brother Beats Giants on Pass" ran the headline of one Chicago newspaper. Gardie retired from football after the 1931 and went into the printing business. He died in Miami in 1981.[16]

Westbrook Pegler wrote a satirical article about the game in which he attempted to educate fans on the high quality of pro football with respect to the college game. He described three spectacular Chicago forward pass plays "which had they been 'tossed and ketched' in a famous college game, would have sent echoes ringing down for weeks" and added that "it looked as though some of the boys were actually willing to die, or at any rate be very ill, for dear old Mr. Mara and the dear old George Halas, manager of the Chicago Bears, Inc." Reflecting on the criticism heaped on college football in the wake of the Carnegie Report, Pegler noted that "professional football had a difficult time for several seasons in New York, owing to popular disinterest and bad weather, but this year patrons have seen little difference between teams which play to support expensive college plants, including coaches, press agents, and graduate managers and the kind that play to support such as Mr. Mara."[17]

The Bears completed their eastern trip with a convincing 26-0 win over Brooklyn, with Grange initiating the scoring on "a remarkable catch of a pass." They returned home to defeat the Cardinals 18-7. Grange's forty-five-yard, second-period touchdown run was the highlight of the day. The victory gave the resurgent Bears a four-game winning streak and an outside chance to catch league-leading Green Bay. Chicago was knocked out of the championship race the following Sunday, however, when Portsmouth shut them out 3-0 as the Spartans' defense held Grange in check all afternoon. A late-season Chicago victory over the champion Green Bay Packers, who won their third straight NFL title, was small consolation in what had to be considered a disappointing season. The Bears finished third in the league, with an 8-5 record.[18]

Grange had another sound year as an all-purpose halfback. He scored forty-two points on seven touchdowns, fifth-best in the league, and rushed for more than six hundred yards—about 5.4 yards per carry. In addition, he contributed nearly two hundred more yards to the Bears' offense by throwing and receiving passes. What a number of NFL veterans from that era recall, however, was Grange's superb defensive play. Remembering his comeback years, Jimmy Conzelman emphasized at the 1984 Pro Football Hall of Fame induction ceremonies that Red, although always dangerous on offense, "distinguished himself on defense." For the second consecutive year Grange was selected as left halfback on the all-NFL team. After the regular season ended, he went on another barnstorming tour before resuming his job as master of ceremonies at the 77 Club. During the summer, he announced that he was retiring from pro football. The retirement was only temporary. George Halas convinced him to return to the Bears for one more season. "I retired every year, you know," Grange remembered. "Half the guys retire every year, and then they come back the next year." A newspaper story in September reported that NFL salaries for the 1932 season were being cut by one-third and listed Grange's wages for the upcoming year at $8,000. In one of the worst years of the depression that income no doubt served as a powerful inducement for Grange to reconsider retirement and return to the NFL.[19]

By 1932 the full impact of the depression was being felt from the dust bowl of the Great Plains to the streets of every major city where the unemployed lined up for a daily ration of bread and soup. As the fall football season approached amid reports of rising bank failures, the nation faced its gravest crisis since the Civil War. Like many other institutions, the NFL teetered on the brink of financial disaster. When the regular season began, only eight teams competed for the championship in the league's thirteenth year, and all eventually sustained economic losses. Despite the continuing criticism of college football in the press, the professional game remained lackluster by comparison. One of the common complaints continued to be the large number of dull, low-scoring NFL games. In 1931 half of the league's teams averaged seven points or less per game, and the 1932 season provided little improvement. During a desolate autumn for many Americans, NFL games averaged only 16.4 points for both teams, the lowest per-game scoring standard since 1926. The Chicago Bears would contribute to the offensive drought, at least in their first four games.[20]

In one of the most unusual seasons in their long history, the Bears began the season with three scoreless tie games. The following week they lost their home-opener against Green Bay 2-0. Fans wondered if their team would ever score again. Few took consolation in the fact that no one had crossed the Chicago goal line or that the Packers had scored just two points

against them in two games. The scoreless streak was broken on October
23 when the Bears pushed across four touchdowns (Grange scoring the
first on a pass reception) in a 27-7 victory over Staten Island. After a 7-7
tie with Boston, Chicago again scored four touchdowns in a 28-8 win over
the New York Giants. The Bears were finally displaying some offensive
potency, but by midseason most experts were predicting a fourth straight
championship for Green Bay, who led the league with a 8-0-1 record.
Chicago completed its first eight games with a somewhat unusual record
of 2-1-5. After the Giants upset the Packers at the Polo Grounds in mid-
November, however, Portsmouth surged to the top of the NFL standings
by defeating Green Bay in its final game of the season. Under existing NFL
regulations, tie games were discounted and the league championship was
awarded to the team with the best winning percentage. With the defeat at
the hands of the Spartans, Green Bay was eliminated from the title race
but had one game remaining with the Bears. Meanwhile, Chicago had
accumulated three more victories and a tie for a 5-1-6 record. A Bears'
victory against the Packers would give them the identical winning percentage as Portsmouth, who had finished the season at 6-1-4.[21]

Grange remembered the 1932 season as his best as a pro after his comeback in 1929. He mistakenly recalled that he scored nine touchdowns and
was named to the all-NFL team. In fact, Grange had a respectable year
but was clearly slowing down and contributing less to the Bears' offense.
He did score seven touchdowns for forty-two points, second-best in the
league, but gained only three yards per carry in seventy-seven rushes and
failed to make the all-pro team. Nagurski, who was selected to the all-NFL
team at fullback, became the Bears' primary rusher, and Grange was used
increasingly as a decoy and pass receiver. Four of his touchdowns came
on pass receptions. That is not to say that Grange was ineffective. He still
produced almost six hundred yards in total offense for the Bears and remained a stalwart on defense. His best days with the Bears were clearly
behind him, but he continued to make an important contribution to the
team.[22]

On December 11 Grange and his teammates prepared for the showdown
game with the Packers that would determine whether they would gain a
share of the NFL championship. The game was played in the worst weather
conditions many players on both teams could remember. A fierce storm
had covered Chicago with more than a foot of snow, and at Wrigley Field
it was plowed into banks along the sidelines. As the game progressed, a
chilling wind blew the snow into clouds that enveloped the field. Only five

thousand hardy fans braved the twenty-four-degree temperature, blustery wind, and blowing snow to watch both teams slip and slide through three periods of scoreless football. In the final quarter, however, Chicago drove to the Green Bay fourteen-yard line, where Tiny Engebretsen kicked a field goal. Shortly thereafter, Nagurski broke loose on a fifty-six-yard touchdown run to secure a 9-0 Bears' victory. Chicago and Portsmouth ended the season with identical .857 winning percentages and apparently shared the NFL championship.[23]

George Halas was delighted by the outcome of the game, but the sparse crowd created a financial problem. He could not meet the Packers' $2,500 guarantee. Green Bay coach and founder Curly Lambeau agreed to accept $1,000 and a note for the rest payable in six months. The following September, Halas made good on the note plus $71.25 in interest. After the season both Grange and Nagurski also received promissory notes of $1,000 from Halas as part of their salaries. Not satisfied with a co-championship, Halas and Sternaman, the Portsmouth owners, and their coach Potsy Clark agreed to play a championship play-off game in Chicago on December 18. Joe Carr sanctioned the game to be played at Wrigley Field. Portsmouth was particularly anxious to play the Bears. The previous season, Green Bay had canceled a "tentatively" scheduled season-ending game with them, which, had the Spartans won, would have made them NFL champions. The Spartans were intent on winning the league title outright. Given their competitive nature and the Bears' precarious financial situation, Halas and Sternaman were also eager to play the first play-off game in NFL history.[24]

Arctic-like conditions gripped Chicago the week before the game. With snow continuing on and off and temperatures plunging below zero, Halas and Sternaman concluded that only very hardy or foolhardy fans would attend a game at Wrigley Field under such conditions. The league office and Portsmouth's management provided permission to play the game indoors at Chicago Stadium, where the Bears had successfully played an exhibition game against the Cardinals after the 1930 season. Because of the limited playing surface at Chicago Stadium, both teams agreed upon a number of modifications. The field would be eighty yards long, including the end zones, with a single goalpost placed at one goal line. Kickoffs would originate from the defensive team's ten-yard line, the ball would be re-spotted to compensate for the shorter field, and field goals were prohibited. Because of the narrowness of the playing surface, the sidelines were only about fifteen feet from the stadium walls in most places. To avoid injuries, it was agreed that the ball would be moved fifteen yards in-bounds on any out-of-bounds plays with a loss of down. The following February the NFL adopted a modified hash-mark rule similar to the play-off game provision. Fortunately for the players, a circus had performed in the arena the week before and left a six-inch bed of dirt on the cement floor. Sod was laid over it, but more than a few players and fans noted the peculiar aromatic quality of the playing surface.[25]

The play-off game was held at night and attracted a near-capacity crowd of about eleven thousand. Grange was among those who predicted that night games would attract large crowds in pro football. Although the teams were evenly matched (they played two tie games during the regular season), Portsmouth began the game with two serious handicaps. Dutch Clark, their top offensive player and the league's leading scorer, was unavailable to play. He had signed a contract to coach basketball at Colorado College and begin his duties as soon as the Spartans' regular season ended. When the college's president insisted that he meet the letter of the contract, Clark complied and was en route to Colorado when the game began. In addition, the lighter Spartans brought only sixteen players to Chicago (the league limit was twenty-two) because of injuries and the expense involved. Chicago sportswriters predicted that the Bears would wear down the smaller, undermanned Spartans in a high-scoring game.[26]

The compressed field, however, gave the advantage to the defense. Portsmouth advanced the ball more effectively than Chicago in the first half but neither team could score. Grange was knocked out by a hard tackle and left the game after making a fifteen-yard run in the second period, but he would return to action in the final quarter. During the second half, Chicago appeared to be wearing down the Spartans, but the game remained scoreless with five minutes to play. At that point, the Bears' Dick Nesbitt intercepted a Portsmouth pass and returned it to the Spartans' seven-yard line before being knocked out of bounds. Because of the special out-of-bounds rule, Chicago started its attack on second down. Nagurski plunged through center for six yards to the Portsmouth one-yard line but lost a yard on his third-down rush. The next play was one of the most dramatic and controversial in the early history of the NFL.[27]

Portsmouth players massed near their own goal line, expecting another desperate plunge by Nagurski. They appeared to be right as Grange went in motion and Brumbaugh took the snap and handed off to his bruising fullback. Nagurski surged forward toward the line, but, as he remembered, "There was no way I could get through. I stopped. I moved back a couple of steps. Grange had gone around and was in the end zone, all by himself.

I threw him a short pass." Grange remembered being flat on his back in the end zone. "Someone had knocked me down. But I got the ball and hung on to it." The referee immediately signaled a touchdown. Portsmouth coach Potsy Clark stormed onto the field, protesting that Nagurski was not five yards behind the line of scrimmage when he threw the pass as the rules required. Referee Bobby Cahn was unmoved, and the touchdown stood. Before the game ended Chicago forced a Portsmouth safety, making the final score 9-0. As an indication of the still tenuous state of pro football, the *New York Times* buried a brief account of the game on the second page of its sporting section.[28]

Following the game, the Spartans not only continued to protest Nagurski's touchdown pass but also claimed that the Chicago Stadium game was not a championship contest and they still retained a share of the NFL title. When NFL owners met in Pittsburgh in February, however, they awarded the 1932 championship to Chicago. They also approved four rules changes, three of which related directly to the play-off game: forward passing was permitted from any point behind the line of scrimmage, a hash-mark procedure was implemented, and the goalposts were to be moved forward to the goal lines. "We hoped the new rules would open up the game," Halas recalled years later. "I believe the record will show that we were right." During the 1933 season, field goal scoring increased dramatically and there were half as many tie games as in the previous season; there were none at all in 1934. Total offense for virtually every team rose over the next several seasons. For their participation in the first NFL play-off game each member of the Bears received $240 while Portsmouth players earned $175.[29]

After the play-off game Grange played several exhibition games with the Bears before once again announcing his retirement. Sportswriter Bill Braucher regarded the retirement as the end of an era. He wrote somewhat lyrically that "Grange, a little fat now, nearly thirty, finds that the flame that swept him to greatness unparalleled by any other player since the World War, has burned itself to an ember." "Though I'm quitting the game, I'm quitting as a player only," Grange explained. "I've had several coaching offers, and I'm considering several propositions right now." When asked about professional football, he predicted a bright future for the sport and added, "I have an idea it would be a good thing to break up the league [the NFL] into two leagues, an eastern and western division." The restructuring of the NFL into divisions with a play-off game between the two regional champions (another fallout from the Chicago-Portsmouth title game), which Boston Redskins owner George Preston Marshall proposed and the other owners approved at the NFL summer meeting, was already being widely discussed during the winter of 1933. In April, Grange returned to Urbana-Champaign for only the second time since he left the University of Illinois to appear in a vaudeville show at the Virginia Theater. He also made an appearance on campus accompanied by Bob Zuppke. When asked about his stage career, Grange remarked somewhat defensively, "Oh, I know some people think it's awful, but I like it and I'm making a pretty fair living. Everywhere I go I hear that people are sorry for me. It really is laughable in a way." He conceded, "I made some mistakes but who hasn't. I've made lots of money and lost a great deal but so have others. It hasn't made me sour on the world." Eddie Jacquin, who interviewed Grange, noted in a postscript to his article that "Red says he has a lot of real estate and if we know of anyone that's in the market for some, just to tell them to get in touch with him."[30]

Public perception of Grange during his comeback years varied depending on what aspect of his life was being evaluated, who made the judgment, and at what stage of his career the evaluation was made. Those sportswriters (clearly a minority) who focused on the corrupt state of college football and applauded the reforms suggested by the Carnegie Report regarded Grange as a symbol of the excesses of the intercollegiate game and its apparent decline by the early 1930s. They appeared to delight in dwelling on his financial woes and his pedestrian off-season jobs as well as his diminished athletic ability. Other writers and most football fans, however, viewed Grange as one of the game's greatest players and revered him in the same way that baseball fans idolized Babe Ruth, even in his last years as a player. Some fans no doubt felt sorry for Grange, and a few may have pitied him because of his financial problems or declining skill on the field, but most continued to see him as the biggest name in football. Throughout the 1932 season, Grange received top billing in both newspaper stories and pregame advertising in most cities in which the Bears played, despite the fact that he was not the team's best player. Grange's reputation and drawing power clearly exceeded other NFL stars of the day, such as Benny Friedman and Ernie Nevers. By 1933 and 1934, as his skills rapidly diminished, it is probable that more fans did feel sorry for or pity Grange, as some did Ruth or Willie Mays in their final seasons. How the general public who did not closely follow football perceived Grange is less certain. It is safe to say that most people became less interested in both his personal life and athletic exploits as his playing career came to a close.[31]

Grange's continuing financial problems may have convinced him to return to the Bears for another season, but more likely it was his attachment to the game. Although he had tentatively retired after each of his comeback seasons, Grange remembered that after "that year [1932] I had had it, and I didn't see any great future out of being a defensive football player. But George wanted me to come back, and I did." In September, he joined the Bears at their training camp on the Notre Dame campus in South Bend, Indiana. It was the first time the team had conducted preseason drills outside of Chicago. During the off-season Halas had bought out his partner Dutch Sternaman and not only became the Bears' sole owner but also returned as head coach, primarily to save on expenses. He strengthened Chicago's line by acquiring tackle George Musso of Milliken College and end Bill Karr of West Virginia. Jack Manders from the University of Minnesota proved to be another valuable acquisition. He served as an all-purpose back and became the most accurate field goal kicker in the league, earning the nickname "Automatic Jack." To spell Grange at halfback, Halas signed Gene Ronzani from Marquette.[32]

In his autobiography, Grange recalled that "my speed was gone by 1933—as attested by the fact that I made only one touchdown that year." One recent commentator on Grange's career has compared his post-1931 football performance to those painful seasons (for spectators) in the early 1970s when Willie Mays unwisely extended his baseball career with the New York Mets. James Mark Purcell argues that Grange "was too big a name for the depression-struck league to afford to let go when his goodbye time would seem to have come." Although Grange and Purcell are correct—Red had slowed down and was by 1933 a part-time player—NFL statistics for that year indicate that he was far from ineffective. Nagurski remained the Bears' leading rusher, but Grange was still the team's second-leading ball carrier in both number of attempts (79) and yards gained (297). He averaged a respectable 3.8 yards per carry, completed two touchdown passes in addition to his one rushing, and had two touchdown runs called back because of penalties. At thirty, he continued to make a contribution to the defending NFL champions on both offense and defense.[33]

The Bears got off to a fast start in 1933 by winning their first six games. Although the offense had improved from the previous season, defense, which limited opponents to 5.5 points per game during the early season winning streak, was the hallmark of the Bears. As a result of the string of cliffhanging victories opening the season, the Chicago press began referring to the team as "the storybook Bears." A three-game eastern road trip in early November removed some of the Frank Merriwell aura. The Bears lost two close games to the Boston Redskins and the Giants and had to settle for a tie with the Philadelphia Eagles, one of two new NFL teams in Pennsylvania. Chicago rebounded, however, by winning their last four games, including two pivotal contests with Portsmouth, their chief competitor in the western division. Finishing the season with a 10-2-1 record, the Bears won their division and faced the New York Giants at Wrigley Field in the first NFL championship game.[34]

The two teams were evenly matched (splitting two regular-season games), and coaches Halas and Steve Owen would pull out all the stops in directing their teams in one of the most memorable postseason games in NFL history. "We had no special strategy," Grange remembered, "as we had played each other twice during the season so we pretty much knew each other's strengths and weaknesses." On December 17, a foggy and misty day in Chicago, twenty-six thousand spectators and a substantial media corps remained on the edge of their seats for most of the afternoon as the lead in the game changed hands six times and the final outcome remained in doubt until the last few moments of play. The tone of the game was set early, when the Giants ran a center-sneak play that netted thirty yards but failed to produce a score. Jack Manders kicked field goals in the first and second periods for Chicago before a Harry Newman–to–Red Badgro touchdown pass and conversion gave the Giants a 7-6 half-time advantage. The lead seesawed back and forth in the third period, and the Bears led 16-14 going into the final fifteen minutes of play. With time running down, the Giants scored on a bizarre broken play in which tailback Newman handed off to halfback Ken Strong on a reverse. Strong promptly found himself trapped in his own backfield at the Chicago fifteen-yard line and passed the ball back to a startled Newman. The Giants' tailback sprinted to his right, regained his composure, and threw a forward pass to Strong, who stood uncovered in the end zone, resulting in a 21-16 Giant lead. The Bears countered with a bit of trickery of their own when Nagurski took a hand-off on the Giants' thirty-three-yard line, faked a rush, and then lobbed a short pass to Bill Hewitt, who was closely covered by Strong. Hewitt quickly turned and tossed a lateral to Bill Karr, who sprinted for a touchdown behind a fine block by Gene Ronzani. With less than two minutes to play the Bears led 23-21, but the excitement was far from over.[35]

New York returned the Bears' kickoff to their own forty-yard line. Once again Newman called a trick play similar to the one he had run in the first period. All the Giant linemen positioned themselves to the right of center

Mel Hein, making him an eligible pass receiver. Newman took the snap from Hein, but instead of handing the ball back to his center he kept it and lateraled to wingback Dale Burnett. The Bears' defenders ignored Hein once they realized he did not have the ball, and after sprinting downfield he stood alone on the Chicago fifteen-yard line, waving his arms. As Burnett prepared to pass to Hein the ball inexplicably slipped out of his hand and was batted down by Keith Molesworth. On the next play, with only seconds remaining, Newman completed a desperate twenty-eight-yard pass to Burnett behind the Bears' secondary defense. Hein was running just a few steps behind Burnett, ready to accept a lateral if the wingback were tackled. Grange, who had been inserted into the game for defensive purposes, was the only Chicago player between Burnett and Hein and the Bears' goal line. "I knew that as soon as I tackled him," Grange recalled, "Burnett was going to lateral to Mel Hein, the great Giant center, who was trailing him. So I grabbed Burnett around the chest and held his arms so he couldn't lateral. And we went down, and the whistle went off, and the Bears won the championship."[36]

"Red Grange saved the game for Chicago," Giants owner Tim Mara stated flatly. George Halas remembered the game-saving tackle as "the greatest defensive play I ever saw." Although he rated the first divisional play-off game as "probably the greatest football game I ever participated in," Grange also remembered that at the time, "The Bears regarded the game as just another pay day for we were paid by the game. Our big incentive to win was the fact that the winner was to get more money." Chicago guard Joe Kopcha agreed, pointing out that "we got about 70 bucks more than the Giants [$210.36 to $140.22], but to me, paying my way through medical school, it was a great windfall. Neither my teammates nor I ever dreamed this game would become what it has."[37]

After the championship game, the Bears played a few exhibition games before disbanding for the season. Grange decided to extend his season by joining the Green Bay Packers for two games on the West Coast in January. He recalled rooming with Packers' halfback Johnny Blood (a.k.a. McNally), one of the most colorful characters in pro football. In order to preserve his college eligibility, McNally had played under the name Blood when he joined a semipro team in Minnesota in 1924, a name he had chosen after spotting an advertisement for Rudolph Valentino's *Blood and Sand*. He liked the name and kept it. What Grange remembered most about the barnstorming games in California was the day some young women wanted Blood to sign their scorecard after the first game. Blood said, "I'll do better than that, I'll sign it in blood. He cut his wrist with his knife and had about four stitches in his wrist" for the final game.[38]

When he returned from the West Coast, Grange again decided to retire as a pro player. He continued to operate and serve as master of ceremonies at the 77 Club. In the summer Halas urged him to return for one more season with the Bears. He reluctantly agreed and announced that he had sold his interest in the 77 Club. "I can't run a nightclub and try to play football, too," Grange maintained, "and I'd rather play football." It seems likely that financial concerns also influenced him to return for a ninth season in pro football. When the season began, Grange took a job as a football commentator for the Columbia Broadcasting System (CBS) radio network. In three broadcasts a week that were carried over fourteen CBS stations he discussed important games and players, interviewed coaches, and predicted scores. At the time he had little idea that the new job would lead to a career in broadcasting and make him one of the first celebrity athletes to make a mark in the radio and later television industries.[39]

The 1934 Chicago Bears would prove to be one of the greatest teams in NFL history. Rookie halfback Beattie Feathers of the University of Tennessee was an explosive runner who, with the help of Nagurski's blocking, became the first NFL player to rush for a thousand yards. To take advantage of Feather's talent, Halas brought back the single wing and used it along with the split-T formation. The introduction of a slimmer ball helped improve the Bears' passing game, and the legalization of the kicking tee aided Jack Manders in becoming the first NFL player to kick ten field goals in a season. All told, the Bears scored 286 points, twenty-two per game and almost double their offensive output during the 1932 championship season.[40]

Chicago's offensive potential was not apparent, however, in their performance in the first-ever College All-Star game. The brainchild of Chicago *Tribune* sports editor Arch Ward, who had promoted the first major league baseball All-Star game the year before, the game was played between outstanding college seniors of the previous season and the reigning NFL champions. All proceeds went to charity. Dutch Sternaman considered the College All-Star game one of the important developments in early pro football, just behind Grange's tours with the Bears in 1925–26, and maintained that it demonstrated just how good pro football really was. Grange helped promote the idea of a college-pro all-star game by creating a controversy over the relative merits of the two brands of football. Ward was a vociferous supporter of college football and considered collegiate players and their game far superior to the pros. Late in the 1933 season, Grange wrote a friendly but provocative letter (most likely solicited) to Ward that appeared in the *Tribune*. In it he compared professional football favorably with the college game. "I say that a football player after three years in college doesn't really know anything about football," he stated. Grange's conclusion was that "pro football is just the difference between seeing the New York Giants play baseball and watching an amateur nine." The first College All-Star game attracted great interest and was a financial success, drawing 79,432 fans to Soldier Field. Grange started for the Bears and after being injured in the first period returned to complete a twenty-two-yard pass to Johnny Sisk in the final quarter, setting up one of Chicago's few scoring opportunities of the day. The game ended in a scoreless tie, and most agreed it was "deadly dull." Until it was cancelled in 1976 the game remained a major preseason attraction. The college all-stars won nine games, the pros thirty-one, and two games ended in ties.[41]

When the NFL season began, the "powerhouse" Bears, as they came to be called, went on an offensive rampage and outscored their first nine opponents by at least two touchdowns. During that streak Chicago scored 230 points to the opposition's forty-eight. The Bears' defense was as strong as their offense was potent. In the midst of the winning streak, Grange returned to the University of Illinois, where he was an honored guest at Homecoming. When asked years later if there were anything special about his triumphant return, Grange hesitated and said, "I suppose it did represent a tremendous change in attitude in a fairly short period of time, because all they had done before was to give me hell for being in the pro league." In November 1934, however, he was focused on extending the Bears' winning streak as the team traveled to New York to oppose the Giants. Although Chicago had easily defeated New York earlier at Wrigley Field, fifty-five thousand fans turned out at the Polo Grounds to watch the rematch. Chicago's 9-0 record was in jeopardy as the Giants took a 7-0 half-time lead and expanded the margin to 9-0 in the third period. The Bears stormed back during the final quarter when Feathers scored with three minutes remaining to play. After Chicago recovered a Giants' fumble, Jack Manders kicked a twenty-three-yard field goal with seconds remaining to preserve the Bears' unblemished record with a 10-9 victory. Halas remembered the game as "the roughest, most vicious game [I] ever saw." After an easy win over the Cardinals, the Bears finished the season with two narrow victories over the western division second-place Detroit Lions, who had played the previous season in Portsmouth. Chicago registered the first undefeated and untied season in NFL history—a 13-0 record.[42]

Grange remembered the 1934 season as one in which he "hardly played at all on offense. I usually went in when the Bears were deep in their own territory." League statistics bear him out. Grange carried the ball only thirty-two times from scrimmage, less than three times a game, for 136 yards and one touchdown. He attempted twenty-five passes but only completed six, including one for a touchdown. Seven (28 percent) of his passes were intercepted. The only bright spot in his offensive game was pass-receiving, where his three receptions resulted in two touchdowns. Grange had clearly slowed to the point that he was ineffective, especially on offense. "The heaviest I ever played with the Chicago Bears my last few years was 187," he remembered. "I was a defensive halfback and eating pretty good in those days." He decided to retire as a player, for good this time, before the season ended. "I got out when it started to become a drudge to me. I didn't like practice anymore. The things that I had been able to do, I couldn't do anymore, and I knew."[43]

Grange played only sparingly in the second NFL championship game against the Giants on December 9, which became known as the "sneakers game." With the temperature at nine degrees and the field at the Polo Grounds frozen solid and covered with ice in places, both teams slipped and slid through the first half, with the Bears somehow managing to score a touchdown and field goal for a 10-3 half time lead. By the beginning of the second half the Giants had managed to obtain basketball shoes from a local college, and nine of their players came out for the third period clad in the indoor footwear. "When they came out wearing those sneakers, we thought they were crazy," Grange recalled. "But the second half of that game was probably the funniest, most ridiculous game ever played. There we were, running along with our cleated football shoes, and our feet were going out from under us. And the Giants, although not running fast, were just trotting along, doing all the things we couldn't do." The Bears expanded their lead to 13-3 in the third period before the Giants staged one of the great comebacks in NFL play-off history by scoring four touchdowns in the final quarter for an incredible 30-13 victory. Although popular wisdom holds that the sneakers provided traction to enable the Giants to overwhelm the Bears, New York halfback Ken Strong, who scored eighteen points, disagreed. He was convinced that by the final period the Bears' new pointed cleats made of brakelite had worn down to nubs, which caused them to lose traction. "If they had had new cleats for the second half," Strong believed, "they would have walloped us."[44]

Before the championship game with the Giants, Grange publicly announced his retirement. The *New York Times* reported that nine seasons in the NFL had left him "battered and worn," noting that the "circuit has become a little too fast for the galloping red-head and he has seen little action this year." Grange might have been well advised to have quit right after the championship game, but he decided to participate in several Bears' exhibition games during late December and January. In a game against the Brooklyn Dodgers in Nashville, he became the center of a controversy between Halas and Brooklyn co-owner and tailback John "Shipwreck" Kelly, who remembered that in the game "the only thing that looked bad was Grange." According to Kelly, Halas went to Dodgers' defensive back Chris Cagel before the game and said, "I wish you all would let Grange intercept a pass and make a good run or something like that because these people in Nashville never have seen him, just heard about him." Without him being aware of it, Kelly contended, Cagel complied with Halas's request and let Grange catch a pass and make a long run. When Halas later told Kelly that the Bears let him get away on a touchdown run in exchange for Cagel's courtesy to Grange, the Dodgers' owner was incensed. "I don't believe in that you know," Kelly fumed many years later. "If you can do it, do it, if you can't, you can't."[45]

Although Grange was likely unaware of the alleged Halas-Cagel arrangement in Nashville, it did highlight an issue some sportswriters had raised beginning with Grange's first barnstorming tours in 1925 and 1926. Would not promoters of such games be tempted to arrange for star players to break away for long runs to satisfy the fans? When asked in 1974 if he had ever heard of a fixed game in pro football, Grange replied, "Nobody ever suggested it to me, and I never heard of a player that ever came in contact with it at all." He played in his last football game at Hollywood's Gilmore Stadium on January 27, 1935, a rematch between the Bears and the NFL champion Giants. Players on both teams realized that it was Grange's last game. He played briefly in the first half before returning to the field late in the fourth period. The Bears, who led 21-0, planned to break Grange loose for one final touchdown run so he could lay the ball down in the end zone and walk off the field. "I almost made it, too," he remembered. From the Bears' twenty-yard line, Grange ran off tackle and broke into the New York secondary. "Although I can't prove it," he later said, "I think the Giants let me loose." Number 77 lumbered down the field pursued by the Giants' 230-pound tackle Cecil Irvin, who Grange described as "so slow you could have timed him with a calendar." At the Giants' thirty-nine-yard line, however, Irvin caught up with him and brought him to the ground. "I know he didn't want to tackle me, but he had to," Grange recalled. After the game he stated, "I'm earnest about it. I'm through, definitely through this time. I'm getting out of the game before I get killed." Sportswriter Paul Zimmerman wrote, "So often had Grange announced his retirement that no one took him seriously. But those who saw his valiant effort at Gilmore Stadium yesterday were certain that this time he meant it."[46]

Grange signed with the Chicago Bears the day after his final college game. Left to right: Bears owners Edward "Dutch" Sternaman and George Halas, Red, and Charles C. Pyle. (Red Grange Collection [SC-20], Special Collections, Buswell Memorial Library, Wheaton College)

The Wheaton Iceman with an admirer in his hometown. Grange continued his summer job delivering ice even after he turned professional. (Red Grange Collection [SC-20], Special Collections, Buswell Memorial Library, Wheaton College)

Babe Ruth and Grange in New York after the Chicago Bears–New York Giants game during the 1925 tour. (Courtesy of University of Illinois Athletic Public Relations)

With the help of Charlie Pyle, Grange was the first pro football player to endorse commercial products. A doll was also named after him. (Red Grange Collection [SC-20], Special Collections, Buswell Memorial Library, Wheaton College)

Grange loved fast cars almost as much as football. Sporting a racoon coat, he sits behind the wheel of this 1920s' roadster with Charlie Pyle at his side. (Red Grange Collection [SC-20], Special Collections, Buswell Memorial Library, Wheaton College)

Grange's last film was a twelve-part talking picture produced by Nat Levine, the king of the serials. It was standard fare on Saturday morning television during the early 1950s. (Red Grange Collection [SC-20], Special Collections, Buswell Memorial Library, Wheaton College)

Chicago Bears backfield stars of the early 1930s: Carl Brumbaugh, Johnny Sisk, Bronko Nagurski, and Red Grange. (Courtesy of Chicago Bears)

Grange publicity photos near the end of his professional career as a player with the Chicago Bears. (Courtesy of Chicago Bears)

Grange was one of the first professional athletes to go into sports broadcasting. Here, he prepares for his weekly football show on CBS radio during the 1930s. (Courtesy of University of Illinois Athletic Public Relations)

After his playing career, Grange did promotional work for a number of companies, including American Airlines. (Red Grange Collection [SC-20], Special Collections, Buswell Memorial Library, Wheaton College)

Three heroes of the golden age of sport photographed in 1966: Red Grange, Jack Dempsey, and Bobby Jones. (Red Grange Collection [SC-20], Special Collections, Buswell Memorial Library, Wheaton College)

Red standing next to his bust at the Pro Football Hall of Fame. He was inducted in 1963 with the first group of enshrinees. (Red Grange Collection [SC-20], Special Collections, Buswell Memorial Library, Wheaton College)

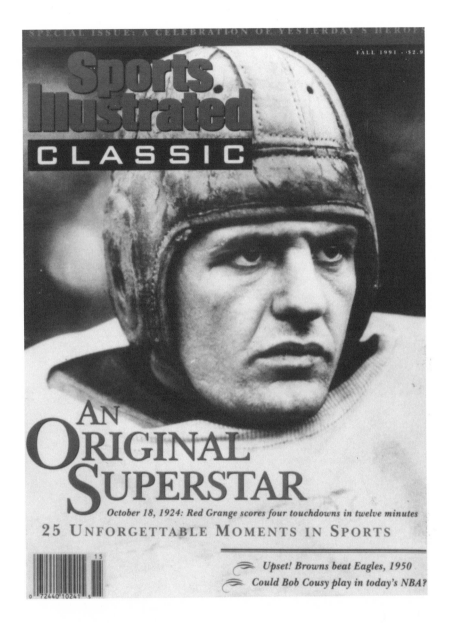

Sports Illustrated

CLASSIC

AN
ORIGINAL
SUPERSTAR

October 18, 1924: Red Grange scores four touchdowns in twelve minutes

25 UNFORGETTABLE MOMENTS IN SPORTS

Upset! Browns beat Eagles, 1950
Could Bob Cousy play in today's NBA?

In 1991, sixty-seven years after his greatest feat, Grange was featured on the cover of a special issue of *Sports Illustrated*. (Courtesy of Culver Pictures, for *Sports Illustrated*; copyright © Time, Inc.)

Grange acknowledging the crowd at Memorial Stadium, University
of Illinois, during festivities in 1974 that marked the fiftieth anniversary of his memorable game against Michigan. (Courtesy of
University of Illinois Athletic Public Relations)

11

Finding a Niche

IN DECEMBER 1934 WHEN HE ANNOUNCED his intention to retire as a football player, there was speculation that Grange was being considered for the head coaching position at the University of Missouri. After his final pro game he confirmed that he had an interest in coaching and "was considering two offers" as well as "several promising business ventures." But he added, "I won't know definitely what my next move will be for several months." Not until June did Grange announce that he had accepted the position of backfield coach with the Chicago Bears. Newspaper reports stated that Halas had offered him the head coaching job, which he declined because "he would rather have a less responsible job as a starter." In his autobiography, Grange recalled that Halas had first offered him the head coaching position after his first season as an assistant. He had declined because he lacked enough experience. "I never had any ambition to be a head coach in either the professional or college ranks," he said. "A coach puts in four times as many hours as a player, is under considerable strain to produce a winning team and must be prepared to take considerable abuse if he is unsuccessful in turning out a winner. It wasn't in my physical make-up to push myself that hard or work under such pressure."[1]

Despite what he said in the 1950s, in 1935 Grange, like many other prominent former football players, had viewed a head coaching position as a natural extension of his athletic career. He was uncertain about what to do with the rest of his life, and a continued association with football appeared safe and appealing. In an article in the *Saturday Evening Post* during the fall of that year, he wrote, "The next best thing to playing football is coaching it—passing on to kids bursting out of their skins with health, vigor and bounce, some of the things you pick up about the game as you go along." Modesty prevented him from accepting Halas's head coaching offer, most likely wisely, whether it was proposed before or after the 1935 season. He chose to begin his coaching career with the Bears because of his familiarity with the team and his business ventures and extensive contacts in and around Chicago. Grange was banned from coaching at any nearby Big Ten school because of a conference rule (prohibiting former pro football players from coaching) that had been established as a result of his turning pro in 1925. As one of Chicago's two assistant coaches, Grange admired Halas's coaching skills and total dedication to the game but found coaching onerous and time-consuming. "I didn't want to work that hard at it," he remembered. "Halas was the coach, and he had us in there from 8 A.M. to midnight, which wasn't my idea of a normal working day. Besides, I didn't want to have to kick some kid in the pants to make him play."[2]

During Grange's first season coaching under Halas, the Bears, plagued by injuries, struggled through their worst season since 1929 with a 6-4-2 record. The following year Chicago rebounded with nine victories in twelve games for a second-place finish in the western division behind the eventual NFL champion Green Bay Packers. In 1937 the Bears won the western division with a 9-1-1 record before losing a dramatic NFL championship game to the Washington Redskins. During his coaching tenure, Grange witnessed some important changes in the pro game he had been instrumental in popularizing. National Football League attendance rose from a record 820,000 in 1934 to more than a million by 1937. In 1936 a new American Football League challenged the NFL but collapsed after only two seasons. That same year the NFL adopted a system to draft college players in order to create more parity in the league. Washington owner George Preston Marshall pioneered in introducing showmanship and gala half-time entertainment to the NFL, a form of spectacle Pyle had haltingly experimented with as head of the New York Yankees during the 1920s. Marshall is also believed to have been responsible for a gentlemen's agreement among NFL owners that led to banning African American players from 1934 until after World War II. Although Grange had been sympathetic toward and supportive of African American athletes during his career, race is one of the few subjects pertaining to pro football that he never discussed publicly.[3]

Grange had launched a career as a public commentator on football well before his professional playing days ended. He wrote a few newspaper articles for national news services during the late 1920s before signing a contract with the *Saturday Evening Post* in 1932 to write, with the assistance of advertising executive George Dunscomb, periodic pieces on football highlights and strategy. Between 1932 and 1935 he and Dunscomb turned out six articles that appeared in the autumn, usually revolved around some point of strategy or nuance of the game, and reviewed the ongoing season, its star players, and important games in both the college and pro ranks. One persistent theme concerned Grange's strong conviction that pro football was superior to the college game. "It is hard to see how any college eleven would have much chance against a leading pro team," he concluded in 1932, "when all the foregoing facts are added up." He and other pro players believed there was "almost as wide a gap between professional and college football as between major and minor league baseball." As football's most widely heralded player, there can be little doubt that Grange's views contributed to the increasing popularity of pro football in the 1930s. He terminated his contract with the *Saturday Evening Post* after he began coaching for the Bears but continued as a football commentator on the CBS radio network.[4]

When Grange began his broadcasting career in 1934, play-by-play coverage and football commentary shows were still relatively new, and the print media held them in low esteem. Most football fans followed the game in the newspaper and either got the latest scores from special "sporting finals" or found them posted at the local gas station. One expert on early sports broadcasting has suggested that Grange's sudden rise to prominence in 1924 helped launch the national broadcasting of college football. By 1932 radio coverage of college games, which most stations broadcast as a public service, had come under attack by many college officials convinced that the transmission of games over the airwaves was responsible, in part, for declining attendance. That year the Eastern Intercollegiate Association, made up of twelve colleges and eighty-three affiliated institutions, announced that it was discontinuing the radio broadcast of games but reversed its decision following a storm of public protest. The following year a group of midwestern universities signed agreements with industrial companies and significantly expanded the commercial broadcasting of college football games. When major eastern colleges followed suit in 1936 nearly twenty-four football programs nationwide had commercial sponsors for their games on radio. The commercial broadcast of football games was still so novel, however, that some leading magazines and newspapers satirized the broadcasters who attempted to sell pancake mix or motor oil during pauses in a game.[5]

Little is known about Grange's early broadcasting career except that he was popular and well paid. His weekly shows, which many CBS stations carried until the early 1940s, attracted a wide national audience. George Dunscomb maintained in 1937 that the power of Grange's name "was indicated last season when some forty-two million of the 'Red Grange score sheets' were requested by customers of the company sponsoring his radio broadcasting, *a world's record!*" CBS paid Grange the then-handsome sum of $7,000 for three weekly radio shows during the football season.[6]

He observed significant changes in the college game during the depression. After experiencing a decline in attendance and revenue due to the severity of the economic slump and inflated ticket prices, major intercollegiate football powers faced a crisis. Football, after all, was the engine that powered intercollegiate athletic programs and paid the mortgage on many of the newly constructed stadiums. To continue their athletic programs at anything like the pre-depression level, many colleges reduced ticket prices and, putting the Carnegie Report aside, embraced commercialism with a vengeance. One indication of a new economic strategy was the increase in the number of bowl games. The Orange Bowl (1933), the Sugar Bowl (1935), and the Cotton Bowl (1937) were the most successful of the nine bowl games inaugurated during the 1930s. A more pernicious development in the evolution of the avowedly amateur sport, however, was the introduction of athletic scholarships in order to obtain the best athletes who might help fill stadiums and college coffers. Although some schools preferred to offer financial enticements to athletes secretly through their coaches and alumni, an increasing number of institutions adopted formal, aboveboard athletic subsidies for players, a practice one writer described as akin to "offering financial inducements to promising athletes, regardless of the candidate's proficiency in scholarship." The search for the "next Red Grange" continued at an accelerated pace.[7]

While continuing to work as a broadcaster and coach Grange accepted a job with Hinckley & Schmitt, a Chicago water and soft drink company, in 1937. Jim Peterson, an Illinois alumnus and president of the company, admired Grange greatly and had seen nearly every game he had played in college and pro football. When Grange told him that he had no ambition to continue in coaching, Peterson recruited him as a sales promotion manager for Hinckley & Schmitt. A short time later Grange underwent an emergency operation on his bladder. Following his recovery and after nearly five weeks of trying to cope with his duties under Halas and his new job, he realized he was overextended and resigned his coaching position (although he continued as a consultant to Halas for several more seasons) to devote more attention to working with Hinckley & Schmitt. Peterson reportedly paid Grange an annual salary of $7,500.[8]

During 1937 Grange also found time to contribute to a book about Bob Zuppke, his former college coach. Entitled *Zuppke of Illinois*, the book listed Grange as the author but it was ghostwritten by George Dunscomb, who included sizable sections on Grange's football career. Grange and Dunscomb heaped praise on Zuppke, who was experiencing a string of disappointing seasons at Illinois, and included a tribute to former Illini athletic director George Huff, who had died a few years earlier. The book, published with Peterson's financial backing, appeared to be Grange's way of improving relations with his former university and coming to terms with two men who had treated him rather harshly when he turned pro in the mid-1920s. If the book was intended as a kind of peace offering to Zuppke and the University of Illinois, it succeeded. In November 1940 Grange was the special guest of the University of Illinois president at the school's Homecoming game against Notre Dame.[9]

The following summer Grange became embroiled in a controversy involving an attempt to replace Zuppke, who continued to oppose athletic scholarships although most other conference schools offered them. He would later admit that "the quality of Illinois football became less and less [in the 1930s] when other schools began to subsidize and we did not." Two months before the start of the 1941 season, Illinois athletic director Wendell S. Wilson announced that Grange would be willing to accept Zuppke's job. Grange was indignant at his name being used as part of a plan to force the university's board of trustees to fire his former coach. At a meeting of the Chicago Illini Club that summer he stated emphatically, "I'll not coach anywhere in the world except my present little job with George Halas." A reporter observed that "when he walked to the 'mike' Red was almost speechless with rage. He brushed past his old colleagues without a word, took his place and started his talk (supporting Zuppke) abruptly and with unaccustomed fire." Grange sued Wilson for $50,000, alleging that the athletic director's statement was "malicious, false, slanderous and defamatory" and had "greatly injured" his reputation. He dropped the libel action only after Wilson retracted his statement two weeks later. Grange's support of his former coach was in vain, however, because Zuppke resigned under pressure following the 1941 season.[10]

The year was a pivotal one in Red Grange's life. On October 13 he married Margaret Hazelberg in Crown Point, Indiana. Although he reportedly had received more than two hundred thousand letters from female admirers in 1925 and later was rumored to be romantically involved with a number of Hollywood starlets, Grange had never married. Little is known about his relationships with women. He met Margaret on an airline trip to Omaha in the fall of 1940 en route to do a radio interview in Lincoln before the Nebraska-Kansas game. His future wife was a stewardess on the flight, and Grange invited her to attend a Bears game in Chicago. Although she wouldn't get to a game for five years, they began to date. In 1953 Grange described his wife, whom he affectionately called Muggs, as "a wonderful pal to me, a constant source of inspiration and unquestionably the finest 'manager' a man could have." Grange's friend Richard Crabb agreed. The Granges' marriage "changed everything," he said in 1992. "If there was ever a major change in his life, it occurred then. Because he didn't ever save any money until he married Muggs. And after that he was never poor." Elmer Hoffman, Grange's friend since childhood, wrote during the 1950s that "his wife Margaret is a very charming person and also has had a great effect on Red's life."[11]

About the time of Grange's marriage, Jim Peterson suggested that he might be better off in the long run if he went into business on his own. Sometime later Grange met Peterson's friend Howard Porter, a successful insurance man, who recommended that he enter the insurance business. Grange began studying for the brokers examination and, after passing it in 1942, left Hinckley & Schmitt to begin an insurance business. In his autobiography he recalled that "it turned out to be the best thing that ever happened to me from a business standpoint." Two decades later, after he had retired, he remembered his career as an insurance broker with pride. "During the depression, though, I really took a licking. Finally I got into the insurance business," he told columnist Loren Tate. "I almost starved to death for three years, but I never once tried to use my football reputation. I was as good an insurance man as there was in Chicago. On the football field I had ten other men blocking for me, but I'm more proud of what I did in the insurance business, because I did it alone."[12]

After America entered World War II, Grange struggled to build his insurance business and also found time to make public appearances around the country during the football season. Wartime mobilization seriously disrupted college football. Scores of schools had disbanded their teams by 1942–43, but Grange continued to broadcast radio commentary shows until 1944. He also contributed to the war effort by serving on the Chicago Selective Service Board's reemployment committee and as a physical fitness teacher for the city's Junior Army Victory program. In 1944, after his radio contract with CBS expired, he began doing play-by-play commentary for short movie highlights of selected NFL games that were shown to travel-restricted military personnel at home and to U.S. forces overseas.[13]

That same year Grange accepted the presidency of the newly formed United States Football League (USFL), an upstart professional league organized by Arch Ward of the Chicago *Tribune*. Organizers envisioned eight franchises from Boston to Chicago and, surprisingly, included a team in Honolulu. "We are not going to fight any other professional league nor are we going to try to steal players already under contract to other teams," Grange announced in November 1944. He also indicated that the league would build covered stadiums, an idea that had fascinated him since he and Pyle first discussed it during the 1920s. Within six months, however, Grange had resigned as USFL president because "the office requires a big promotional job and my insurance business prevents me from giving it the necessary time. . . . I wouldn't advise anybody to start in pro football now," he cautioned other promoters. "Players are holding out for between $400 and $600 a game when they used to get $150." The new league failed to begin play in 1945 as promised and was reorganized under Ward's direction as the All-America Football Conference in 1946. As he approached his forty-second birthday, Grange seemed unable to reestablish a satisfactory connection with the game he loved and that had brought him so much fame.[14]

After the war, Grange continued a busy schedule that included weekly football commentary shows in Chicago and speaking engagements in the fall in addition to selling insurance. His business was beginning to prosper, and he usually put in a ten-hour day at the office but still found time to devote to civic affairs. He was particularly committed to supporting youth groups and trying to combat the growing problem of juvenile delinquency. In early 1947, when the Chicago Cardinals signed former University of Georgia halfback Charlie Trippi to a four-year contract for the then fabulous sum of $100,000, the media again focused on Grange's glory days. According to a news article by Chicago sportswriter Charles Chamberlain, Grange telephoned him to emphasize that Trippi's $100,000 over four seasons was "absolutely peanuts." He then recounted earning $35,000 for one game at the Polo Grounds in 1925 and $50,000 for another game in Los Angeles in 1926. "Pyle and I split a million dollars from gate receipts from 1925 through 1927," he said. He approved, however, of Trippi getting all the money he could.[15]

During the same year Grange began helping the University of Illinois raise money for athletic scholarships. As part of that effort he wired to invite Bob Zuppke to a scholarship awards banquet in 1947. Zuppke scribbled three responses on the back of the telegram, declining the invitation. Two included the statement, "I do not believe in athletic scholarships." He evidently sent the third message, which indicated that he could not attend but wished Grange well. The men apparently had made their peace, but it was an uneasy one.[16]

In 1947 Grange expanded his broadcasting activities to include play-by-play descriptions of football games over radio as well as his first venture as a sports announcer on television. During the early period of radio sports broadcasting (1921–45) most leading play-by-play football announcers, including Graham McNamee, Ted Husing, and Bill Stern, usually did the entire broadcast themselves, aided only by technical assistants and spotters. After World War II, producers of football broadcasts increasingly included an expert analyst ("color man") to assist the play-by-play announcer in the booth. Grange was one of the first of these color men in football broadcasting and the first prominent former athlete in that sport to become a play-by-play sportscaster. He would soon be joined by former all-American halfback Tom Harmon of Michigan, Missouri's outstanding tailback Paul Christman, and many others. In the early postwar years Grange did a good deal of play-by-play broadcasting, but as time passed he served more often as an expert commentator. By 1949 he was involved in the broadcast of thirty football games a year, including intercollegiate games in the Midwest, postseason bowl games, and NFL contests. He also did three weekly football commentary shows that originated in Chicago. The following year he signed a five-year contract with the American Broadcasting Company (ABC) to do the fifteen-minute "Red Grange Show," which was transcribed and sent across the country to network radio affiliates. He replaced Notre Dame football coach Frank Leahy, who had signed a $25,000 contract with CBS to do a weekly show with Arthur Godfrey. Already scheduled to do another thirty live football broadcasts that year, Grange described 1950 as "my biggest and best season on the radio."[17]

Grange also announced football games on the relatively new medium of television. The first telecast of a football game took place in 1939, but sports broadcasting on television did not make much headway until after World War II. Programming was scarce, and producers found that sporting events were a cheap and proven way of filling air time and attracting viewers. Because many early network producers considered television an extension of radio, they often televised sporting events carried on radio, including the World Series and college and pro football games. In 1947 television stations began to air some of the Big Ten and Notre Dame football games, which Bob Elson and Grange usually broadcasted nationwide over radio. "I was one of the first television football announcers," he remembered many years later. "I began in 1947."[18]

The Chicago Bears pioneered taking advantage of the new market. George Halas signed a contract with Chicago television station WBKB in 1947 to broadcast six home games and received a fee of $5,400. In subsequent years, as more Chicagoans purchased television sets and Halas became concerned about competition from the new medium in terms of attendance, only a few home games were carried live. To fill the void, excerpts from the official movies of Bears' home games of the previous Sunday were broadcast on television in Chicago during the week. Beginning in 1949 Grange and Bears' assistant coach Luke Johnsos provided commentary for the games on "The Bears Quarterback Club," which aired on Tuesday nights. Meanwhile, Halas arranged for Chicago's home games to be shown on television in selected cities in the Midwest, hoping to attract additional fans and ticket sales. By the early 1950s the games were carried over a fifteen-city network and eventually were expanded to a number of southern cities such as Birmingham, Tampa, and Miami. Grange provided the play-by-play description for these games and the occasional home game (usually against the Cardinals) that was televised in Chicago. Toward the end of his career as a Bears' broadcaster he did the postgame show until he retired in 1963. When the Bears played on the road, he sometimes did play-by-play descriptions of Chicago Cardinal home games televised on the network Halas developed in the early 1950s. Beginning in 1950 Grange also began to broadcast a few NFL games (primarily in the East) with New York sportscaster Joe Hasel over the ABC television network.[19]

When Grange became a regular play-by-play sportscaster in 1947 the profession was dominated by announcers who were masters of the gee-whiz style of broadcasting. Starting with Graham McNamee in the 1920s, most were less concerned with precision in play-by-play accounts than with engaging the audience through the use of drama and hyperbole. Bill Stern, the leading practitioner of the gee-whiz school by the late 1940s, once asked

Grange's permission to fabricate a story for his weekly radio show. Stern thought it would make a good yarn to recount that a University of Illinois alumnus and former gambler had paid for Grange's college education. Red refused. By outlook and temperament he was not well suited to gee-whiz broadcasting and was fortunate to have been paired primarily with sportscasters who were more reflective and precision-oriented. In 1974 Grange briefly reviewed his television broadcasting career: "I didn't talk too much. Now announcers hold a clinic after every play to show how smart they are. And they're 90 per cent wrong."[20]

During the late 1940s and 1950s Grange admired many of the improvements and innovations in modern football but continued to believe that the game had not changed radically since the 1930s, when the ball was streamlined, forward passing regulations relaxed, and the hash-mark rule implemented. He also readily agreed that free substitution (adopted during World War II) and improved equipment made for a better game. The most prominent change he saw in the modern game concerned the substantially increased size and strength of players, particularly linemen. In the postwar era of general prosperity and exciting technological change, most Americans (including football fans and broadcasters) automatically assumed that American athletes and the games they played were better and more innovative than ever before. Grange was one of only a few voices that generally questioned conventional wisdom. When asked about the new breed of coaches supposedly revolutionizing the game, he replied, "How much football is there to know? Every coach knows enough football." Another time, when a sportswriter carried on about new formations that were transforming football, he responded, "There's only so many places you can stand on the field to do any good."[21]

Grange's sometimes deflating commentary combined with a monotone delivery and laconic style left some listeners and viewers perplexed. I was ten or eleven when I first heard him on national college football telecasts during the early 1950s, and I found the gray-haired, elderly gentleman—about whom I knew little or nothing—to be dull and uninformed about the game. Many others who had seen Grange play or knew of him by reputation, however, respected his analysis and opinions and were charmed by his quiet modesty. "We were the voices of college football," Lindsey Nelson, Grange's broadcasting partner for five years on NBC television during the 1950s, recalled. "Everywhere we went, fans formed long lines to meet or just see Red Grange, perhaps the greatest star the game of football has ever known. His magnitude was immense."[22]

Announcers have been criticized for lack of enthusiasm, alleged partisanship, inaccuracy, grammatical mistakes, and tortured syntax since the beginning of play-by-play sports broadcasting. After sitting beside Graham McNamee at a World Series game in 1933, for example, Ring Lardner reported, "The Washington Senators and the New York Giants must have played a double-header this afternoon—the game I saw and the game Graham McNamee announced." During the 1940s and 1950s former St. Louis Cardinal pitcher Jerome "Dizzy" Dean was assailed by educators yet became a broadcasting legend for his innovative although incorrect use of the language. Grange also received substantial criticism for his torpid style, inaccurate commentary, alleged favoritism of one team over another, midwestern accent, and grammatical errors. A Chicago detractor once wrote, "It is considered a masterpiece of achievement when Grange has the right team in possession of the ball." He once "diagramed" a forward pass play on a televised game by sketching a straight line. Although his grammatical lapses and mispronunciation of words were less noticeable than Dizzy Dean's country drawl and mangled syntax, one sportswriter observed that Grange's "sometimes unique use of the language gave critics the impression he was self-educated." To Grange, athletes were "athaletes" and sometimes made tackles from their "reinbacker" position. He had particular difficulty with collective nouns. Listeners were informed, for example, that "Army *are* now on the five-yard line." When an NBC executive complained about Grange's inability to use a singular verb on such occasions, Lindsey Nelson defended him by pointing out, "That's the way they do it in England." Unmoved, the executive replied, "Damnit Lindsey, Red didn't go to Oxford. He went to Illinois!"[23]

Grange remained unperturbed when fans or the press criticized his broadcasting. In 1956 he volunteered that he did receive some unfavorable mail from viewers but didn't "care much one way or the other. Sometimes they accuse me of favoritism, too. I'm glad I have a thick skin." He no doubt agreed with veteran baseball and football announcer Red Barber, who maintained that football was the most difficult game to follow. Barber held that "football is organized confusion" and "not even the coaches know much about what is happening until they study the films after the game is played." Grange insisted that "a quarterback that doesn't fool you at least a couple times in a ball game is not a good quarterback. If he doesn't fool you, he's not fooling the defense." He advised viewers to watch the line play: "By watching the line and seeing which team has the advantage there, you often can tell early in the game who's going to win."[24]

Lindsey Nelson maintained that Grange was extremely knowledgeable about the finer points of the game and modest about his knowledge. The night before their first telecast together in 1954 Grange happened to mention seeing a game in Canada in which a player had come off the bench to make a tackle. It was one of the few rule infractions, he explained, that allowed a referee to award a touchdown if he judged that the tackled player would have scored. The following day in the Cotton Bowl game, which Nelson and Grange were broadcasting, Rice's Dickie Moegle (later, Dickie Maegle) broke into the clear and raced down the sideline en route to a near-certain touchdown when Alabama's Tommie Lewis jumped off the bench and tackled him near midfield in one of the most famous and bizarre plays in college football history. After the play, Grange smiled at Nelson and turned his palms upward as if to say, "It's all yours, take it and run." Nelson received much praise for promptly reporting that the referee would award Moegle a touchdown and explaining the rule. Grange never asked for the credit he deserved. He became convinced by the mid-1950s that television was the main force in popularizing pro football on a national basis. When he traveled around the country trying to convince people that pro football was a good game during the 1920s and 1930s, "They'd laugh at you. No, they never saw a game" but "they'd say that the pros don't tackle and they don't block and that there was no spirit." That changed once television brought the game into people's homes. Despite occasional criticism of his broadcasting technique, Grange remained in demand and covered nearly five hundred football games, including thirty-two bowl games, on television and radio before his full retirement in 1969.[25]

Grange's enduring fame and status stemmed in part from the recognition he received from the sports media in polls conducted around mid-century to determine the nation's all-time greatest football players. As early as 1943 *Esquire* asked a cross-section of football coaches and sportswriters to name "the greatest football player you ever saw in action." Grange won top honors. That same poll also listed his ninety-five-yard return of the opening kickoff for a touchdown against Michigan in 1924 as the single greatest play in football history. Around 1950 wire services and prominent sportswriters began to publish selections of the greatest athletes since 1900. Invariably, Grange was chosen as either the greatest or one of the greatest football players or was included on mythical all-time all-American teams. In 1949 Grantland Rice named him along with Jim Thorpe, Bronko Nagurski, and Sammy Baugh to his all-time dream backfield. Two years later the

Associated Press in conjunction with the College Football Hall of Fame polled a hundred leading sportswriters to determine the best twelve men ever to play football. Grange received more votes than any other player. To the older generation, the results of these polls came as no surprise. For younger Americans, the name "Red Grange" became linked with other legendary athletes of the nation's sporting heritage. His popularity as a sports broadcaster and public speaker in the 1950s was enhanced by America's nostalgic glance back to an earlier era of athletic achievement.[26]

Grange's hectic work schedule, which included radio and television broadcasting, public speaking engagements, and tending to his insurance business, increased in 1950 when he reluctantly entered politics. While he and Harry Wismer were broadcasting the College All-Star game at Soldier Field in early August rebellious Illinois Republicans overturned the party's slate of candidates and nominated Grange to stand for the position of University of Illinois trustee. He had occasionally expressed conservative political views on his commentary shows and in public speeches but had never indicated any interest in holding elective office. The *New York Times* reported that his backers believed "he would attract thousands of extra votes for the state ticket and would oust 'Red sympathizers' from the university faculty." Grange's supporters were led by delegates hostile to university president George Stoddard, who, they claimed, "had hired and tolerated left-wing teachers." Democrats immediately countered by nominating former Illinois football star Harold Pogue to run against Grange. Despite his refusal to campaign, Grange was easily elected and "received more votes that year than anyone in the state, including Governor Adlai Stevenson."[27]

At the time, Grange "felt it a great privilege to be able to serve my old school," but that attitude soon changed. "I didn't enjoy being on the board," he later related. "I hadn't been a trustee more than a couple of days, and I started getting phone calls from politicians, telling me to put this guy or that guy to work or else you won't get your budget through. I don't believe it's the right way to run a university, and I got out as soon as I could." Grange would remain on the board for five years. In 1962 an Urbana-Champaign newspaper reported that "he served on the board without distinction and resigned in 1955 after participating actively in a midnight board session which resulted in the resignation of the president of the university, Dr. George D. Stoddard."[28]

During the 1951 football season Grange later admitted that he "literally burned the candle at both ends. . . . Instead of slowing down as I got older, I quickened the pace." In addition to his insurance business and new duties as a University of Illinois trustee, he spoke at nearly fifty football banquets a year and carried on with what he described as a normal schedule of radio and television broadcasts. Typically, Grange would transcribe a radio show on Monday that was syndicated in about fifty cities and on Tuesday and Thursday did live television shows in Chicago. On Friday night he would leave for some midwestern city to broadcast a Big Ten or Notre Dame football game on Saturday with Bob Elson. After that game, he normally flew to an eastern city, where he and Joe Hasel covered an NFL game on Sunday. "It was a killing pace," Grange remembered, "but I didn't realize it because I so enjoyed what I was doing." Near the end of the season he felt fatigued and agreed to heed his wife's advice to take "a good rest immediately after the season."[29]

On December 14 Grange traveled to Kirksville, Missouri, accompanied by Mark Cox, an executive with Wilson Sporting Goods Company for which Red served as a consultant, to speak at a football banquet at Northeast Missouri State Teachers College. He became ill during the trip but insisted on attending the banquet and delivering his speech. When he got home, Grange had a high temperature and went right to bed, where he was attended to by his wife, who had once been a nurse. When his condition did not improve, she summoned a doctor who rushed Grange to a hospital when he discovered that Red's blood pressure was dangerously low. Grange had suffered a heart attack. Although he had incurred numerous injuries during his playing career, he was shocked at the news. He had never been "seriously ill before." He remained in the hospital for five weeks, Margaret Grange as his nurse. For the next three months he recuperated at home "as a semi-invalid." Upon the advice of his doctor he improved his diet and dropped from 210 pounds to 170, his weight as a sophomore halfback at Illinois. The following autumn Grange reduced his broadcasting and public-speaking commitments as well as the time spent at his insurance office. "I consider myself lucky for having had that heart attack," he wrote in 1953. "I've been given a warning. Now that I'm cutting down on my activities and have learned the secret of relaxation, I hope to live on to a ripe old age."[30]

As Grange sensed, the heart attack was a major turning point. Within a year he had given up his insurance business, and he and Margaret moved to Florida. Grange continued to broadcast football games each autumn but reduced the workload to a more manageable number. He also worked part-time during the football season as a public relations representative for the

Falstaff Brewing Company. His heart attack, however, resulted in more than Grange changing just his diet, work habits, and life-style. It gradually brought about a change in his view of life and how to cope with being a sporting legend. Grange, in effect, would reinvent himself. In the process, he would fascinate, charm, and sometimes confound a new generation of sportswriters and broadcasters who in an age of increasingly flamboyant and outspoken athletic celebrities could hardly fathom such a reluctant sports hero.

12

A Reluctant Hero

★ ★

IN AN ARTICLE HE WROTE about a year after Grange's heart attack, sportswriter Al Stump related an apocryphal story that underscored Red's generosity and compassion. Members of a rural Illinois high school football team had written to Grange. One of their teammates was gravely ill and wanted to meet him. Grange got out of his sickbed and "drove two hundred miles through a snowstorm to get there." When he walked into the boy's room, the youngster was overcome with emotion and burst into tears. If Stump concocted the story, which seems likely, it was to emphasize what people close to Grange already knew: He was an unselfish and sympathetic individual who was also shy and unassuming. For more than two decades Grange had given generously of his time and energy to support worthy civic projects, institutions, and causes in Chicago and throughout the Midwest and the nation. He was also a soft touch when it came to assisting former football colleagues who were down on their luck. In 1950, for example, he appealed to NFL commissioner Bert Bell on behalf of his former teammate Earl Britton, who was seeking a position as a pro football game official. In the view of his friend Richard Crabb, Grange's personality and character traits remained constant throughout his life, other than in those heady days during the mid-1920s when he briefly reveled in his new-found wealth and the swirl of publicity that enveloped him. His heart attack in

1951, a year and a half before his fiftieth birthday, appeared to change his outlook and cause him to take stock and confront mortality. It also reinforced character traits such as patience and modesty.[1]

The first public indication that Grange's serious illness had prompted a transformation in his outlook and demeanor came in the fall of 1952, when with the aid of Bill Fay he wrote an article for *Collier's:* "I Couldn't Make the Varsity Today." There, he related being among a group of "fat and fortyish" former football players who were discussing the modern specialized game. One had asked him how badly his 1923 team would have beaten the 1951 University of Illinois varsity. After heaping praise on his former college teammates, Grange admitted that his "reluctant but honest answer to the embarrassing question" was that the 1951 Illini would have won the hypothetical game 50-0. "What's more," Grange added, "the 1951 Illini could have beaten any of the outstanding teams of the 1920s, including Notre Dame's famous Four Horsemen and Seven Mules, by at least fifty points." He summarized the numerous improvements in the modern game and then stated, "I'll frankly admit that I don't think the Grange of 1923 could land a halfback job on the 1952 Illinois varsity." Responding to the article, for which he had been interviewed, Bob Zuppke maintained that Grange's remarkable statements were designed to stir controversy: "Red must have got talked into something." Grange's former coach was convinced that "Red over-emphasized his modesty, a good man is always a good man, 1923 or 1952." Regardless of Grange's motives for writing the article, his restrained and humble assessment of his ability as a college player stands in marked contrast to his spirited, somewhat boastful rebuttal in 1947 of the claim that Charlie Trippi was the highest-paid pro football player in history.[2]

During the 1950s Grange's colleagues in sports broadcasting were also struck by his self-effacing modesty, shyness, and gentle disposition. Such traits were not new to him but became more pronounced in the years following his heart attack. Lindsey Nelson came to admire him not so much for his expert commentary, which he valued, but as the ideal role model for a public figure. At five points in his autobiography Nelson remarked on Grange's modesty. "He was the most modest hero I ever knew. I tried to learn all I could from him about how one charts a course, without controversy and furor, when cast into the glare of the public spotlight. No one ever did it more becomingly." Of all the broadcasters with whom Nelson had worked, Grange "left the greatest imprint. . . . I hope that I learned a lot from him about how to maintain proper values in a world of mounting egos." Grange's calm and polite demeanor were also impressive. "Red had such a wonderful way of handling things that he could make the worst situations seem O.K." One night in Chicago, Nelson relates, "A waitress dropped a bowl of Roquefort dressing on my new blue suit," and "I hopped up and was dancing around, all excited, and there sat Red, looking at me ever so sweetly. 'I thought you ordered Thousand Island,' Grange calmly said."[3]

Former Bears' lineman George Connor, Grange's color man on Chicago's televised games in the late 1950s, remembered him in much the same way. "The surprising thing about him," Connor recalled, "was that for all the publicity he retained his simplicity. On airplanes, he traveled coach. He was never too busy to sign autographs. He was the most down-to-earth person and the greatest friend I ever met in my life." Richard Crabb was in close contact with Grange during the 1970s and also remarked on what he described as "this *tremendous* humbleness." When strangers approached Grange in restaurants or other public places, they invariably inquired about how he was able to score four touchdowns in one period against Michigan. "There wasn't too much to it," Red would expain, "and I never did anything unusual and all that sort of thing." Crabb emphasized that Grange "really believed it. He really did." The response, however, was also what Crabb described as a "pat" and allowed Grange to deflect attention and politely end conversations quickly. He would sometimes say, "Your grandmother could have done it. And I know she could because I know mine could have." "How do you keep a conversation going after that?" Crabb asked pointedly.[4]

In 1954 Red and Margaret left Chicago and resettled in Florida, a move they had contemplated for some time. They lived in Miami for five years while planning their dream house, which they had built in Indian Lakes Estates near the town of Lake Wales. Grange designed the sprawling green and white ranch constructed of concrete blocks and situated on the edge of a lagoon fed from nearby Lake Wheohyakapka. Red planned the dwelling, according to Margaret, "to take advantage of every inch" of space, and each room expanded into the next. There were no halls, and the windows and glass patio doors opened onto a screen-enclosed pool to take advantage of summer breezes. The house was comfortable but not ornate. Although Indian Lake Estates was advertised as a "country club community," the Lake Wales area of central Florida, as one sportswriter described it in 1985, "is one of those fortresses of underdevelopment around which time did not pass as much as it got rerouted." The interstate highways that now allow tourists to race from Tampa and Orlando to Miami run well to either side of the Lake Wales region. Although Grange could not have anticipated that pattern of development in the mid-1950s, he must have been well pleased to be isolated from the onrush of tourists and new residents who would engulf the state.[5]

In Florida, Grange maintained a relatively busy schedule that kept him in the public view, especially during the football season. He continued to do play-by-play for Chicago Bears' televised games, served as Lindsey Nelson's expert analyst for NBC's college games on television until 1959, and covered at least one college bowl or all-star game each season. During the 1950s, however, he did begin to curtail the number of public speaking engagements and appearances he had routinely made before moving to Florida. Yet he continued to be recognized as a football personality and expert. In 1957 the U.S. House of Representatives began an investigation on the applicability of federal antitrust laws to organized professional sports. The inquiry was prompted by a bill proposed by Rep. Emanuel Celler of New York that sought to apply antitrust laws to major league baseball, exempt from such legislation since 1922. When hearings began in a House Judiciary subcommittee that Celler chaired, he expanded the scope of the inquiry to include all organized professional sports. Professional football received special attention because of a recent Supreme Court decision, *Radovich v. National Football League* (1957), which held that the sport came within the scope of federal antitrust laws.[6]

On July 25, 1957, the House Judiciary subcommittee summoned five witness to testify on the applicability of antitrust laws to pro football. Grange was the principal witness in a group that included retired NFL players George Connor and Sid Luckman, who had played for the Bears, and active players Chuck Bednarik of Philadelphia and Jack Jennings of the Chicago Cardinals. Representative Celler was convinced that pro football should come under federal antitrust statutes, and he attacked the NFL draft system, "a dead hand, a dead weight upon the boys who want to go into football." He further argued that "the players should be able to form an association for 'collective bargaining' with the league owners." Under questioning, Grange described the draft as "absolutely essential" and added that "the only reason we have professional football as we know it is because of the draft." He rejected Celler's suggestions that the draft forced some players to sign with teams for whom they did not wish to play. He "had never heard any such complaints." His conservative views on labor-management relations and other issues, not unusual among pro athletes at the time, appeared to spring from a long association with corporate executives and the impact of the cold war. The other witnesses supported Grange's testimony. Only Jennings suggested that players "ought to have a minimum salary," but otherwise he saw little need for collective bargaining. No new antitrust legislation was passed as a result of the House investigation, but later that summer the ongoing inquiry played a role in convincing NFL commissioner Bert Bell to recognize the newly organized NFL Players Association. The players' union would remain largely dormant until after the NFL merged with the rival American Football League in 1966.[7]

By the end of the 1950s Grange had cut back on the number of college football games he helped broadcast on national television and found more time to savor semiretirement. He enjoyed taking out his cabin cruiser on the nearby lake, Margaret as co-pilot, and doing routine household chores such as gardening, lawn care, and feeding the abundant variety of wildlife that inhabited the area. During his early years in central Florida, Grange also fished on the lake and played golf. After a time he gave up fishing because he disliked cleaning the catch. He continued to play golf into the early 1980s but found something lacking in the game. "It's like kicking field goals," he told a sportswriter. "You don't have to be a football player to kick field goals; you just have to be precise." The game might be better, he thought, "if someone came up from behind and tackled you when you were swinging."[8]

Grange also maintained an interest in politics. In 1960 he became a charter member of an organizing committee for a national Republican group called Volunteers for Nixon-Lodge. Under the chairmanship of attorney Charles S. Rhyne, Volunteers for Nixon-Lodge consisted of groups of prominent Americans in entertainment and professional and academic life who were recruited to sway independents and wavering Democrats into the Republican camp during the 1960 presidential campaign. Grange and Jesse Owens were the only prominent former athletes among the charter members of the organization. There is no record that Grange contributed to the 1960 Republican campaign other than a letter from Vice-President Richard Nixon on the eve of the 1961 presidential inauguration thanking him for his support in the campaign. "Losing the election was naturally a disappointment from a personal standpoint," Nixon wrote, "but I shall always be proud of the fact that I was privileged to have your friendship and support."[9]

Nearly two decades after the 1960 election Grange sent three scrapbooks of newspaper clippings to Richard Crabb, who was helping to organize a heritage museum in DuPage County. Grange explained that the views articulated in the articles "coincide with my [political] thinking." He added, "I have been around a long time, and I am very interested in the way our great country is governed." The clippings, primarily from Florida newspapers, indicate that Grange was a conservative Republican. He selected articles that supported free enterprise, an all-out attack on communism, restraints on big government, and a reduction of the national debt. Grange also included items attacking labor unions, foreign aid, the United Nations, and the Democratic-controlled Congress. He informed Crabb that collecting clippings for the scrapbooks was one of his hobbies.[10]

In 1963 Grange was selected as a charter member of the Pro Football Hall of Fame and attended induction ceremonies at the newly constructed facility in Canton, Ohio. He had been chosen among the initial inductees into the National Collegiate Football Hall of Fame in the early 1950s. At the Canton festivities he was joined by a number of the surviving pioneers of the game, who made up the first class of seventeen former players, coaches, owners, and administrators. Pro Football Hall of Fame director Dick McCann honored the enshrinees by describing them as "the milestone men of pro football. Their deeds and dogged faith wrote the history of this great game." Among the Class of 1963 were two of Grange's former Chicago Bears teammates, George Halas and Bronko Nagurski. During the next decade he remained in contact with both former and active NFL players and officials and returned to Canton in 1973 for a special reunion of the surviving members of the initial class of inductees. Grange charmed and awed many former pro players who came to know him at Canton. Meeting him, Sid Luckman said, was "one of the greatest honors I've received in sports," and Mel Hein called him "the nicest, dearest man I ever met." During the years when he was active in promoting pro football, particularly the hall of fame (to which he donated a large part of his football memorabilia), however, Grange did more than socialize. He became the leading advocate of extending the NFL pension plan to earlier generations of league players. When the NFL Players Association did not respond to his pleas on behalf of the old-timers, Grange called the modern players "cheap." John Underwood described him as "adamant in his futile support of a pension plan for those who had played pro ball when he did and were not as well off as he was. But he always made his case politely."[11]

The summer after the 1963 football season Grange retired as a television broadcaster for the Chicago Bears, thus ending a weekly sportscasting career that dated back to 1934. He continued to serve as a commen-

tator for a few college games over the next several years before severing
ties with sports broadcasting altogether. In 1969 he announced his full
retirement when he ended a more-than-twenty-year association with the
Falstaff Brewing Company as a public relations representative. He was
determined to enjoy a peaceful life with Margaret in their quiet hideaway
in Florida. Grange had experienced all the ups and downs of being a sports
celebrity and had had enough. "I don't particularly like looking back and
reliving the past," he said. "All I did was handle a football well. And the
woods are full of those kind of people now. I never bought that celebrity
bunk." Commenting on the drawbacks of "having your name known,"
he pointed out with an uncharacteristic touch of bitterness that "right away
people start bitching at you about everything that happens. Then they want
to borrow money. Then they want to do this and that. If you take a drink,
everybody knows it. It's nice to read how great you are and all that, but
being in the limelight isn't always the good life."[12]

Despite his inclination to avoid public notice and acclaim, Grange could
not escape media attention in an era of escalating salaries in professional
sports and expanding coverage of athletic celebrities (especially on television) that brought back memories of the 1920s. Soon after he retired in
1969 the Football Writers Association of America selected an all-time all-
American team to commemorate the hundredth anniversary of intercollegiate football. Grange was not only named to the first team but also was
the only unanimous choice for the select team. University of Southern
California halfback sensation O. J. Simpson made the second team. When
a sportswriter contacted him by telephone to elicit his reaction, Grange
was cordial but far from elated. He politely recounted a number of changes
and improvements in modern football but noted with some dismay that
many contemporary players and some coaches were wrapped up in their
own importance. They lacked the kind of respect for one another and loyalty to the team that was more common in his day. He admired some of
the players and coaches but added, "I don't think anybody has any respect
for anybody else nowadays." When asked about his retirement, Grange
explained that he did some boating and fishing and played a little golf and
had "a lot of time to take it easy. My time's not too valuable now," he said.
"I don't watch much football any more, though. I just don't see anything
new, when you come down to it." He admitted that he'd sometimes "watch
a game and turn it off at half-time. I wouldn't go very far to watch two
teams play football. It just doesn't mean an awful lot to me."[13]

At a time when American sports were in a period of transition from the

more sedate years following World War II, when sports idols were typically perceived as clean-cut, modest, all-American boys (like Johnny Uni-
tas in pro football), to an era of highly paid, flamboyant, brash, and often
boastful young athletes (like Joe Namath) who thrived in the glare of publicity, Grange's seeming indifference to contemporary athletics both con-
founded and fascinated the sports media. In some ways he had been a
prototype of athletes such as Namath, Muhammad Ali, and later John
McEnroe who in part had built careers on the same type of notoriety Pyle
had orchestrated for Grange in the mid-1920s. They were products of an
innovative and intense style of television sports coverage that Grange knew
well, and he believed they should get every dollar they could from the sports
and television establishments. Without mentioning names, however, he
decried their egotism and lack of civility. During the 1920s Grange had
felt the exhilaration and sting of unbridled publicity but in his own mind
had maintained a sense of modesty and integrity. Now he had little interest in reflecting on that bygone era or contemplating the changes in modern sports. He'd just as soon mow the lawn as watch a football game on
television. He was polite and indulgent to members of the sports media,
who viewed him as one of the few surviving links to an era that appeared
to be a precursor of the contemporary transition in sports, but had scant
interest in dwelling on a distant past, which, he said, meant little to him.
Yet reporters continued to visit Indian Lake Estates or contact him by telephone in an effort to gain better insight into the transformation of modern sports. They were intrigued and charmed by Grange but often concluded interviews with more questions than answers.[14]

During the 1970s the Granges enjoyed tranquility and only rarely left
Florida to attend major functions that celebrated Red's football career. In
October 1974 he agreed to participate in the Homecoming weekend at the
University of Illinois commemorating the fiftieth anniversary of the dedication of Memorial Stadium and the 1924 Michigan game that had forever changed his life. Starting several weeks before the highly publicized
event, Grange was besieged by telephone calls from inquisitive reporters
trying to set the stage for what was being billed as the "Golden Anniversary Game" between Illinois and Michigan State on October 19. Grange
responded to a multitude of mostly familiar questions about his past glory and upcoming visit with dry humor and typical modesty. He told an
Urbana-Champaign sportswriter that he was not traveling a thousand miles
to see Illinois lose and added glibly that despite his pride in the Illinois team,
"It's the first time in awhile that I've been able to go out and face people.

Not many years ago the Illini lost all their games and the Chicago Bears lost all but one. I had to stay in the house that year." Grange informed another reporter, "The only tough part of my visit is that I'll see guys I haven't seen for forty or fifty years. They'll say, 'Do you remember me?' and I won't." During the course of numerous long-distance telephone interviews, Grange reeled off a string of stories and anecdotes about his college and pro playing days that reporters who had followed his career had heard many times over the years. One wrote perceptively, although understating Grange's place in football history, that "the Red Grange story has become a series of anecdotes that reinforce his statistical position as one of the greatest football players in Illinois history."[15]

From the time he arrived in Urbana-Champaign on the Thursday evening before Homecoming weekend until he left on Sunday, Grange graciously attended nearly a dozen separate functions, including an alumni tailgate party, a reunion at his fraternity, and a formal banquet in his honor attended by the state's governor and George Halas among other notables on the eve of the game. He readily agreed to help boost a fund-raising drive for shoring up and restoring the fifty-year-old stadium. "I'm happy," he declared, "to help out with the Stadium if they think I can." A journalist who tracked Grange's movements during the long weekend reported that before it was over "he had signed books, programs and scraps, shaken every hand in sight, and listened—with a direct and steady gaze—to re-tellings of the now-too-familiar tale of the fan who was in Memorial Stadium THAT DAY, Oct. 18, 1924." At the banquet, Halas paid him perhaps the highest tribute of the weekend: "I'll go on record saying that Red Grange, Old 77, had more impact on the game of college and pro football than any other single man in this century."[16]

On the following afternoon, Red Grange Day at Memorial Stadium, Grange made a half-time appearance at midfield to the delight of more than fifty-five thousand fans who strained to catch a glimpse of him amid a throng of official greeters, cameramen, and reporters. The New York Times ran a story on the ceremony and a follow-up interview with Grange as the lead article in its Sunday sporting section. "Spry and wry, carrying his exact playing weight of fifty years ago, 170 pounds, Harold (Red) Grange bounded out of the stands yesterday at half-time of the Illinois-Michigan State game at Champaign, Ill., to receive yet one more award," the story began. The writer went on to describe the distinguished service medallion presented to Grange by the university's board of trustees as "an understatement by half a century." Few readers grasped the irony that Grange's short walk to midfield rated front-page coverage although his long runs before the historic Michigan game in 1924 had seldom rated more than a few inches of print in the prestigious newspaper. On the same day in South Bend, Indiana, Notre Dame celebrated the fiftieth anniversary of another singular event in college football history by defeating Army 48-0 on Four Horsemen Day. Grantland Rice might have smiled had he seen the following day's sporting headlines: The Galloping Ghost eclipsed the immortal Four Horsemen in most national newspapers. Grange returned to Florida confident that he would be "able to go out and face people" because Illinois had rallied to gain a 21-21 tie with Michigan State. He was less secure with the thought that he was the only surviving member of the 1924 Illinois backfield. As he admitted to a reporter, "That's kind of scary to be the only one left."[17]

As part of the Golden Anniversary weekend, community leaders in Wheaton had hired several buses so residents from Red's hometown could attend the celebration in Urbana-Champaign. Richard Crabb remembered that Grange, during his formal address at the Friday-night banquet, laid down his prepared manuscript on the podium about halfway through the speech, looked around, and spoke informally to the overflow audience. "By the way, there is one thing I want you to know this evening," he said, "and that is that there are more people here from my hometown of Wheaton than there are from Urbana and Champaign combined." During the course of that evening and at a reception organized by Wheaton admirers the following day, which he attended, leaders of the city's contingent led by publisher D. Ray Wilson prevailed upon Grange to visit his hometown later that year. He had not done so in several decades. When Wheaton joined the state pension program (likely in the 1940s), Lyle Grange, who had retired as the town's chief of police in 1937, was not afforded a pension although the three patrolmen under his command were. Crabb implied that the town council had made the decision to exclude Lyle, and, he added, "It's hard to think it was an oversight." It was "very controversial" locally for many years. As a result, Lyle Grange left town and resettled in northeastern Pennsylvania, where he died in the early 1950s. He never returned to Wheaton, and neither had his famous son.[18]

In late 1974 Grange did visit Wheaton, where he renewed old friendships and became involved in discussions to build a heritage museum in DuPage County. Crabb became a driving force behind the project and credited Grange with promoting the idea, stating that he "was responsible for starting it." Over the next several years Grange provided Crabb with scrapbooks, memorabilia, and written and oral testimony on his career that might be suitable for inclusion in the proposed museum. In the fall of 1978 the Granges made another trip to Wheaton, where Red was honored and became the first former county resident enshrined in what became known as the DuPage Heritage Gallery. His speech, which capped the weekend's ceremonies, was described as "warmly informal, neither chronological nor memorized, but most compelling and entertaining. He touched many yardlines, and scored again and again with graciousness and modesty rarely encountered in sports heroes of today." When a question from a man in the audience revealed that more than thirty people in the crowd of about 1,500 had actually seen Red play, he was visibly moved. "It's been great coming back to Wheaton," he concluded. "I just wish I could come back and play for you again."[19]

After returning to Florida, Margaret wrote to Richard Crabb and expressed appreciation for the impressive ceremony honoring her husband. "All I can say is you are going to have a heck of a time topping what you all did for the first Enshrinee into the Heritage Gallery. As Red told you yesterday, words cannot express how overwhelmed he was at the reception he received." When the gallery was formally dedicated two years later and four additional inductees were honored, Illinois governor James Thompson praised Grange as a hero, an exemplar "of those rare men and women whose spirit transcends any category." Grange's support for the Heritage Gallery project and his heartfelt reaction to the honor of being selected the first enshrinee revealed a side he seldom displayed in his retirement years. Throughout much of his life he had been in the public spotlight and knew both the exaltation and rigorous demands that being in such a position entailed. In his declining years he primarily wanted to enjoy a more measured and tranquil life yet was not immune from occasionally reflecting on past achievements and contemplating how he might be remembered in annals of twentieth-century sports. For the casual journalist who asked familiar questions that Red had heard many times before, he reduced his career to a series of quips and charming anecdotes, which, combined with his disarming modesty, usually satisfied the reporter and quickly ended the interview. When confronted by more knowledgable and persistent interviewers, however, Grange sometimes could be coaxed into going beyond the anecdotes and filling in some of the details of his multi-faceted life. However haltingly or unconsciously, he seemed to sense the importance of setting the historical record straight as he saw it.[20]

After his return to Wheaton Grange seldom traveled far from his Florida home. He could not stay out of the limelight for long, however, because the media continued to focus on him as a reference point for the golden era of the 1920s. In June 1980 Grange celebrated his seventy-seventh birthday, coincidentally, the number he had worn on his uniform and made famous during his playing days. Over the years, millions of golfers and sports commentators had etched the number in the public consciousness—those who completed a round in seventy-seven strokes were said to have shot a "Red Grange." Grange, who planned to observe the day quietly at home by sharing a bottle of champagne with Margaret, was inundated by telephone calls from well-wishers and scores of reporters who would write stories on what they considered a milestone in sports. "All I've been doing is answering the telephone—and trying to smile," he complained mildly to one visiting columnist. His response to the birthday was typically understated. "I've finally arrived at my football number. And I don't know whether that's good or bad. I do know it means I'm one year older." Another reporter who visited with him noted, "Time has not changed Grange's gentlemanly manner, though. He is almost a cliche of the fictitious old-time sports hero, but his modesty and grace are quite real."[21]

By the time his age equaled the number he had worn on his football jersey, Grange and his storied career had become part of Americana. In 1979 Michael Cristofer, who had won both the Pulitzer Prize and Tony Award for *The Shadow Box*, wrote another play, *C. C. Pyle and the Bunion Derby*, which evoked memories of the Jazz Age, its bizarre stunts and extravagant publicity, and the memorable partnership between Pyle and Grange. Paul Newman directed the play in a trial run at Kenyon College, but plans to stage the production on Broadway in 1980 never materialized. Two years later Luke Salisbury, a sport historian and advocate of fans' rights in organized athletics, delivered a lecture at numerous college campuses and highlighted the once-famous collaboration between Pyle and Grange. His focus was on whether Pyle had cheated Grange out of large sums of money during their partnership. Grange continued to defend Pyle, however, who after going bankrupt as a result of a second Bunion Derby in 1929 recouped his fortune as a promoter at Chicago's Century of Progress Fair and as head of a radio transcription company. He died in Los Angeles in 1939 at age fifty-six. The nostalgia for the 1920s that began to intensify in the 1970s was, according to Robert Cowley, based on the perception that the two decades had much in common. During the 1920s, "We were too infatuated with the novelty of modern life," Cowley wrote. "The consequences would be easier to dismiss if the process were not again duplicating itself: a society out of control, an environment endangered, and a financial system on the verge of collapse. It suddenly seems so familiar."[22]

Although members of the sports media may not have shared Cowley's interpretation, they were aware that the "golden decade" was a watershed in the development of modern athletics and that the number of surviving sports luminaries from that era was dwindling. When Grange made what would be his last trip out of Florida in 1981 to receive the prestigious Walter Camp Man of the Year Award for outstanding national service, reporters descended on him to pose many of the questions he had answered politely for years. "For the sportswriters, the great things in Grange's career were rising at the time," Crabb maintained. "Had he not lived so long, that would not have happened. And that's one reason why the Four Horsemen, for instance, are virtually unknown. They command very little attention, but they didn't live that long." He hesitated and then asserted emphatically, "And in addition to that they weren't Grange."[23]

When Jack Dempsey died at the age of eighty-seven in 1983, Grange was practically alone as one of the once-ballyhooed sports legends of the Jazz Age. Shortly after Dempsey's death on the eve of Grange's eightieth birthday, *New York Times* columnist Dave Anderson reminded readers that the Galloping Ghost was now the last survivor of the "five athletes adored by a nation" during the 1920s. Other than Dempsey, Babe Ruth had died in 1948, Bill Tilden in 1953, and Bobby Jones in 1971. In a telephone interview, Grange accepted Anderson's birthday greeting with a chuckle. "I never thought I'd make it," he said. "Margaret and I are still speaking." After reviewing his career, he offered a brief appraisal of sports during the 1920s: "Those were great years. Some of the finest writers and editors were building up sports right after World War I when people wanted to relax a little bit, when the country was ready to expand. Maybe it was all built out of proportion but I'm glad to have been part of it. And I'm glad to be eighty."[24]

During the 1980s Grange continued to receive numerous telephone calls and periodic visits from sportswriters when some athletic event or milestone evoked memories of the 1920s. In general, however, he wanted to be left alone. When a Chicago reporter made a visit to Indian Lakes Estates on the eve of the 1983 Illinois-Michigan football game and inquired why Grange had chosen the steamy midriff of Florida for retirement, he replied, "I like it here where we can be alone." The reporter came away with the impression that "life is best when he can just be Harold Grange, out mowing the lawn in his khakis." In his last in-depth interview with John Underwood in 1985 Grange said he still read books (most of them on baseball) and did chores around the house, but "mainly I do nothing, if that's what I want to do. It's what happens when you have enough dough." Although he politely answered questions about his career, Grange complained that "I got footballed to death after it became a job." When people asked whether he might be "the guy who played football," Underwood wrote, "Grange tells them, 'That was my uncle.'"[25]

Grange's world had receded to his home on North Amaryllis Drive in Indian Lakes Estates by the late 1980s. When a *New York Times* correspondent visited on the eve of the 1988 Orange Bowl, Grange was increasingly housebound because of a back injury suffered six decades before during his playing days: "Age and aching bones have narrowed the world of a man who was once the toast of the nation." In 1990 he was diagnosed as having Parkinson's disease. "He won't be going dancing," Margaret informed the media resolutely, "but he's going to outlive all of us." When University of Illinois halfback Howard Griffith, who had recently broken Grange's records for most touchdowns in a game, season, and career at Illinois, visited him in a Lake Wales nursing home in early 1991, Grange counseled him not to worry about those who were disappointed to see his records surpassed. Griffith remembered being "overwhelmed for him to say that he was honored to meet me." It was vintage Red Grange.[26]

Grange could not overcome the effects of the debilitating disease. He died peacefully of complications from pneumonia at Lake Wales Hospital on January 28, 1991. It was perhaps fitting that he died only a few hours after millions of football fans had watched the New York Giants defeat the Buffalo Bills in the Super Bowl, a game that originated in the first NFL playoff contest of 1932, in which Grange scored the winning touchdown by catching a pass while flat on his back in the end zone. Most of the tributes that poured into the sleepy town of Lake Wales and appeared in the national media echoed the thoughts of Grange's former college teammate Dwight Follett: "I had a lot of respect for him. He was a great athlete. He was a very cheerful and friendly person, but his greatest asset was his modesty." Reflecting on Grange's "humble, pleasant and courteous" manner, Timothy Dwyer emphasized that it was "a part of his prototype many modern athletes have not adopted." No doubt Grange would have liked to be remembered more simply. As he reminded a gathering of old friends and former teammates during his visit to Wheaton in 1978, "Hell, I'm not that great. I'm just an ordinary guy." Bob Zuppke may have had the last word several decades earlier: "They can argue all they want about the greatest football player who ever lived. I was satisfied I had him when I had Red Grange."[27]

Epilogue:
Red Grange in Perspective

★ ★

DURING THE 1920S, especially after he retired as a football player in 1935, the sports media routinely referred to Red Grange as a football hero. Historians and scholars who study popular culture now debate whether sports figures of that era or today are legitimate American heroes or simply well-publicized celebrities. Peter Williams and Michael Oriard argue, for example, that popular sports are manifestations of archetypal myths, and a select few of the participants should be regarded as heroes. Other scholars such as Richard Schickel and Richard Crepeau question the idea of sports idols as authentic heroes. Schickel, a film historian, maintains that by the 1920s, at least, "The public ceased to insist that there be an obvious correlation between achievement and fame. It was no longer absolutely necessary for its favorites to perform a real-life heroic act, to invent a boon for mankind, to create a business enterprise." Beginning around World War I, it was possible to become a celebrity by just becoming famous—in Daniel Boorstin's phrase, to be "known for your well-knownness." Despite their disagreement on the distinction between a sports hero and a sports celebrity, most scholars agree that the hero-celebrity in athletics was a phenomenon of the early twentieth century and that the 1920s was a germination period for this new type of sports figure.[1]

Grantland Rice provided an uncomplicated explanation for the rise of the sports idol in the postwar years. Assessing the phenomenon from the perspective of the late 1940s, he stated, "The answer is a simple one. It is because the postwar period gave the game the greatest collection of stars, involving both skill and color, that sport has ever known since the first cave man tackled the mammoth and the aurochs bull." Two more recent studies of heroes and hero-worship in the 1920s hold that it was not the sports stars but the mass media itself, including Rice, that created sports idols during the decade. In a study of Grantland Rice, Mark Inabinett maintains that "the sportswriters of the Golden Age worked in a time when they had a virtual monopoly on sports news" and "the image of unsurpassed greatness attained by the leading athletes of the Golden Age is more attributable to the influence of sportswriters than to the caliber of the sportsmen." Bruce J. Evensen, in a book on the mass media of the 1920s and the rise of Jack Dempsey, is more cautious: "the cultivation of sports celebrity and mass-mediated hero worship during the 1920s" resulted from "a generation's search for significance during a period in American history when for many the world seemed increasingly insensible." Grange himself acknowledged many times that sportswriters played an important role in building up sports personalities during the 1920s and conceded that maybe "it [sport] was built out of proportion."[2]

Richard Schickel has suggested that the press was only one element in a changing postwar society that helped usher in the age of celebrity. The 1920s brought together the emerging forces of modernization that allowed the public to become intimate with outstanding (and sometimes not so outstanding) individuals. Rapid development or improvements in motion pictures, transportation, photography, advertising, and radio, to but name a few areas, created an environment in which "almost anyone could be wrested out of whatever context had originally nurtured him" and turned into a celebrity. Schickel traces the great transformation in modern society to World War I and views developments in the motion picture industry as a precursor to the rise of the cult of celebrity during the 1920s. Many scholars would agree with much of that analysis but quickly point out that not many of the numerous celebrity-heroes of the 1920s have become enduring symbols of the period. In sports, Ruth, Dempsey, Tilden, Jones, and Grange are familiar figures, yet Gertrude Ederle and Gene Tunney, to name two, were celebrities of the golden decade who are less widely known now.[3]

Benjamin Rader argues that the emergence of numerous athletic heroes in the 1920s "went deeper than the skillful ballyhooing of the promoters and journalistic flights of fancy." They were a creation of the public itself. "The athletes as public heroes served a compensatory function," Rader maintains. He explains that "as the society became more complicated and systematized as success had to be won increasingly in bureaucracies, the need for heroes who leaped to fame and fortune outside the rules of the system seemed to grow. No longer were the heroes the lone business tycoon or the statesman, but the 'stars'—from the movies and sports." Those in the public domain who were obsessed with their individual powerlessness gained the most satisfaction from "the athletic hero who presented an image of all-conquering power"—Babe Ruth's titanic home runs, Dempsey's crushing knockout blows, and Grange's dramatic acceleration on long touchdown runs. Less admired were those athletes who, like Tunney and Ty Cobb, employed a more "scientific style" to achieve victory.[4]

Beyond their personification of raw power, which also symbolized America's emergence as a world economic and political force, many of the enduring sports idols of the era represented traditional Victorian virtues and the ideal of the self-made man. The public image of Grange as a shy, modest, and clean-cut youth who toted heavy chunks of ice to pay his way through college helps explain his appeal as a sports hero. Although not every enduring sports hero-celebrity of the era embodied all the qualities associated with traditional values (Ruth was anything but modest and clean-cut and Bobby Jones came from a wealthy background), most possessed at least some. Grange's stature was enhanced by the popular perception created by the media that he was a product of the West and represented frontier values that were being threatened in an increasingly industrial and urban nation. Although his hometown of Wheaton was rapidly evolving into a suburb of Chicago, the eastern media typically portrayed it as a rustic village. Like Dempsey, Bronko Nagurski, and above all Charles Lindbergh, Grange came to epitomize those virtues of farm, village, and frontier life that many Americans prized but believed to be endangered by the process of modernization. It is also noteworthy that the press focused an inordinate amount of attention on Grange's passion for fast automobiles and his frequent brushes with the law for driving at excessive speeds. John W. Ward has suggested that the extraordinary public acclaim for Lindbergh as the quintessential hero of the 1920s might be partially explained by the fact that he represented both frontier values and the triumph of the machine during a decade in which those issues were central to the lives of many Americans. To a lesser degree, Grange's public image touched on these fundamental concerns of the 1920s.[5]

During his retirement years, Grange occasionally offered ideas on why the 1920s produced so many sports heroes. Like Grantland Rice, he emphasized that many sports celebrities "had great personalities" and acknowledged that a talented group of sportswriters and promoters had given them enormous publicity. Grange particularly focused on the impact of World War I, which he described as a trying time. Sports seemed to provide a natural outlet for the release of pent-up energy and tension as "everyone seemed to let their hair down after World War I." In terms of his emergence as the nation's premier football hero, Grange perceptively pointed out that few outstanding players had preceded him in that category. "I don't think there were any outstanding names in football in those days," he told Richard Whittingham. "Starting with Jim Thorpe and a lot of them the names were made after most of these people were out of school and the writers wrote about them, and guys that never saw them play started telling how good they were." Grange was undoubtedly correct. Early stars of the game such as William "Pudge" Heffelfinger, Willie Heston, Ted Coy, Eddie Mahan, and even Thorpe became more widely known in the 1920s and after than they had been in their collegiate days, when football was more a regional sport. It was not until after World War I that the mass media began to promote truly national football heroes.[6]

Although Bruce Evensen and others have emphasized the mass media's responsibility for the rise of numerous sports heroes during the 1920s, a number of other factors also set the stage for this development in the case of football. America's involvement in World War I helped elevate football from a game that had a sometimes-sordid past to one that became associated with fitness, fortitude, and even patriotism. The war also hastened the development of better highways, which made many rural state universities more accessible to students as well as football fans. Universities responded by constructing large stadiums, many of them war memorials, to accommodate the overflow crowds. An increase in automobile ownership, better roads, and new or expanded stadiums combined to make a dramatic impact in the Midwest, South, and Pacific Coast and to make football a genuinely national game. New technology and the further development of radio and newsreels, along with improvements in photography, helped provide the basis for football enthusiasts to closely follow outstanding teams and star players. These innovations, combined with a more nationally oriented print media and an increase in intersectional games, created more interest in football outside the eastern region of the country.[7]

Although midwestern football was played conservatively by today's standards, in the 1920s it was considered an open game that featured more passing and scoring than the more established eastern game. In general, the eastern press remained skeptical of highly regarded teams and players from outside the region where the game was developed. Red Grange changed the minds of many eastern reporters when he almost single-handedly defeated a highly rated University of Pennsylvania team in Philadelphia on a rain-soaked field in 1925. It may have been the most significant game he played as a collegian. Grange's central place in football history can be attributed to timing. He began his college career just as football was reaping the benefits of being associated with the war effort and the media was perfecting a formula for focusing national attention on hero-celebrities, from Balto the dog to Floyd Collins and Jack Dempsey.[8]

It is not clear whether Grange was the best football player of all time or of the 1920s, but he was a gifted athlete who had enormous natural ability, a willingness to work hard, and a great desire to succeed. He competed at a time when fewer of the nation's best athletes played college football (compared with today) and many did not have sound training at the preparatory level. During Grange's years at Illinois, Bob Zuppke complained, "I wish you kids hadn't played in high school—then I wouldn't have to waste so much time correcting the bad habits you've developed." It is not surprising that Grange, with a natural talent for the game, excelled in college football. What helped make him a household name in the 1920s was the fact that he played three of his best college games (against Michigan and Chicago in 1924 and Penn in 1925) at pivotal times, when, for various reasons, the media focused great attention on him and his team. Grange's extraordinary individual performances also came at a time when some sportswriters were questioning the prevailing view that college coaches were the most important factor in creating winning teams. Although coaches would continue to be revered by football experts and still are (Knute Rockne's exalted stature in the 1920s is a case in point), a number of postwar writers began to emphasize that overpaid coaches were of less importance in producing victories than gifted individual performers. Chicago sportswriter Ralph Cannon made the point in 1923, when he wrote that "a couple of halfbacks like Grange are more to be desired than a genius of even a Haughton," a reference to Percy Haughton, the famed Harvard coach of the 1910s. Grange's spectacular feats on the gridiron came at a time when the pendulum was swinging, for the moment at least, toward more emphasis on individual performers rather than field generals who directed the game from the bench.[9]

When he signed a professional contract after his final college game, Grange became, at least temporarily, the most written about man in America. Many former collegians played pro football at the time, and a number of them had begun playing before their college classes graduated. College officials made Grange's decision to turn pro a cause célèbre because they were smarting over perceived past abuses by the pros against college football. They were also concerned about the renewed attack against the alleged corruption in the collegiate game that would eventually culminate in the Carnegie Report of 1929 and, above all, by the fact that Grange had come to symbolize college football. Despite the then widely held view that Grange rescued the struggling pro game from the verge of extinction, college coaches and administrators were more concerned about the relative strength of pro football than its weaknesses. Using a strategy perfected by boxing promoter Tex Rickard, C. C. Pyle orchestrated a public relations campaign centered around a near-suicidal schedule of games that embedded Grange's name into the national consciousness. He and Grange helped popularize pro football, but Pyle's strategy of relying on the star system to fill stadiums, emulated by other pro owners, was not in the long-term interest of the game. His reckless scheduling methods designed to maximize profits, which Grange did not oppose, contributed to Red's career-threatening injury and his fall from public grace.[10]

Grange reached his nadir as a football player and public idol in 1928. Forced into the role of nightclub barker to make a living and pay his debts, he was ridiculed by some journalists and depicted as a fallen hero. After he had gone through a short period of moodiness and defensiveness with the media, his finer qualities reasserted themselves. He admitted making mistakes, refused to blame Pyle for his misfortune, declined public pity, and carried on as an impaired but effective pro football player. Relying on integrity, modesty, and stick-to-itiveness, Grange persevered, and the public forgave him. When the onset of the depression deflated public interest in spectator sports and fascination with star performers, Grange was almost instantly portrayed in the press as a throwback to a bygone era. Faced with declining attendance and gate receipts, college coaches and their allies searched diligently for the next Red Grange who might reverse their economic fortunes. Ironically, as Grange's effectiveness as a player diminished he joined the media guild, which had once gloated over his tarnished image, and emerged as one of football's most trusted spokesmen. After World War II he became a pioneer in television broadcasting and served as a link between the perceived glory days of football in the 1920s and its resurgence in the postwar years. He remained in broadcasting long enough to become a celebrity to a new generation of sports fans and witness the emergence of a new breed of athletes who flouted the traditional norms of behavior for sports idols.

In the 1950s and 1960s, Grange's popularity as a broadcaster and celebrity can be explained by the fact that he provided a connection between the 1920s and the public persona adopted by contemporary athletic heroes. He approved of their acquisitive instincts but criticized their lack of humility and civility. A symbol of an earlier era, Grange provided a reference point in evaluating more recent changes in modern sports. In retirement he became an anachronism. The media was fascinated by a man who had helped usher in an age of flamboyance and excess yet had little apparent regard for his considerable achievements, was humble to a fault, and displayed minimal interest in the contemporary sports scene. The fact that Grange outlived most of the important sports heroes of the 1920s made him a focal point for media attention and an enduring symbol of the Jazz Age.

Grange's career as a collegiate and professional player both paralleled and contributed to the rise of modern football and made him an essential element in explaining and understanding the game's important place in American culture. For more than five decades after his playing days ended Grange continued to associate himself with football as a coach, commentator, broadcaster, and eventually an elder statesman, highlighting and reinforcing his central role in shaping the modern sport. He would have been impatient with and dismissive of being assigned such an exalted position in the game's history. "I could carry a football well," he once admitted, "but I've met hundreds of people who could do their thing better than I. I mean engineers, and writers, scientists, doctors—whatever." Grange would have preferred to be remembered as "a poor kid who was lucky to have a good opportunity. I could run, and that was the basis of any success I ever had."[11]

Notes

Prologue

1. A. M. "Tony" Ulrich, "The Greatest Game Ever Played: 1924 Revisited," *University of Illinois Souvenir Football Program,* Oct. 19, 1974, iii, University of Illinois Archives, Urbana.

2. *Illinois Alumni News,* Nov. 1924, 43, 56, University of Illinois Archives, Urbana; Roger Ebert, ed., *An Illini Century: One Hundred Years of Campus Life* (Urbana: University of Illinois Press, 1967), 93–94; James Crusinberry, "Grange Thrills Huge Crowd by Racing to Five Touchdowns," Chicago *Tribune,* Oct. 19, 1924.

3. L. H. Baker, *Football: Facts and Figures* (New York: Farrar and Rinehart, 1945), 365–75, 389–94, 621–23; George W. Rockwood to Editor, *Sunday Journal* (DuPage County, Ill.), July 29, 1974.

4. During this era, Big Ten teams did not play one another each season. Baker, *Football,* 389–90; Joe Marcin, "Magic Moment in Sports: Illinois' Grange Runs Wild," undated newspaper clipping, and "Red Grange Alone Beats Wolverines," Associated Press game account, Oct. 18, 1924, both in the University of Illinois Archives, Urbana.

5. *Memorial Stadium Notes,* July 1922, David Kinley Papers, University of Illinois Archives, Urbana. On stadium building during the 1920s, see Philip J. Lowry, "College Green Gridirons," *College Football Historical Society* [bulletin] 4 (Feb. 1991): 13–15.

6. *Memorial Stadium Notes,* Sept. 1922, Feb. 1923, David Kinley Papers, University of Illinois Archives, Urbana; *The Stadium Story,* 1, 26, David Kinley Pa-

pers, University of Illinois Archives, Urbana; "A Memorial through the Years," *Athletic Journal* 26 (Dec. 1945): 23, 38.

7. *Illinois Alumni Journal,* Oct. 1924, 8, Nov. 1924, 43, 56; box marked "Stadium Drive, 1921–27," David Kinley Papers, University of Illinois Archives, Urbana.

8. *Illinois Alumni News,* Oct. 1924, 8, 9, University of Illinois Archives, Urbana; Wheaton *Illinoian,* Oct. 24, 1924; *Memorial Stadium Notes,* Dec. 1923, Oct. 1924, David Kinley Papers, University of Illinois Archives, Urbana; Bill Marsteller, "Quin Ryan Says Grange Placed Football on Air," April 4, 1937, newspaper clipping, University of Illinois Archives, Urbana. Grange incorrectly states that the Michigan game was the first Illinois game broadcast on radio. Harold E. Grange, as told to Ira Morton, *The Red Grange Story: An Autobiography* (Urbana: University of Illinois Press, 1993), 52.

9. Maureen McKernan, "New Illinois Stadium Riot of Color and Noise as Grange Runs over Wolverines," Chicago *Tribune,* Oct. 19, 1924; George W. Rockwood to Editor, *Sunday Journal,* July 29, 1974; Ulrich, "Greatest Game," iii.

10. Marcin, "Magic Moment in Sports"; Lizbeth Lemke, "The Day Red Grange Became a Hero," *Illinois Magazine* (Sept.–Oct. 1985): 3; Grange, *Red Grange Story,* 52–54; Maynard Brichford to Author, June 15, 1993; article by Red Grange, undated newspaper story on the 1924 Michigan game, University of Illinois Archives, Urbana; Crusinberry, "Grange Thrills Huge Crowd."

11. Harold E. "Red" Grange, *Zuppke of Illinois* (Chicago: A. L. Glaser, 1937), 1–29; Baker, *Football,* 370; *Memorial Stadium Notes,* Oct. 1924, David Kinley Papers, University of Illinois Archives, Urbana; David Condon, "Galloping Ghost Rambles toward Seventy-seven," Chicago *Tribune,* June 12, 1980; Grange, *Red Grange Story,* 49–50. Without mentioning Yost or Michigan by name, Chicago's Coach Stagg alluded to how Zuppke took advantage of the boastful and insulting comments coming out of Ann Arbor in the months preceding the 1924 game. See Amos Alonzo Stagg, as told to Wesley Winans Stout, *Touchdown!* (New York: Longmans, Green, 1927), 257–58.

12. "The Story of the Game," undated clipping, and *Illinois Alumni News,* Oct. 1924, 9, both in University of Illinois Archives, Urbana.

13. Ulrich, "Greatest Game," iv; Grange, *Red Grange Story,* 50, 54; "The Story of the Game"; Champaign-Urbana *News-Gazette,* Nov. 22, 1978.

14. Crusinberry, "Grange Thrills Huge Crowd"; George W. Rockwood to Editor, *Sunday Journal,* July 29, 1974.

15. Crusinberry, "Grange Thrills Huge Crowd"; Paul Gallico, "Red Grange: Houdini of the Gridiron," *Esquire,* Nov. 1944, 42.

16. Crusinberry, "Grange Thrills Huge Crowd"; Grange, *Red Grange Story,* 56–57.

17. "Ten Local Men Recall Grange's Six-Touchdown Performance vs. Michigan," Urbana-Champaign *Courier,* Oct. 18, 1974; John H. Schacht, "A Man No

One Could Forget," *Illinois Alumni News,* March 1974, 14–16, University of Illinois Archives, Urbana.

18. Richard Whittingham, *Saturday Afternoon: College Football and the Men Who Made the Day* (New York: Workman, 1985), 178–79.

19. Crusinberry, "Grange Thrills Huge Crowd"; *Illinois Alumni News,* Nov. 1924, 51, University of Illinois Archives, Urbana; George W. Rockwood to Editor, *Sunday Journal,* July 29, 1974; Lon Eubanks, "Circus Mood Prevailed in '24 Game," Urbana-Champaign *Courier,* Oct. 17, 1974; Grange, *Red Grange Story,* 58–59. Grange's statistics for the game are taken from a tabulation by L. M. Tobin of the University of Illinois Athletic Association, University of Illinois Archives, Urbana.

Chapter 1: An Odd Kind of Family

1. In its autumn 1991 special issue on "Yesterday's Heroes," *Sports Illustrated* featured Red Grange on the cover and selected his 1924 performance against Michigan to lead off a photo essay on "Unforgettable Moments in Sports." The editors noted that the selections were "not the twenty-five greatest achievements in sports, nor are they the twenty-five most important moments, though some would certainly fall into those categories. They are, simply put, our twenty-five Classic Moments." "Unforgettable Moments in Sports," *Sports Illustrated,* Fall 1991, cover, 20–29; Douglas A. Noverr and Lawrence E. Ziewacz, *The Games They Played: Sports in American History, 1865–1980* (Chicago: Nelson-Hall, 1983), 80.

2. John Underwood, "Was He the Greatest of All Time?" *Sports Illustrated,* Sept. 4, 1985, 115.

3. Bill Kehoe, "Fodder Visits the Home of a Ghost and Finds Red Grange's Father Was a Man of Sinewy Limbs," undated newspaper clipping, Wheaton College Archives, Wheaton, Ill.; Grange, *Red Grange Story,* 3, 5.

4. Grange, *Red Grange Story,* 3–4, 7; Kehoe, "Fodder Visits the Home of a Ghost"; author interview with Richard Crabb, June 15, 1992.

5. *Wheaton: Sesquicentennial, 1988* (Wheaton: City of Wheaton, 1989), 7–9, 21; Jean Moore and Hiawatha Bray, *DuPage at 150 and Those Who Shaped Our World* (West Chicago: West Chicago Printing, 1989), 254; Richard A. Thompson et al., *DuPage Roots* (Wheaton: DuPage County Historical Society, 1985), 56, 252.

6. Grange, *Red Grange Story,* 5–6; author interview with Richard Crabb, June 15, 1992. Norma died in her teens, and as an adult Mildred lived for many years in Binghamton, New York. W. C. Heinz, "The Ghost of the Gridiron," in Red Smith, *Press Box: Red Smith's Favorite Sports Stories* (New York: W. W. Norton, 1976), 49.

7. Grange, *Red Grange Story,* 6.

8. *City Record, City of Wheaton,* vol. 4, 424–25, 434, 438, 460–61, 483; author interview with Richard Crabb, June 15, 1992; Wheaton *Illinoian,* May 24, 1918.

9. See, for example, "The First All-American Iceman," *Literary Digest,* Nov. 15, 1924, 64–68. Grange remarked, "I was a green country punk who had stagged most of the time in college because I seldom had 15 cents to buy a girl a soda." Chicago *Tribune,* Jan. 28, 1991; Grange, *Red Grange Story,* 11; *City Record, City of Wheaton,* vols. 4, 6; *City of Wheaton, Council Proceedings,* vol. 1; *Abstract of the Fifteenth Census of the United States* (Washington D.C.: Government Printing Office, 1933), 742.

10. *City Record, City of Wheaton,* vol. 4, 198; Robert S. Gallagher, "The Galloping Ghost: An Interview with Red Grange," *American Heritage* 26 (Dec. 1974): 22. The estimated annual income is based on Red Grange working ten weeks during the summer and does not include any earnings that Garland might have contributed.

11. Chicago *Tribune,* Jan. 28, 1991; Elmer J. Hoffman, "Red Grange—Little-Known Items," undated manuscript, Wheaton College Archives, Wheaton, Ill.; author interview with Richard Crabb, June 15, 1992.

12. Chicago *Tribune,* Jan. 28, 1991.

13. Hoffman, "Red Grange."

14. *Wheaton High School Orange and Black, 1922* (Wheaton: Wheaton High School, 1922), 18 (first quotation); Grange, *Red Grange Story,* 19–20 (second quotation); *Bumstead's Directory of Wheaton City and DuPage County, 1915–1916* (Chicago: Bumstead, 1915), 70. See also Charles D. Weldon to Mike Hawkins, July 31, 1974, Wheaton College Archives, Wheaton, Ill.

15. Charles D. Weldon to Mike Hawkins, July 31, 1974, Wheaton College Archives, Wheaton, Ill.; Richard Crabb, "Ex-Wheaton Coach Dies," *Daily Journal* (DuPage County), Aug. 8, 1974; Grange, *Red Grange Story,* 11.

16. Grange, *Red Grange Story,* 16; *City Record, City of Wheaton,* vol. 4.

17. *City Record, City of Wheaton,* vol. 4. From 1914 to 1919, Lyle Grange had a deputy only for special events and, for a time, during the Chicago Race Riot of 1919. On the U.S. homefront in World War I, see David M. Kennedy, *Over Here: The First World War and American Society* (New York: Oxford University Press, 1980). Author interview with Richard Crabb, June 15, 1992.

18. Richard Crabb to Red Grange, Oct. 12, 1981, Wheaton College Archives, Wheaton, Ill.; Underwood, "Was He the Greatest?" 130; Gallagher, "Galloping Ghost," 22.

19. Richard Crabb to Red Grange, Oct. 12, 1981, Wheaton College Archives, Wheaton, Ill.; Underwood, "Was He the Greatest?" 130

20. Thompson et al., *DuPage Roots,* 253; author interview with David Malone, June 17, 1992; Wheaton *Illinoian,* 1917–21, see especially, May 24, 1918 and Oct. 8, 1920.

21. Wheaton *Illinoian,* March 21, May 24, June 28, 1918, Oct. 8 (quotation), Nov. 19, 1920; Paul Carter, *Another Part of the Twenties* (New York: Columbia University Press, 1977), 12–13; Christopher Finch, *Highways to Heaven: The Auto*

Biography of America (New York: Harper Collins, 1992), 80–81; *City Record, City of Wheaton*, vol. 6, 330. On the Chicago Race Riot, see William M. Tuttle, Jr., *Race Riot: Chicago in the Red Summer of 1919* (New York: Antheneum, 1970).

22. Wheaton *Illinoian*, Oct. 8, 1920, Jan. 14, March 28, 1921. The January 14, 1921, headline read: "Fortnightly Raid on Hiatt's Store Tuesday Night." *City Records, City of Wheaton*, vol. 6, 375, 428.

23. Gallagher, "Galloping Ghost," 22.

24. Author interview with Richard Crabb, June 15, 1992; Grange, *Red Grange Story*, 5.

25. Underwood, "Was He the Greatest?" 130 (first quotation); Wheaton *Illinoian*, July 23, 1920 (second quotation); Gallagher, "Galloping Ghost," 22 (third quotation).

26. "What, Ho Grange Says He Doesn't Like Football," undated newspaper clipping, 1924, Wheaton College Archives, Wheaton, Ill.

27. Nelson is quoted in Underwood, "Was He the Greatest?" 122.

Chapter 2: Football and the Emergence of Red Grange

1. Stephen Jay Gould, "Dreams That Money Can Buy," *New York Review of Books*, Nov. 5, 1992, 41; Steven A. Riess, *City Games: The Evolution of American Urban Society and the Rise of Sports* (Urbana: University of Illinois Press, 1989), 55–56.

2. Ronald A. Smith, *Sports and Freedom: The Rise of Big-Time College Athletics* (New York: Oxford University Press, 1988), 77–82; Glenn C. Altschuler and Martin W. LaForse, "From Brawn to Brains: Football and Evolutionary Thought," *Journal of Popular Culture* 16 (Spring 1983): 79–89; Michael Oriard, *Reading Football: How the Popular Press Created an American Spectacle* (Chapel Hill: University of North Carolina Press, 1993), 89–101; George B. Kirch, "Payoffs, Ringers, and Riots: Princeton and the Rise of Intercollegiate Football, 1880–1895," *Princeton Alumni Journal*, Sept. 11, 1991, 12–17.

3. Kirch, "Payoffs, Ringers, and Riots," 14; Smith, *Sports and Freedom*, 88–95; Frederick Rudoff, *The American College and University: A History* (New York: Alfred A. Knopf, 1962), 373–93. On colleges banning football in the 1890s, see Jim L. Sumner, "John Franklin Crowell, Methodism, and the Football Controversy at Trinity College, 1887–1894," *Journal of Sport History* 17 (Spring 1990): 5–20, and Hal D. Spears, "The Moral Threat of Intercollegiate Sports: An 1893 Poll of Ten College Presidents, and the End of 'The Champion Football Team of the Great West,'" *Journal of Sport History* 19 (Winter 1992): 211–26.

4. A excellent case study of the development of a college football program and its attendant problems is Robin Lester, *Stagg's University: The Rise, Decline, and Fall of Big-Time Football at Chicago* (Urbana: University of Illinois Press, 1995). See also Benjamin G. Rader, *American Sports: From the Age of Folk Games to the*

Age of Spectators (Englewood Cliff: Prentice-Hall, 1983), 81, 157; Patrick B. Miller, "Athletes in Academe: College Sports and American Culture, 1850–1920," Ph.D. diss., University of California, Berkeley, 1987, 85; Smith, *Sports and Freedom*, 158, 246n9; C. W. Hackensmith, *History of Physical Education* (New York: Harper and Row, 1966), 393–94; and George B. Wingate, "The Public Schools Athletic League," *Outing* 57 (May 1910): 166. Some sources cite the Oneida Club of Boston as being the first football team composed of secondary school students. Miller, "Athletes in Academe," 175.

5. Lester, *Stagg's University*, 20–21; Hackensmith, *History of Physical Education*, 393; Miller, "Athletes in Academe," 260–61, 270–71, 273.

6. "Sixth Annual Field Day of the Cook County High School Athletic Association, June 16, 1894," Neighborhood Research Collection, Sulzer Regional Library, Chicago, Ill.; Smith, *Sports and Freedom*, 188–89; Lester, *Stagg's University*, 50–56; *The Oski Wow Wow: A History of Hyde Park High School Athletics* (Chicago: Hyde Park High School, 1924), 8–19, Chicago Historical Society; Gerald R. Gems to author, Sept. 5, 1989.

7. Oriard, *Reading Football*, 132; Baker, *Football*, 455–528; J. Thomas Jable, "The Public Schools Athletic League of New York City: Organized Athletics for City Schoolchildren, 1903–1914," in *The American Sporting Experience: A Historical Anthology of Sport in America*, ed. Steven A. Riess (New York: Leisure Press, 1984), 219–38; Rader, *American Sports*, 159–61; Wingate, "Public Schools Athletic League," 166.

8. Ronald A. Smith, "Harvard and Columbia and a Reconsideration of the 1905–06 Football Crisis," *Journal of Sport History* 8 (Winter 1981): 5–19; Guy Lewis, "Theodore Roosevelt's Role in the 1905 Football Controversy," *Research Quarterly* 40 (Dec. 1969): 718–24; John S. Watterson, "Inventing Modern Football," *American Heritage* 39 (Sept.–Oct. 1988): 103–10; Altschuler and LaForse, "Brawn to Brains," 87.

9. Smith, *Sports and Freedom*, 202–6; Rader, *American Sports*, 142–43; Smith, "Harvard and Columbia," 5–19. Until 1910, the NCAA was called the Intercollegiate Athletic Association of the United States.

10. Watterson, "Inventing Modern Football," 106, 110 (quotation); Miller, "Athletes in Academe," 440, 449; John S. Watterson, "The Football Crisis of 1909–1910: The Response of the Eastern 'Big Three.'" *Journal of Sport History* 8 (Spring 1981): 33–37; *New York Times*, Nov. 21, 1909.

11. *New York Times*, Nov. 19, 20, 21 (first quotation), and Dec. 9, 1909. In addition, the Rochester, New York, school board banned football for a year in the spring of 1910. *New York Times*, April 26, 1910.

12. Watterson, "Football Crisis," 39–47; Watterson, "Inventing Modern Football," 110. Watterson notes that in 1912 the committee "added a fourth down to make ten yards, raised the value of the touchdown to six points, and reduced the field goal to three points. The twenty-yard restriction on forward passes was also

eliminated, though the pass still had to be thrown from five yards behind the line of scrimmage."

13. Parke H. Davis, *Football: The American Intercollegiate Game* (New York: Charles Scribner's, 1911), 117; Roberta J. Park, "From Football to Rugby—and Back, 1906–1919: The University of California-Stanford Response to the 'Football Crisis of 1905,'" *Journal of Sport History* 11 (Winter 1984): 10–18; Miller, "Athletes in Academe," 438–39; *New York Times*, Sept. 15, 1910.

14. Watterson, "Football Crisis," 45; Baker, *Football*, 44, 56; *New York Times*, Nov. 26, 1911.

15. The concept of Progressive reform being more conservative than liberal is examined in Gabriel Kolko, *The Triumph of Conservatism: A Re-interpretation of American History, 1900–1910* (New York: Free Press, 1963). See also Watterson, "Inventing Modern Football," 110–11; Baker, *Football*, 16–20, 166, 261, 271, 483, 505; and James Mennell, "The Service Football Program of World War I: Its Impact on the Popularity of the Game," *Journal of Sport History* 16 (Winter 1989): 250. On Thorpe and Carlisle, see Robert W. Wheeler, *Jim Thorpe: World's Greatest Athlete* (Norman: University of Oklahoma Press, 1979), and John S. Steckbeck, *Fabulous Redmen: The Carlisle Indians and Their Famous Football Teams* (Harrisburg: J. Horace McFarland, 1951).

16. "Army and Navy Condemnation of Football," *Literary Digest*, Nov. 15, 1913, 941 (quotation); "Ban Competitive Athletics," *New York Times*, May 16, 1915.

17. For an example of criticism of highly competitive sports in 1914 and 1915, see Alfred E. Stearns, "Athletics and the School," *Atlantic Monthly* 113 (Feb. 1914): 148–52; William T. Foster, "An Indictment of Intercollegiate Athletics," *Atlantic Monthly* 116 (Nov. 1915): 577–88. "Fewer Athletes Are Lost," *New York Times*, Oct. 14, 1917; Mack Whelan, "Will the War Kill Athletics?" *Outing* 68 (June 1916): 278–88; Ewald O. Stiehm, "Athletics in Wartime," *Outing* 70 (Aug. 1917): 672–75; and Baker, *Football*, 232, 273.

18. Kennedy, *Over Here*, 253–56; Raymond B. Fosdick, *Chronicle of a Generation: An Autobiography* (New York: Harper and Brothers, 1958), 136–41, 143–54; Guy Lewis, "World War I and the Emergence of Sport for the Masses," *Maryland Historian* 4 (Fall 1973): 109–12; Mennell, "Service Football Program," 248–60, esp. 259.

19. Timothy P. O'Hanlon, "School Sports as Social Training: The Case of Athletics and the Crisis of World War I," *Journal of Sport History* 9 (Spring 1982): 14–21; F. L. Kleeberger, "Essentials of Physical Education in Relation to Military Training in Public Schools," *School and Society*, Nov. 2, 1918, 529–31; F. L. Kleeberger, "Athletics and the War Game," *School and Society*, May 11, 1918, 541–45; "What the Draft Should Teach Us," *Literary Digest*, Aug. 2, 1919, 39.

20. Mennell, "Service Football Program," 250; Richard Whittingham, interview with Red Grange, 1984, Pro Football Hall of Fame (first quotation); Grange, *Red*

Grange Story, 7; Thompson et al., *DuPage Roots,* 58; John Donley, "Happy Birthday, Red Grange!" St. Petersburg *Times,* June 13, 1980 (second quotation); Underwood, "Was He the Greatest?" 129 (third quotation).

21. Underwood, "Was He the Greatest?" 129; Grange, *Red Grange Story,* 7, 8; Hoffman, "Red Grange."

22. Jean Moore, *From Tower to Tower: A History of Wheaton, Illinois* (Mendota, Ill.: Wayside Press, 1974), 72; Crabb, "Ex-Wheaton Coach Dies"; Norman T. Moline, *Mobility and the Small Town, 1900–1930: Transportation Change in Oregon, Illinois* (Chicago: University of Chicago Department of Geography, 1971), 116–19.

23. Grange, *Red Grange Story,* 11, 13, 14; Wheaton *Illinoian,* Sept. 20, 1920; *Wheaton High School Orange and Black, 1922,* 50.

24. Grange, *Red Grange Story,* 12; "Wheaton High School Football Record, 1918–1921," Wheaton College Archives, Wheaton, Ill.; Wheaton *Illinoian,* Oct. 18, Nov. 1, 22, 29, 1918.

25. Author interview with Richard Crabb, June 15, 1992; Grange, *Red Grange Story,* 21; Underwood, "Was He the Greatest?" 129.

26. Grange, *Red Grange Story,* 12–13, 16–17; "Wheaton High School Football Record, 1918–1921," Wheaton College Archives, Wheaton, Ill.; Ray Schmidt, "Red Grange of Wheaton," *College Football Historical Society* [bulletin] 4 (May 1991): 11; Wheaton *Illinoian,* Dec. 5, 1919.

27. Crabb, "Ex-Wheaton Coach Dies"; Wheaton *Illinoian,* Sept. 17, 1920; Gallagher, "Galloping Ghost," 22; Grange, *Red Grange Story,* 23–24.

28. Schmidt, "Red Grange of Wheaton," 11–12; "Wheaton High School Football Record, 1918–1921," Wheaton College Archives, Wheaton, Ill.; Wheaton *Illinoian,* Oct. 22 (quotation), Nov. 5, 1920; *Wheaton High School Orange and Black, 1921* (Wheaton: Wheaton High School, 1921), 55, 57.

29. Wheaton *Illinoian,* Aug. 26, 1921; *Wheaton High School Orange and Black, 1922,* 50–51; Grange, *Red Grange Story,* 19; Schmidt, "Red Grange of Wheaton," 12; undated newspaper clipping, Wheaton College Archives, Wheaton, Ill.

30. Wheaton *Illinoian,* Nov. 7, 1921; Grange, *Red Grange Story,* 19 (first quotation); Schmidt, "Red Grange of Wheaton," 12 (second quotation).

31. Grange, *Red Grange Story,* 14, 15, 179; Chicago *Tribune,* Jan. 28, 1991; Charles Dunkley, "Dream Player Gallops Gridiron," Nov. 2, 1937, newspaper clipping, Pro Football Hall of Fame; Wheaton *Illinoian,* May 17, 1921; Wheaton *Progressive,* May 26, 1922.

32. O'Hanlon, "School Sports," 7; "Cardinal Principles of Secondary School Education," *U.S. Bureau of Education Bulletin* 35 (1918): 8.

33. Stan Grosshandler, "Was He That Good?" *College Football Historical Society* [bulletin] 5 (Nov. 1991): 11.

34. "Wheaton Football Record, 1918–1921," Wheaton College Archives, Wheaton, Ill.; Wheaton *Illinoian,* Jan. 31, 1919.

35. Wheaton *Illinoian*, Oct. 8, 1920. Profiles on Wickhorst and Baker provided by Pat Harmon, curator of the College Football Hall of Fame.

Chapter 3: Grange and the Golden Age of Sport

1. Myron Cope, interview with Red Grange, 1974, Pro Football Hall of Fame.

2. Lewis, "World War I and the Emergence of Sport for the Masses," 109–10; Fosdick, *Chronicle of a Generation,* 154 (quotation).

3. Lewis, "World War I and the Emergence of Sport for the Masses," 112–14. Also see Baker, *Sports in the Western World,* 209–10.

4. *Literary Digest,* Aug. 2, 1919, 39 (first quotation); Lewis, "World War I and the Emergence of Sport for the Masses," 114–16 (second quotation); Kleeberger, "Athletics and the War Game" (third quotation); Riess, *City Games,* 154.

5. Grange, *Red Grange Story,* 19–20; Donley, "Happy Birthday, Red Grange!" On scholarships, see for example Underwood, "Was He the Greatest?" 129, and Gallagher, "Galloping Ghost," 23.

6. Grange, *Red Grange Story,* 20 (first quotation); Lon Eubanks, "'Galloping Ghost' Had a Humble Beginning with Illini," undated newspaper clipping, Urbana-Champaign *Courier,* University of Illinois Archives, Urbana (second quotation); Wheaton *Progressive,* May 26, 1922; author interview with Richard Crabb, June 15, 1992; Richard Whittingham, interview with Red Grange, 1984, Pro Football Hall of Fame.

7. Grange, *Zuppke,* 1–29 (quotation on 14–15); "Robert C. Zuppke—Football," *Memorial Stadium Drive,* 1922, 8–10, David Kinley Papers, University of Illinois Archives, Urbana; Mervin D. Hyman and Gordon S. White, Jr., *Big Ten Football: Its Life and Times, Great Coaches, Players and Games* (New York: Macmillan, 1977), 110–11.

8. "Robert C. Zuppke," 8–10; Grange, *Zuppke,* 15 (quotation); Zuppke to Mr. Applequist, July 1943, Pro Football Hall of Fame.

9. Carol F. Pullen, interview with Robert Zuppke, undated, box 8, Robert Zuppke Papers, University of Illinois Archives, Urbana; *Memorial Stadium Notes,* Dec. 1924; and Zuppke to Applequist, July 1943, all in David Kinley Papers, University of Illinois Archives, Urbana; John D. McCallum, *Big Ten Football since 1895* (Randor: Clinton Book, 1976), 225–26, 236, 251–52.

10. Gallagher, "Galloping Ghost," 23.

11. "Shall Intercollegiate Football Be Abolished?" *Literary Digest,* Oct. 10, 1925, 68–76 (quotation on 68). For an overview on college recruiting, see John F. Rooney, Jr., *The Recruiting Game: Toward a New System of Intercollegiate Sports* (Lincoln: University of Nebraska Press, 1980), 10–21.

12. "How Football Fosters Fair Play and Clean Living," *Literary Digest,* Oct. 31, 1925, 57–58.

13. "Football as the 'Goat' of College Sports," *Literary Digest,* Jan. 15, 1927,

80–81; Howard J. Savage, *American College Athletics*, Bulletin 23 (New York: Carnegie Foundation for the Advancement of Teaching, 1929), 297. For background on the events leading to the Carnegie Report and its contents, see John Thelin, *Games Colleges Play: Scandal and Reform in Intercollegiate Athletics* (Baltimore: Johns Hopkins University Press, 1994), 11–37.

14. "The Big Scrimmage over College Football," *Literary Digest*, Nov. 9, 1929, 58–70 (first quotation); Savage, *American College Athletics*, 241–42 (second quotation).

15. Savage, *American College Athletics*, 225.

16. Huff is quoted in *An Illini Century*, ed. Ebert, 64. Winston U. Solberg, *The University of Illinois, 1867–1894: An Intellectual and Cultural History* (Urbana: University of Illinois Press, 1968), 382; Ray Allen Billington, *Frederick Jackson Turner: Historian, Scholar, Teacher* (New York: Oxford University Press, 1973), 275–280; Miller, "Athletes in Academe," 442–43. From 1896 to 1913, the Western Conference had nine teams and was known as the Big Nine. Thereafter, it was known as the Big Ten until Chicago dropped football in 1939. A tenth team was added later.

17. On Yost, see Rader, *American Sports*, 139–40, and Lester, *Stagg's University*, 46–51, 108–12, 134–37; Ebert, ed., *An Illini Century*, 108–9, 155–56; Hyman and White, *Big Ten Football*, 115; Carol F. Pullen, interview with Robert Zuppke, undated, box 8, Robert Zuppke Papers, University of Illinois Archives (quotations).

18. Savage, *American College Athletics*, 63, 242; Miller, "Athletes in Academe," 398.

19. Grange, *Red Grange Story*, 31–32; Grange, *Zuppke*, 88. Grange often told this story, and his accounts over the years varied in detail. See, for example, Underwood, "Was He the Greatest?" 130–31, and Eubanks, "'Galloping Ghost.'"

20. Savage, *American College Athletics*, 239, 261–62; Chicago *Tribune*, Jan. 28, 1991; author interview with Richard Crabb, June 15, 1992.

21. Solberg, *University of Illinois*, 59, 99; Ebert, ed., *An Illini Century*, 1; *Memorial Stadium Notes*, Nov. 1922, David Kinley Papers, University of Illinois Archives, Urbana; Paula Fass, *The Damned and the Beautiful: American Youth in the 1920's* (New York: Oxford University Press, 1977), 124.

22. Myron Cope, interview with Red Grange, 1974, Pro Football Hall of Fame; Gallagher, "Galloping Ghost," 23; *Memorial Stadium Notes*, Nov. 1922, David Kinley Papers, University of Illinois Archives, Urbana.

23. Hyman and White, *Big Ten Football*, 166; Underwood, "Was He the Greatest?" 131 (quotation); material provided by Pat Harmon, curator, College Football Hall of Fame; Lon Eubanks, undated newspaper clipping, Wheaton College Archives, Wheaton, Ill.; Eubanks, "'Galloping Ghost.'"

24. Grange, *Red Grange Story*, 31–34 (first and third quotations on 32); Gallagher, "Galloping Ghost," 23; Underwood, "Was He the Greatest?" 131; Eubanks, "'Galloping Ghost'"; Grange, *Zuppke*, 87 (second quotation).

25. Grange, *Red Grange Story,* 32–33; Gallagher, "Galloping Ghost," 23; University of Illinois Football Display, University of Illinois Archives, Urbana; Eubanks, "'Galloping Ghost.'"

26. Urbana-Champaign *Courier,* Oct. 4, 1923 (first quotation); Grange, *Red Grange Story,* 35–36; Grange, *Zuppke,* 88–89; Carol F. Pullen, "Outline of Master's Thesis," box 8, Robert Zuppke Papers, University of Illinois Archives, Urbana (second quotation); Chicago *Tribune,* Oct. 7, 1923. Eckersall was both a football official and sportswriter.

27. Grange, *Red Grange Story,* 36–37; Underwood, "Was He the Greatest?" 131; Grange, *Zuppke,* 90–91.

28. Grange, *Red Grange Story,* 37–38 (first quotation); *New York Times,* Oct. 28, 1923 (second quotation); McCallum, *Big Ten Football since 1895,* 248, 252, 271 (third quotation).

29. *Memorial Stadium Notes,* Oct., Dec. 1923, Jan. 1924, David Kinley Papers, University of Illinois Archives, Urbana; *New York Times,* Nov. 4, 1923.

30. *Illinois Alumni News,* Dec. 1923, University of Illinois Archives, Urbana (first quotation); *Memorial Stadium Notes,* Dec. 1923, David Kinley Papers, University of Illinois Archves, Urbana (second quotation).

31. Grange, *Red Grange Story,* 38 (first quotation); *New York Times,* Nov. 4, 1923 (second quotation). Despite the popular wisdom that Grantland Rice gave Grange his famous nickname, the term was first used by Brown of the Chicago *Herald and Examiner.* Champaign-Urbana *News-Gazette,* Nov. 22, 1978.

32. *New York Times,* Nov. 10, 11, 25, 1923; Grange, *Red Grange Story,* 38–39.

33. *New York Times,* Nov. 25, 26, Dec. 18, 1923; Grange, *Red Grange Story,* 179; Alexander M. Wayland, *The Saga of American Football* (New York: Macmillan, 1955), 467–76.

34. *New York Times,* Dec. 18, 1923; Baker, *Football,* 601, 35.

35. Grange, *Zuppke,* 91–92; Donley, "Happy Birthday, Red Grange!"

Chapter 4: Football and Mass Society

1. Warren I. Susman, *Culture as History: The Transformation of American Society in the Twentieth Century* (New York: Pantheon Books, 1984), 105–6, 108; William E. Leuchtenburg, *The Perils of Prosperity, 1914–32* (Chicago: University of Chicago Press, 1975), 272–73.

2. On baseball stadiums, see Philip J. Lowry, *Green Cathedrals* (Cooperstown: Society of American Baseball Research, 1986); Lowry, "College Green Gridirons"; Ronald A. Smith, ed., *Big-Time Football at Harvard, 1905: The Diary of Coach Bill Reid* (Urbana: University of Illinois Press, 1994), 268n67; and Elliott J. Gorn and Warren Goldstein, *A Brief History of American Sports* (New York: Hill and Wang, 1993), 140.

3. Myron W. Serby, *The Stadium: A Treatise on the Design of Stadiums and their Equipment* (New York: American Institute of Steel Construction, 1930), 52; *The Illinois Stadium* (Urbana: University of Illinois, 1922), 8, University of Illinois Archives, Urbana; Riess, *City Games,* 14–44, 208; McCallum, *Big Ten Football since 1895,* 233.

4. Paul Gallico, *A Farewell to Sport* (Freeport: Books for Libraries Press, 1970), 210–11; Pullen, "Outline of Master's Thesis"; *Illinois Stadium,* 8; Grange, *Zuppke of Illinois,* 77 (quotation).

5. "A Memorial through the Years," 23; W. J. Chubb, "Ohio Stadium, Ohio State University, Columbus, Ohio," *American Architect,* Sept. 5, 1926, 203–12; Miller, "Athletes in Academe," 475–76.

6. Susman, *Culture as History,* 70–73; *Illinois Stadium,* 26; "The Stadium Story," box marked "Stadium Drive, 1921–27," David Kinley Papers, University of Illinois Archives, Urbana.

7. Frederick Lewis Allen, *Only Yesterday: An Informal History of the 1920's* (New York: Harper and Row, 1964), 172; John R. Tunis, "The Great God Football," *Harper's* 157 (Nov. 1928): 743. For a brief overview of the sports mania of the 1920s and its causes and meaning, see Robert L. Duffus, "The Age of Play," *The Independent,* Dec. 20, 1924, 539–40, 557, and "Sport Is Elected," *The Nation,* Sept. 17, 1924, 278.

8. *Memorial Stadium Notes,* Jan. 1924, David Kinley Papers, University of Illinois Archives, Urbana. Illinois used most of its football profits for the remainder of the decade to pay off the stadium debt. Basketball courts were later built under the stadium stands. Figures on Ohio State are in Tunis, "The Great God Football," 749.

9. Gallico, *Farewell to Sport,* 211–21; twelve folders marked "Complimentary Football Tickets, 1923–30," David Kinley Papers, University of Illinois Archives, Urbana.

10. Underwood, "Was He the Greatest?" 132.

11. Carter, *Another Part of the Twenties,* 11–12; John D. Hicks, *Republican Ascendancy, 1921–1933* (New York: Harper and Row, 1960), 8; Moline, *Mobility and the Small Town,* 52, 74; Donald R. McCoy, *Coming of Age: The United States during the 1920's and 1930's* (Baltimore: Penguin Books, 1973), 83; Merle Miller, *Ike the Soldier: As They Knew Him* (New York: G. P. Putnam's, 1987), 176–77; "Illinois Breaks World Record," Wheaton *Progressive,* March 23, 1923.

12. Hicks, *Republican Ascendancy,* 115, 169; Paul Goodman and Frank O. Gatell, *America in the Twenties: The Beginnings of Contemporary America* (New York: Holt, Rhinehart, and Winston, 1972), 37.

13. Ellis Kriekhaus, "The Stadium Will Be a Noble Memorial," *Memorial Stadium Notes,* May 1923, David Kinley Papers, University of Illinois Archives, Urbana; "The Greatness of the Stadium," *Illinois Alumni News,* Nov. 1924, 1, University of Illinois Archives, Urbana.

14. James Mark Purcell, "A Legend and a Research Problem: Red Grange of

Illinois," *College Football Research Association Bulletin* 2 (Nov. 1983): 1–3, and 2 (Dec. 1983): 1–6 [parts 1 and 2 of three-part series]; Grange, *Zuppke,* 90, 94–95; Grange, *Red Grange Story,* 50.

15. *Memorial Stadium Notes,* Oct. 1924, David Kinley Papers, University of Illinois Archives, Urbana; Grange, *Red Grange Story,* 60, 179; Purcell, "A Legend and a Research Problem," Dec. 1983, 3; *New York Times,* Oct. 5 and 12, 1924.

16. Jerome Brondfield, "The Immortal Galloping Ghost," *Readers Digest,* Sept. 1973, 151; Purcell, "A Legend and a Research Problem," Dec. 1983, 3.

17. Gallagher, "Galloping Ghost," 24; *New York Times,* Oct. 19, 1924; *Memorial Stadium Notes,* Oct. 1924, David Kinley Papers, University of Illinois Archives, Urbana; Charles Fountain, *Sportswriter: The Life and Times of Grantland Rice* (New York: Oxford University Press, 1993), 11–14.

18. Gilman M. Ostrander, *American Civilization in the First Machine Age, 1890–1940* (New York: Harper and Row, 1970), 230–31.

19. Ostrander, *American Civilization,* 232–33; Bruce J. Evensen, *When Dempsey Fought Tunney: Heroes, Hokum, and Storytelling in the Jazz Age* (Knoxville: University of Tennessee Press, 1996), 50–53; John Stevens, "The Rise of the Sports Page" *Gannett Center Journal* 1 (Fall 1987): 1–11; Don Maxwell, "Speaking of Sports," Chicago *Tribune,* Oct. 9, 1926, Jan. 28, 1991; author interview with Richard Crabb, June 15, 1992.

20. On the importance of magazines in football coverage, see Oriard, *Reading Football,* esp. xix, 142–88; and "The First All-American Iceman," 64–68. Also see Grantland Rice, "Is Grange the Greatest?" *Collier's,* Dec. 20, 1924, 14.

21. Loren Tate, "Grange, Seventy-one, Bright, Witty in Conversation with Press," Champaign-Urbana *News-Gazette,* Oct. 15, 1974; author interview with Richard Crabb, June 15, 1992.

22. Fountain, *Sportswriter,* 196–97, 209; Hicks, *Republican Ascendancy,* 171; McCoy, *Coming of Age,* 128; Raymond Fielding, The March of Time, *1935–1951* (New York: Oxford University Press, 1978), 4; Raymond Fielding, *The American Newsreel, 1911–1967* (Norman: University of Oklahoma Press, 1972), 57–58.

23. Undated newspaper clipping on radio broadcasting, Pro Football Hall of Fame; Hicks, *Republican Ascendancy,* 172; McCoy, *Coming of Age,* 127; Marsteller, "Quin Ryan Says Grange Placed Football on Air."

24. McCallum, *Big Ten Football since 1895,* 33; Maxwell, "Speaking of Sports"; Hicks, *Republican Ascendancy,* 172–73; Gorn and Goldstein, *A Brief History,* 194–95; Marsteller, "Quin Ryan Says Grange Placed Football on Air." For commentary on the impact of radio on boxing in the 1920s, see Evensen, *When Dempsey Fought Tunney,* 84–111.

25. *Illinois Alumni News,* Nov. 1924, 43, 53, 56 (quotation), University of Illinois Archives, Urbana; *New York Times,* Oct. 26, Nov. 2, 9, 1924.

26. Grange, *Red Grange Story,* 60; *New York Times,* Nov. 2, 1924; Purcell, "A Legend and a Research Problem," Dec. 1983, 3. During the 1920s, national cham-

pions were unofficial and usually selected by newspapers or individual sportswriters.

27. Grange, *Red Grange Story,* 60–62 (first quotation); Stagg, *Touchdown!* 341 (second quotation); Lester, *Stagg's University,* 13–122 (third quotation); *New York Times,* Nov. 9, 1924 (fourth quotation).

28. Purcell, "A Legend and a Research Problem," Dec. 1983, 3; Lester, *Stagg's University,* 122–23, 259n87; Grange, *Red Grange Story,* 62. Purcell makes the point about Stagg's recruiting practices.

29. Purcell, "A Legend and a Research Problem," Dec. 1983, 3; *New York Times,* Nov. 9, 1924; Grange, *Red Grange Story,* 62–63; Lester, *Stagg's University,* 122–23; Stagg, *Touchdown!* 345.

30. *New York Times,* Nov. 9, 1924; Purcell, "A Legend and a Research Problem," Dec. 1983, 4; Stagg, *Touchdown!* 345–46.

31. Grange, *Red Grange Story,* 63–64 (quotations); Stagg, *Touchdown!* 346; Purcell, "A Legend and a Research Problem," Dec. 1983, 4.

32. *New York Times,* Nov. 9, 1924; Stagg, *Touchdown!* 346; Grange, *Red Grange Story,* 64–65; Purcell, "A Legend and a Research Problem," Dec. 1983, 4.

33. Purcell, "A Legend and a Research Problem," Dec. 1983, 4; Grange, *Red Grange Story,* 65–66. Notre Dame finished the season as unofficial national champions with a 9-0 record that included impressive road victories over Army and Princeton. See Murray Sperber, *Shake Down the Thunder: The Creation of Notre Dame Football* (New York: Henry Holt, 1993), 163–72. Zuppke is quoted in Lester, *Stagg's University,* 124.

34. Gallagher, "Galloping Ghost," 95; Stagg, *Touchdown!* 348. Camp is quoted in Grange, *Red Grange Story,* 68.

35. Grange, *Red Grange Story,* 66–68, 179; *New York Times,* Nov. 16, 23, 1924; Purcell, "A Legend and a Research Problem," Dec. 1983, 4.

36. Grange, *Red Grange Story,* 68; Wheaton *Illinoian,* Dec. 5, 1924.

37. *Illinois Alumni News,* March 1925, 189 (first quotation), Jan. 1925, 117 (second quotation), University of Illinois Archives, Urbana.

Chapter 5: A Media Frenzy

1. *Illinois Alumni News,* March 1925, 189, University of Illinois Archives, Urbana; Wheaton *Illinoian,* Jan. 23, 1925; Milwaukee *Journal,* May 13, 14, 1925; Gallagher, "Galloping Ghost," 93–94.

2. Wheaton *Progressive,* Feb. 26, 1925; Willard Hansen, "'Hi' Gelvin Wrote of UI Football," Champaign-Urbana *News-Gazette,* Oct. 24, 1985; Heinz, "The Ghost of the Gridiron," 55; *Bulletin of Wheaton College* (Wheaton College, April 1925): 54; Kenneth E. Andersen to Louis D. Liay, July 2, 1984, University of Illinois Archives, Urbana; *Daily Illini,* Jan. 1, 1926. The average grade for football players at Illinois between 1920 and 1925 was 3.25.

3. Allen, *Only Yesterday*, 161–62.

4. Ibid.

5. Wheaton *Illinoian*, Sept. 12, 19, 1924; *New York Times*, June 18, 1925; "Grange Spends Night in City," newspaper clipping (Peoria, Ill.), June 9, 1925, University of Illinois Archives, Urbana; author interview with Richard Crabb, June 15, 1992.

6. Grange, *Red Grange Story*, 69–70; Myron Cope, interview with Red Grange, 1974, Pro Football Hall of Fame; Purcell, "A Legend and a Research Problem," Dec. 1983, 5; D. M. Johnson, "The World's Largest Raincoat," *Dupont Magazine*, May 1926, University of Illinois Archives, Urbana (quotation).

7. Myron Cope, interview with Red Grange, 1974, Pro Football Hall of Fame; Grange, *Red Grange Story*, 69–70, 179; Grantland Rice, "Red Grange Will Make His Debut for 1925 To-day," New York *Herald-Tribune*, Oct. 3, 1925; Grantland Rice, *The Tumult and the Shouting: My Life in Sport* (New York: A. S. Barnes, 1954), 196.

8. *New York Times*, Oct. 4, 11, 18, 1925.

9. Purcell, "A Legend and a Research Problem," Dec. 1983, 4–5; Grange, *Red Grange Story*, 179. Grange's average of 179 yards total offense per game for his last eight college games does not include the 1925 Wabash game in which he made an appearance but did not carry the ball. Tryon was selected to Walter Camp's second team in 1925 and Brown to the third team. Richard Whittingham, interview with Red Grange, 1984, Pro Football Hall of Fame.

10. Purcell, "A Legend and a Research Problem," Dec. 1983, 5; *New York Times*, Sept. 28, 1925, April 28, 1953; Champaign-Urbana *News-Gazette*, June 2, 1983; Heinz, "The Ghost of the Gridiron," 46. The *American Film Institute Catalog* lists only four films with football themes made in the 1920s before 1925.

11. For a sampling of Grange's accounts of meeting Pyle, see Grange, *Red Grange Story*, 90–91; Richard Whittingham, *What a Game They Played: An Inside Look at the Golden Era of Pro Football* (London: Simon and Schuster, 1987), 18; Whittingham interview with Red Grange, 1984, Pro Football Hall of Fame (quotation); and Myron Cope, interview with Red Grange, 1974, Pro Football Hall of Fame.

12. Whittingham, *What a Game They Played*, 18 (first quotation); Larry Engelmann, *The Goddess and the American Girl: The Story of Suzanne Lenglen and Helen Wills* (New York: Oxford University Press, 1988), 241; Alva Johnston, "Cash and Carry," *The New Yorker*, Dec. 8, 1928, 31.

13. Myron Cope, interview with Red Grange, 1974, Pro Football Hall of Fame; Johnston, "Cash and Carry," 31.

14. Johnston, "Cash and Carry," 32–33; Myron Cope, interview with Red Grange, 1974, Pro Football Hall of Fame.

15. Grange, *Red Grange Story*, 91–92; Richard Whittingham, interview with Red Grange, 1984, Pro Football Hall of Fame (quotation); Gallagher, "Galloping Ghost," 94.

16. Grange, *Red Grange Story*, 92.

17. Richard Whittingham, interview with Red Grange, 1984, Pro Football Hall of Fame; Randy Roberts, *Jack Dempsey: The Manassa Mauler* (Baton Rouge: Louisiana State University Press, 1979), 36–37; Kal Wagenheim, *Babe Ruth: His Life and Legend* (New York: Praeger, 1974), 82–83; Robert W. Creamer, *Babe: The Legend Comes to Life* (New York: Simon and Schuster, 1974), 271–73; David S. Neft and Richard M. Cohen, *Pro Football: The Early Years, An Encyclopedic History, 1892–1959* (Ridgefield: Sports Products, 1987), 26.

18. Grange, *Red Grange Story,* 91; Richard Whittingham, *The Chicago Bears: From George Halas to Super Bowl XX* (New York: Simon and Schuster, 1986), 41; Richard Whittingham, interview with Red Grange, 1984, Pro Football Hall of Fame; Milwaukee *Journal,* May 13, 14, 1925. A reproduction of the August 9, 1925, letter from Pyle to Sternaman is in Whittingham, *Chicago Bears,* 41.

19. Milwaukee *Journal,* May 14, 1925; Chicago *Tribune,* Nov. 12, 1925; Champaign *News-Gazette,* March 8, 1932; author interview with Jack McNevin, May 14, 1991. Although Grange's appearance in a film might not have jeopardized his amateur standing under existing Big Ten rules, starring in an "athletic" film might have. Other Big Ten players had lost eligibility for receiving money while appearing or working at athletic events.

20. "Gelvin Sells His Contract with Grange," newspaper clipping (Champaign), Dec. 9, 1925, University of Illinois Archives, Urbana; *New York Times,* Jan. 8, 1926; "Grange Spends Night in City," newspaper clipping (Peoria, Ill.), June 9, 1925, University of Illinois Archives, Urbana.

21. The Big Ten, in fact, did not have a rule in 1925 that disqualified football players from intercollegiate play who signed contracts to play professional football. The conference did have a regulation declaring that athletes lost amateur standing if they signed a contract to play pro baseball. Commissioner John L. Griffith ruled on November 19, 1925, that the rule would apply to pro football as well. *New York Times,* Nov. 20, 1925.

22. Hyman and White, *Big Ten Football,* 198; Wheaton *Illinoian,* Oct. 16, 22, 29, 1925. An estimated four hundred Wheaton residents attended the game despite the inclement weather. *New York Times,* Oct. 25, 1925.

23. Grange, *Red Grange Story,* 70–71; *New York Times,* Oct. 25, 1925.

24. Grange, *Red Grange Story,* 71–78; New York *Herald-Tribune,* Oct. 30, 1925.

25. Paul Gallico, "The Golden People of a Golden Decade," Chicago *Tribune,* March 29, 1964.

26. *Illinois Alumni News,* Oct. 1925, 2, University of Illinois Archives, Urbana; Grange, *Red Grange Story,* 71–78; transcript of a speech by C. E. "Chilly" Brown, former president of the Illinois Alumni Association, Oct. 1974, University of Illinois Archives, Urbana.

27. Grange, *Red Grange Story,* 72–73; Gallagher, "Galloping Ghost," 93.

28. Grange, *Red Grange Story,* 73–74; Grange, *Zuppke of Illinois,* 95–97; *New York Times,* Nov. 1, 1925.

29. Chuck Flynn, "Novelist Played Hookie to See Legend Born," Champaign-Urbana *News-Gazette,* Feb. 11, 1979.

30. Grange, *Red Grange Story,* 75–76; Chicago *Herald-Examiner,* Nov. 1, 1925. Two other excellent accounts of the Penn game are Walter Eckersall, "Grange Shows the East," in *The Greatest Sport Stories from the Chicago* Tribune, ed. Arch Ward (New York: A. S. Barnes, 1953), 215–16, and Damon Runyon, "The Galloping Ghost," in *These Were Our Years: A Panoramic and Nostalgic Look at American Life between the Two World Wars,* ed. Frank Brookhouser (Garden City: Doubleday, 1959), 290–92. For a description of Zuppke's version of the flea flicker play, see Whittingham, *Saturday Afternoon,* 91.

31. Chicago *Tribune,* Nov. 1, 1925; *New York Times,* Nov. 2, 1925; Runyon is quoted in Grange, *Red Grange Story,* 76. Stallings's dilemma is recounted in John D. McCallum, *Ivy League Football since 1892* (New York: Stein and Day, 1977), 81–82. Gallico, "The Golden People."

32. *New York Times,* Nov. 3, 4, 1925.

33. *New York Times,* Nov. 8, 1925; Grange, *Red Grange Story,* 78–79.

34. *New York Times,* Nov. 11, 12, 1925; New York *World,* Nov. 12, 1925; Joe Williams, "Tim Mara Quits Suckers Long Enough to See His Giants," newspaper clipping, Aug. 31, 1939, Pro Football Hall of Fame; Robert W. Peterson, *Pigskin: The Early Years of Pro Football* (New York: Oxford University Press, 1997), 98; Chicago *Tribune,* Nov. 12, 1925.

35. Grange, *Red Grange Story,* 79; "Red Denies Signing Large Contract to Play in Miami, Fla.," Nov. 15, 1925, newspaper clipping, University of Illinois Archives, Urbana (first quotation); *New York Times,* Nov. 15 (second quotation) and 17, 1925; Chicago *Tribune,* Nov. 17, 1925 (third quotation).

36. Grange, *Red Grange Story,* 93; Gallagher, "Galloping Ghost," 94; *New York Times,* Nov. 18, 1925.

37. *New York Times,* Nov. 19 (first quotation) and 20, 1925; Grange, *Red Grange Story,* 93–94; Chicago *Tribune,* Nov. 20, 1925 (second quotation).

38. Chicago *Tribune,* Nov. 20, 1925; *New York Times,* Nov. 20, 1925 (first quotation); Grange, *Red Grange Story,* 94–95 (second quotation). Grange also wrote that "a lot of hogwash has been written that almost everyone, including George Huff, Bob Zuppke, and my father, tried to discourage me from casting my lot with the pros. The plain fact is that no one except the newspapers ever brought up the subject until Zup questioned me about my future plans as we traveled on the train to Columbus for the Ohio State encounter" (94–95). Grange is more critical of Illinois officials in Gallagher, "Galloping Ghost," 94.

39. William D. Richardson, "Grange Plays Last Game Today," *New York Times,* Nov. 21, 1925; Grange, *Red Grange Story,* 95; Al Stump, "The Ghost still Gallops," *Pageant* (Dec. 1952): 148.

40. Richardson, "Grange Plays Last Game"; "Grange Turns Pro; Illinois Wins, 14-9," *New York Times,* Nov. 22, 1925.

41. *New York Times,* Nov. 22, 1925; Grange, *Red Grange Story,* 96 (first quotation); Gallagher, "Galloping Ghost," 94 (second quotation).

42. Gallagher, "Galloping Ghost," 94; Whittingham, *What a Game They Played,* 19.

Chapter 6: The Great Debate

1. Milwaukee *Sentinel,* Nov. 23, 1925.

2. "What, Ho Grange Says He Doesn't Like Football," undated newspaper clipping, 1924, Wheaton College Archives, Wheaton, Ill.

3. "Grange Turns on Those Who Have Criticized Him," Milwaukee *Sentinel,* Jan. 7, 1926.

4. *New York Times,* Nov. 23, 1925.

5. Ibid.; Gallagher, "Galloping Ghost," 94–95; Grange, *Red Grange Story,* 96; Michael Oriard, "Home Teams," *South Atlantic Quarterly* 95 (Spring 1996): 477–78. Although he may have walked out of the banquet, Grange spoke with Zuppke a few months later in Los Angeles.

6. Author interview with Richard Crabb, June 15, 1992.

7. Myron Cope, interview with Red Grange, 1974, Pro Football Hall of Fame.

8. "Shall Intercollegiate Football Be Abolished?"; "How Football Fosters Fair Play and Clean Living."

9. *New York Times Times,* Nov. 24, 1925.

10. Peoria *Journal,* Nov. 24, 1925; Cleveland *Plain Dealer,* Nov. 23, 1925.

11. David Kinley to Edward Keator, Dec. 10, 1925, box 129, David Kinley Papers, University of Illinois Archives, Urbana; "A Tribute to Higher Education," *Christian Science Monitor,* Nov. 23, 1925.

12. Underwood, "Was He the Greatest?" 117; Stagg, *Touchdown!* 293.

13. Lester, *Stagg's University,* 10 (first quotation), 20; Whittingham, *What a Game They Played,* 27–28 (second quotation); Stagg, *Touchdown!* 293 (third quotation).

14. George Halas, with Gwen Morgan and Arthur Veysey, *Halas by Halas: The Autobiography of George Halas* (New York: McGraw-Hill, 1979), 59; Bob Carroll, "Bulldogs on Sunday," *Coffin Corner* 9, no. 3 (1987): 33–34. The Illinois semipro game was between Taylorville and Carlinville. Taylorville, led by University of Illinois star Joey Sternaman, defeated the Carlinville Irish 16-0. Healy is quoted in Myron Cope, "The Game That Was," *Sports Illustrated,* Oct. 13, 1969, 93.

15. On the criticisms and proposals for reform in college football and the rebuttal by college coaches, see the *New York Times,* Dec. 1, 1925–Jan. 17, 1926. For a brief survey of the debate, see "Football a Menace to Colleges, He Says" and "'Tad' Jones Defends Game," *New York Times,* Dec. 8, 1925, and "Roper in Address Defends Football," *New York Times,* Dec. 9, 1925.

16. *New York Times,* Dec. 4, 1925; Stagg, *Touchdown!* 297; Stoney McLinn, "Grid Mentors' Lofty Gesture Will Affect Situation Not at All," newspaper clipping, Dec. 30, 1925, Pro Football Hall of Fame.

17. Herbert Reed, "'De-Granging' Football," *Outlook,* Jan. 20, 1926, 102–3.

18. *New York Times,* Feb. 8, 9, 1926; Neft and Cohen, *Pro Football,* 47.

19. Neft and Cohen, *Pro Football,* 47; Peterson, *Pigskin,* 93; "Pro Football's New Czar: 'Big Bill' Edwards," *Literary Digest,* March 27, 1926, 54; Oriard, "Home Teams," 478.

20. *New York Times,* Jan. 24, April 27, May 24, 1926; Savage, *American College Athletics;* "Big Scrimmage over College Football," 59–62.

21. "Peters Fabled Drop Kicker," undated article, University of Illinois Archives, Urbana; "Picking This Year's Red Grange and Other All-America Timber," *Literary Digest,* Nov. 2, 1929, 61–63; "Rentner's Threat to the Laurels of Red Grange," *Literary Digest,* Nov. 28, 1931, 32–33; Dunkley, "Dream Player Gallops Gridiron"; "Twenty-five Touchdowns in Five Games!" Milwaukee *Journal,* Nov. 2, 1937; "Harmon Top Grange? Zup Roars 'No!'" Chicago *Daily News,* Oct. 24, 1939; "Football Sighs for More Concrete," *The Independent,* Nov. 6, 1926, 525–28.

22. Gallico, "The Golden People."

Chapter 7: The Grand Eastern Tour

1. Whittingham, *Chicago Bears,* 43, 45; "Red Grange Collects $12,000, Teams Tie," newspaper clipping, Nov. 27, 1925, Pro Football Hall of Fame; Jim Muzzy, interview with Red Grange, 1984, Pro Football Hall of Fame.

2. Neft and Cohen, *Pro Football,* 14; Whittingham, *Chicago Bears,* 45 (first quotation), 43 (second quotation); *New York Times* Nov. 27, 1925; "Red Grange Collects $12,000"; Underwood, "Was He the Greatest?" 118.

3. Whittingham, *Chicago Bears,* 43; Riess, *City Games,* 233; Underwood, "Was He the Greatest?" 117.

4. Henry McLemore, "Tim Mara a Cool Hand at Horses, but Football Makes Him Wild Man," Milwaukee *Journal,* Sept. 7, 1938; "George 'Papa Bear' Halas Was Mr. NFL," Dec. 1983, University of Illinois Archives, Urbana.

5. *New York Times,* Nov. 30, 1925; Whittingham, *Chicago Bears,* 46; Chicago *Tribune,* Jan. 28, 1991.

6. Chicago *Tribune,* Dec. 1, 1925; Oriard, "Home Teams."

7. Neft and Cohen, *Pro Football,* 13–14; Dan Daly and Bob O'Donnell, *The Pro Football Chronicle* (New York: Collier Books, 1990), 16–18.

8. Daly and O'Donnell, *Pro Football Chronicle,* 16–18; Grange, *Red Grange Story,* 105.

9. *New York Times,* Dec. 3, 1925; Whittingham, *Chicago Bears,* 47–48; Daly and O'Donnell, *Pro Football Chronicle,* 18, 22; Champaign *News-Gazette,* Dec. 4, 1925.

10. Whittingham, *Chicago Bears,* 48–49; Myron Cope, interview with Red Grange, 1974, Pro Football Hall of Fame; *New York Times,* Dec. 6, 1925; Grange, *Red Grange Story,* 101; Daly and O'Donnell, *Pro Football Chronicle,* 22. John Hennessy, the referee that day at Schibe Park, claimed that Grange scored only one touchdown. According to his account, after a Chicago player plunged over for the second touchdown that resulted in a muddy pile-up near the goal line, a newspaper photographer asked him who had made the score. Before Hennessy could answer, Bears' center George Trafton winked at the official and shouted, "Grange." Hennessy looked around and spotted Grange standing up about ten yards away from the play. The referee was convinced that Trafton believed that a two-touchdown game for Grange would help increase attendance for the game at the Polo Grounds the following day. John Hennessy to the College of Agriculture, University of Illinois, Sept. 21, 1960, University of Illinois Archives, Urbana.

11. Allison Danzig, "Hero Worship Urge Brings Out Throng," *New York Times,* Dec. 7, 1925.

12. "Seventy Thousand May Watch Grange Here Today," *New York Times,* Dec. 6, 1925; McLemore, "Tim Mara a Cool Hand at Horses."

13. Daly and O'Donnell, *Pro Football Chronicle,* 22; Richards Vidmer, "Seventy Thousand See Grange in Pro Debut Here," *New York Times,* Dec. 7, 1925; Whittingham, *Chicago Bears,* 50.

14. Grange, *Red Grange Story,* 101; Westbrook Pegler, "Red Intercepts Pass, Races Thirty Yards to Score," Chicago *Tribune,* Dec. 7, 1925.

15. "Grange Gets $30,000; Says Its Secondary," *New York Times,* Dec. 7, 1925 (first and fifth quotations); Condon, "Galloping Ghost Rambles toward Seventy-seven"; Chicago *Tribune,* June 12, 1980 (second quotation); Gallagher, "Galloping Ghost," 95 (third and fourth quotations); Grange, *Red Grange Story,* 102.

16. Myron Cope, interview with Red Grange, 1974, Pro Football Hall of Fame (first quotation); "Grange's Two Days Here Yield $370,000," *New York Times,* Dec. 8, 1925; Gallagher, "Galloping Ghost," 95 (second quotation); Whittingham, *Chicago Bears,* 52.

17. *New York Times,* Dec. 8, 1925.

18. Daly and O'Donnell, *Pro Football Chronicle,* 18 (first quotation); Whittingham, *What a Game They Played,* 20 (second quotation); Peterson, *Pigskin,* 90; *New York Times,* Dec. 9, 1925 (third quotation).

19. "Football History as Made by the Illinois Iceman," *Literary Digest,* Dec. 26, 1925, 29 (quotation); Earl Loftquist, "Inside-Out," Providence *Journal,* undated newspaper clipping provided by Pearce Johnson; Providence *Journal,* Dec. 9, 10, 1925.

20. Grange, *Red Grange Story,* 103–4 (first quotation); Providence *Journal,* Dec. 10, 1925 (second quotation); Westbrook Pegler, "Boston Jeers as Red Fails to Scintillate," Chicago *Tribune,* Dec. 10, 1925 (third quotation).

21. Transcript of an interview with Red Grange, undated, Wheaton College

Archives, Wheaton, Ill.; *New York Times,* Dec. 11, 1925; Daly and O'Donnell, *Pro Football Chronicle,* 22.

22. *New York Times,* Dec. 12, 13, 1925; Daly and O'Donnell, *Pro Football Chronicle,* 22; Grange, *Red Grange Story,* 106.

23. Champaign *News-Gazette,* Dec. 8, 1925; "Football History as Made by the Illinois Iceman," 32.

24. James Crusinberry, "Tired Bears Drop Contest to N.Y. Team," Chicago *Tribune,* Dec. 14, 1925; Daly and O'Donnell, *Pro Football Chronicle,* 18. The Cleveland Bulldogs later sued Grange and the Bears for breach of contract.

25. For an example of two writers who equate Grange's first pro tour with the rise of professional football, see Heinz, "The Ghost of the Gridiron," 56, and Underwood, "Was He the Greatest?" 118. See also Daly and O'Donnell, *Pro Football Chronicle,* 16 (first quotation); and Oriard, "Home Teams," 471–500 (quotation on 483).

26. James Quirk and Rodney D. Fort have argued that the struggle between the NFL and Grange and Pyle's American Football League in 1926 convinced Joe Carr that his league's future lay in large metropolitan franchises. Although the war with the AFL may have expedited that transition, it seems more likely that Grange drawing huge crowds in New York, Chicago, and Philadelphia in 1925 convinced Carr to concentrate on large urban franchises. James Quirk and Rodney D. Fort, *Pay Dirt: The Business of Professional Team Sports* (Princeton: Princeton University Press, 1992), 337.

27. *New York Times,* Dec. 17, 1925; Daly and O'Donnell, *Pro Football Chronicle,* 21 (first quotation); Grange, *Red Grange Story,* 107 (second and third quotations).

Chapter 8: Barnstorming, Hollywood, and the AFL

1. Chicago *Tribune,* Dec. 16, 1925; *Illinois Alumni News,* Jan. 1926, 142, University of Illinois Archives, Urbana; *New York Times,* Dec. 16, 1925, Jan. 12, 1926; *Daily Illini,* Dec. 24, 1925.

2. Whittingham, *Chicago Bears,* 52; Halas, *Halas by Halas,* 111–12; Earl T. Britton to Dan T. Desmond, undated letter, Wheaton College Archives, Wheaton, Ill.; John M. Carroll, *Fritz Pollard: Pioneer in Racial Advancement* (Urbana: University of Illinois Press, 1992), 144.

3. Allen, *Only Yesterday,* 228–29; Cope, "The Game That Was," 103 (quotation).

4. Earl T. Britton to Dan T. Desmond, undated letter, Wheaton College Archives, Wheaton, Ill.; *New York Times,* Dec. 25, 1925; "Only Eight Thousand See Bears Win," Dec. 27, 1925, newspaper clipping, University of Illinois Archives, Urbana.

5. Grange, *Red Grange Story,* 110; Underwood, "Was He the Greatest?" 134; Daly and O'Donnell, *Pro Football Chronicle,* 23; *New York Times,* Jan. 1, 1926;

"Grange Wins, Fails at Gate," Jan. 2, 1926, newspaper clipping, Pro Football Hall of Fame; Richard O. Compton to the editor of the *Illinois Alumni News*, Feb. 9, 1926, University of Illinois Archives, Urbana.

6. Whittingham, *Saturday Afternoon*, 78; Billy Evans, "Football's Young Frenzied Financiers," Dec. 21, 1925, newspaper clipping, University of Illinois Archives, Urbana; Whittingham, *Chicago Bears*, 53 (quotation); *Daily Illini*, Jan. 12, 1926.

7. "Nevers Fumbles Often, Grange's Team Wins," Jan. 3, 1926, newspaper clipping, Pro Football Hall of Fame; Daly and O'Donnell, *Pro Football Chronicle*, 23 (quotation).

8. Halas, *Halas by Halas*, 112–13; *New York Times*, Jan. 8, April 16, 1926; Chicago *Tribune*, Jan. 8, 1926.

9. Whittingham, *Chicago Bears*, 52–54; Daly and O'Donnell, *Pro Football Chronicle*, 23; Halas, *Halas by Halas*, 113; "Grange Is Great Show Down South," Jan. 11, 1926, newspaper clipping, University of Illinois Archives, Urbana; Oriard, "Home Teams," 480.

10. "Grange Turns on Those Who Have Criticized Him"; "College Game Will Always Be Greatest Says Harold Grange," Jan. 12, 1926, and "'Red' Denies All Manner of Things Papers Say He Said," Jan. 11, 1926, newspaper clippings, University of Illinois Archives, Urbana; Stump, "The Ghost still Gallops," 144.

11. John B. Kennedy, "The Saddest Young Man in America: An Interview with Red Grange," *Collier's*, Jan. 16, 1926, 15; *Illinois Alumni News*, Feb. 1926, 184, University of Illinois Archives, Urbana; Damon Runyon, "L.A. to Welcome Red Grange," Jan. 14, 1926, newspaper clipping, Pro Football Hall of Fame; Halas, *Halas by Halas*, 113; Whittingham, *Chicago Bears*, 54.

12. *New York Times*, Jan. 18, 1926; Charles Chamberlain, "Red Made $50,000 in One Game," Urbana-Champaign *Courier*, Jan. 17, 1947; Whittingham, *Chicago Bears*, 54; *Daily Illini*, Jan. 13 (first quotation), 19, 1926. Zuppke quoted in Daly and O'Donnell, *Pro Football Chronicle*, 20–21 (second quotation). Michael Oriard has suggested that the attendance at the L.A. Coliseum may have been closer to sixty-two thousand and that many newspapers tended to overstate Grange's share of the profits in this and other games on both tours. See "Home Teams," 487–89.

13. "Grange Loafs as Bears Win," Jan. 18, 1926 (first quotation), and "Frisco Tigers Beat Grange," Jan. 25, 1926, newspaper clippings, Pro Football Hall of Fame; Daly and O'Donnell, *Pro Football Chronicle*, 23; Myron Cope, interview with Red Grange, 1974, Pro Football Hall of Fame (subsequent quotations).

14. "Red Grange Bears Defeat All-Stars by 54-3 Score," Jan. 31, 1926, newspaper clipping, University of Illinois Archives, Urbana; "Grange Stars in Victory," Feb. 1, 1926, newspaper clipping, Pro Football Hall of Fame.

15. Daly and O'Donnell, *Pro Football Chronicle*, 24; Whittingham, *Chicago Bears*, 54 (quotations), 56; Oriard, "Home Teams," 471–500, esp. 481–82.

16. Whittingham, *Chicago Bears*, 57; Halas, *Halas by Halas*, 121.

17. Irving Vaughn, "Grange, the Capitalist," in *The Greatest Sports Stories from the Chicago* Tribune, ed. Arch Ward (New York: A. S. Barnes, 1953), 218–19; "The Grange League," *Coffin Corner* 19, no. 2 (1997): 6–8; *New York Times,* Feb. 7, 8, 1926; Neft and Cohen, *Pro Football,* 54; Halas, *Halas by Halas,* 121.

18. James Crusinberry, "Pyle's New Pro Grid League Is Officially Born," Chicago *Tribune,* Feb. 18, 1926.

19. "Edwards Named President of Grange League," March 8, 1926, newspaper clipping, University of Illinois Archives, Urbana (quotation); "Pro Football's New Czar: 'Big Bill' Edwards"; "Grange League," 8–9.

20. Grange, *Red Grange Story,* 122; Peoria *Journal,* March 17, 1926 (on new house and cars); Underwood, "Was He the Greatest?" 132 (first quotation); author interview with Richard Crabb, June 15, 1992 (second quotation).

21. Wheaton *Illinoian,* Feb. 19, 26, 1926; *New York Times,* March 20, 21, 1926.

22. Frazier Hunt, "We Pay Red Grange Ten Times as Much as Coolidge," *Cosmopolitan Magazine* (Feb. 1926): 30–31; Carl Stephens, editor of the *Illinois Alumni News,* to Benjamin Wham, Feb. 24, 1926, University of Illinois Archives, Urbana.

23. *New York Times,* April 6, 1926; David E. Koskoff, *Joseph P. Kennedy: A Life and Times* (Englewood Cliffs: Prentice-Hall, 1974), 30; Bill Henry, "Red Grange Hailed in Screen Debut," Los Angeles *Times,* Feb. 1, 1937; Champaign *News-Gazette,* June 28, 1926.

24. "Wheaton Happy as Red Plans to Return to His Ice Route," May 27, 1926, newspaper clipping, University of Illinois Archives, Urbana; Grange, *Red Grange Story,* 123–26.

25. Gallagher, "Galloping Ghost," 95 (first quotation); Richard Whittingham, interview with Red Grange, 1984, Pro Football Hall of Fame (second quotation).

26. Grange, *Red Grange Story,* 123, 126.

27. *New York Times,* July 18, 1926; author interview with Richard Crabb, June 15, 1992.

28. Champaign *News-Gazette,* June 28, 1926; *New York Times,* July 22, 23 (quotation), 27, 1926.

29. "Red Grange Thrills Folk with Famous Tricks," Aug. 17, 1926, newspaper clipping, and *Illinois Alumni News,* Oct. 1926, 20, both in University of Illinois Archives, Urbana; Mordaunt Hall, "'Red' Grange's First Film," *New York Times,* Sept. 6, 1926 (quotation); Rose Pelswick, "New Pictures on Broadway," Sept. 6, 1926, newspaper clipping, University of Illinois Archives, Urbana.

30. Hall, "'Red' Grange's First Film"; Pelswick, "New Pictures"; Grange, *Red Grange Story,* 127.

31. Raymond William Stedman, *The Serials: Suspense and Drama by Installment* (Norman: University of Oklahoma Press, 1971), 61–62; Jim Campbell, "That's Entertainment, Too," *Game Day* program, National Football League, Oct. 24, 1976, Pro Football Hall of Fame.

32. "How Does It Strike You?" Sept. 9, 1926, newspaper clipping, Pro Foot-

ball Hall of Fame; "Grange League," 9–10; Gallagher, "Galloping Ghost," 96; Grange, *Red Grange Story,* 113; Neft and Cohen, *Pro Football,* 54; Whittingham, *Chicago Bears,* 58; "Nationals Score in Football War," July 22, 1926, newspaper clipping, Pro Football Hall of Fame.

33. Cope, "The Game That Was," 93–94 (quotation); Lyman DeWolf to William T. McIlwain, April 11, 1967, Wheaton College Archives, Wheaton, Ill.

34. Whittingham, *Chicago Bears,* 59–60; Neft and Cohen, *Pro Football,* 56–57; Cope, "The Game That Was," 94–102.

35. *New York Times,* Sept. 27, Oct. 4, 1926; Wheaton *Illinoian,* Sept. 17, 1926; Engelmann, *The Goddess and the American Girl,* 269; Grange, *Red Grange Story,* 117.

36. Gallagher, "Galloping Ghost," 96 (first quotation); Grange, *Red Grange Story,* 116; *New York Times,* Oct. 18, 1926; Whittingham, *What a Game They Played,* 11 (second quotation); Halas, *Halas by Halas,* 127; Neft and Cohen, *Pro Football,* 54–55.

37. Richards Vidmer, "Grange Team Wins on Tryon's Run, 6-0," *New York Times,* Oct. 25, 1926.

38. "Grange and Kreuz Meet on Gridiron," Oct. 30, 1926, newspaper clipping, Pro Football Hall of Fame; *New York Times,* Oct. 31, 1926; Neft and Cohen, *Pro Football,* 54.

39. Engelmann, *The Goddess and the American Girl,* 272; Cope, "The Game That Was," 103; Myron Cope, interview with Red Grange, 1974, Pro Football Hall of Fame.

40. "Pyle Denies Merger," Nov. 9, 1926, newspaper clipping, Pro Football Hall of Fame; Richards Vidmer, "Grangers Roll Up a 35-0 Victory," *New York Times,* Nov. 3, 1926; New York *Age,* Nov. 13, 1926.

41. Richards Vidmer, "Grangers Outromp Horsemen, 21-13," *New York Times,* Nov. 8, 1926; "Red Grange in Canada," *Coffin Corner* 4 (July 1982): 6–7; Neft and Cohen, *Pro Football,* 54.

42. Richards Vidmer, "With Grange Hurt His Team Is Beaten," *New York Times,* Nov. 22, 1926; Grange, *Red Grange Story,* 119; *New York Times,* Nov. 26, 1926.

43. *New York Times,* Nov. 28, 1926; Allison Danzig, "Grange Is Absent but Yankees Win," *New York Times,* Nov. 29, 1926.

44. Grange, *Red Grange Story,* 119–20; Neft and Cohen, *Pro Football,* 56; *New York Times,* Dec. 13, 1926; Gallagher, "Galloping Ghost," 96.

45. Grange, *Red Grange Story,* 120–21; Whittingham, *Chicago Bears,* 62–63; Neft and Cohen, *Pro Football,* 54; *New York Times,* Dec. 21, 1926.

Chapter 9: Down but Not Out

1. Charles C. Pyle to Hal Broda, July 14, 1927, Pro Football Hall of Fame; Underwood, "Was He the Greatest?" 132 (quotations).

2. *New York Times,* March 29, April 28, 1927; Lyman DeWolf to William T. McIlwain, April 11, 1967, Wheaton College Archives, Wheaton, Ill.; James B. Harrison, "Sports of the *Times,*" *New York Times,* April 29, 1927.

3. Chicago *Tribune,* Feb. 4, 1939; Myron Cope, interview with Red Grange, 1974, Pro Football Hall of Fame.

4. *New York Times,* Feb. 6, 7, 1927; "Racing Film," undated newspaper clipping, University of Illinois Archives, Urbana; "'Red' Grange Is the Hero," Chicago *Daily News,* Oct. 25, 1927; Grange, *Red Grange Story,* 130–31 (quotation).

5. "Racing Film"; Grange, *Red Grange Story,* 132.

6. Underwood, "Was He the Greatest?" 126, 132; "Racing Film"; Grange, *Red Grange Story,* 128–31.

7. Neft and Cohen, *Pro Football,* 62; *New York Times,* July 18, Aug. 18, 1927.

8. Grange, *Red Grange Story,* 133.

9. Detroit *Free Press,* Oct. 10, 1927; *New York Times,* Oct. 13, 1927.

10. *New York Times,* Oct. 17, 1927; Daly and O'Donnell, *Pro Football Chronicle,* 31–32 (quotation).

11. *New York Times,* Oct. 17, 1927; Daly and O'Donnell, *Pro Football Chronicle,* 31–32; Grange, *Red Grange Story,* 134–35; "Grange Hurt in Pro Game," Oct. 17, 1927, newspaper clipping, Pro Football Hall of Fame.

12. Daly and O'Donnell, *Pro Football Chronicle,* 32; Jim Muzzy, interview with Red Grange, 1984, Pro Football Hall of Fame; Grange, *Red Grange Story,* 135.

13. Grange, *Red Grange Story,* 135–36; Milwaukee *Journal,* Oct. 24, 1927; *New York Times,* Oct. 31, Nov. 7, 1927.

14. *New York Times,* Nov. 9 (first quotation), 12, 14, 15, 1927; Bryan Field, "Tryon-Baker Hurt as Yanks Win, 20-6," *New York Times,* Nov. 14, 1927 (second and third quotations); Grange, *Red Grange Story,* 136–37.

15. *New York Times,* Nov. 25, 1927; Grange, *Red Grange Story,* 137.

16. *New York Times,* Nov. 28, Dec. 4, 5 (first quotation), 1927; Grange, *Red Grange Story,* 138–39; Whittingham, *Chicago Bears,* 64 (second quotation).

17. *New York Times,* Dec. 11, 12, 1927; Grange, *Red Grange Story,* 139; Evensen, *When Dempsey Fought Tunney,* 116.

18. "Red Grange," Feb. 1928, newspaper clipping, University of Illinois Archives, Urbana; Pat Harmon, "'Era of Nonsense' Produced Bunion Derby," Cincinnati *Post,* March 4, 1978.

19. Grange, *Red Grange Story,* 140–41; author interview with Richard Crabb, June 15, 1992; Harmon, "'Era of Nonsense'"; Allen Bernerd, "The Great Bunion Derby," *Coronet* 33 (Nov. 1952): 150–56.

20. Harmon, "'Era of Nonsense'"; Grange, *Red Grange Story,* 140; Bernerd, "Bunion Derby," 154 (first quotation); Myron Cope, interview with Red Grange, 1974, Pro Football Hall of Fame (subsequent quotations).

21. Bernerd, "Bunion Derby," 154; "Grab Pyle's Palatial Bus; Writ Served," May 4, 1928, newspaper clipping, University of Illinois Archives, Urbana.

22. "Pyle to Pay Note to Defunct Bank," May 6, 1928, newspaper clipping, University of Illinois Archives, Urbana; Bernerd, "Bunion Derby," 154–56; Grange, *Red Grange Story*, 141; Harmon, "'Era of Nonsense.'"

23. *New York Times*, May 20, 27, 30, 1928, Feb. 4, 1939; Bernerd, "Bunion Derby," 156; Myron Cope, interview with Red Grange, 1974, Pro Football Hall of Fame.

24. Grange, *Red Grange Story*, 142; *New York Times*, June 20, 1928; Eddie Jacquin, "In Perspective," Champaign *News-Gazette*, June 7, 1928.

25. Chicago *Tribune*, Feb. 4, 1939 (quotation); Champaign *News-Gazette*, April 29, 1928, Feb. 20, 1930, March 8, 1932; *New York Times*, June 19, 1928.

26. Grange, *Red Grange Story*, 143–44; newspaper clipping, Oct. 18, 1928, University of Illinois Archives, Urbana.

27. *New York Times*, Oct. 25 (first quotation), Nov. 14, 20, 1928, June 8, 1929; "Grange again Faces Court," Peoria *Journal*, Dec. 12, 1928; Daly and O'Donnell, *Pro Football Chronicle*, 24–25 (second quotation).

28. Grange, *Red Grange Story*, 144–45; Ken Weiss and Ed Goodgold, *To Be Continued . . .* (New York: Crown Publishers, 1972), 18.

29. Grange, *Red Grange Story*, 145; Stedman, *The Serials*, 92; Weiss and Goodgold, *To Be Continued*, 18; Henry, "Red Grange Hailed in Screen Debut."

30. Grange, *Red Grange Story*, 147; Gallagher, "Galloping Ghost," 97 (first, second, and third quotations); Ernest L. Cuneo, "Present at the Creation: Professional Football in the Twenties," *American Scholar* 56 (1987): 490–92, 498 (fourth quotation).

31. Gallagher, "Galloping Ghost," 97 (first quotation); Grange, *Red Grange Story*, 147–48; Jim Muzzy, interview with Red Grange, 1984, Pro Football Hall of Fame.

32. Grange, *Red Grange Story*, 148; Neft and Cohen, *Pro Football*, 72–75; Chicago *Tribune*, Oct. 28, 1929; Frankford Yellow Jackets Game Program, Nov. 2, 1929, Pro Football Hall of Fame.

33. Grange, *Red Grange Story*, 148; Chicago *Tribune*, Sept. 6, 1929; Whittingham, *Chicago Bears*, 71; Daly and O'Donnell, *Pro Football Chronicle*, 44.

34. Grange, *Red Grange Story*, 150–51.

35. Chicago *Tribune*, Nov. 4, 1929; "Grange and Bears Are Due Saturday," Nov. 13, 1929, and "Grange and Bears Drill Here Today," Nov. 15, 1929, newspaper clippings, Pro Football Hall of Fame; Frankford Yellow Jackets Game Program, Nov. 9, 23, 1929, Pro Football Hall of Fame (quotation).

Chapter 10: A Solid Pro Player

1. Lyle Abbott, "Grange Fond of Job with Night Club," May 30, 1930, newspaper clipping, University of Illinois Archives, Urbana; Cleveland *Plain Dealer*, May 18, 1930.

2. W. O. McGeehan, "Down the Line," New York *Herald-Tribune,* Jan. 18, 1930; Jim Flagg, "Flaggin' 'Em," May 23, 1930, newspaper clipping, University of Illinois Archives, Urbana.

3. Whittingham, *Chicago Bears,* 71; Grange, *Red Grange Story,* 159–64; Halas, *Halas by Halas,* 136–43.

4. Neft and Cohen, *Pro Football,* 79; Whittingham, *Chicago Bears,* 71; Kevin Britz, "Of Football and Frontiers: The Meaning of Bronko Nagurski," *Journal of Sport History* 20 (Summer 1993): 104–11 (first quotation, 111); Richard Whittingham, interview with Red Grange, 1984, and Jim Muzzy, interview with Red Grange, 1984, both in the Pro Football Hall of Fame (second quotation).

5. Cuneo, "Present at the Creation," 495; Wilfrid Smith, "Bears Held to Tie by Brooklyn Pros," Chicago *Tribune,* Sept. 22, 1930; Daly and O'Donnell, *Pro Football Chronicle,* 50.

6. Grange, *Red Grange Story,* 161–62; Chicago *Tribune,* Oct. 20, 1930. Grange's account of the origin of the man-in-motion feature of the split T differs from that of Halas and Brumbaugh. They maintained that Coach Jones had Grange going in motion to the strong side of the Bears' offensive formation (usually the right) from the beginning of the season. Grange and Brumbaugh added a new twist to the man-in-motion procedure in Green Bay by starting Grange to the right and then having him reverse his direction to the left, causing confusion for the Packers' defense. Halas, *Halas by Halas,* 140; George Vass, *George Halas and the Chicago Bears* (Chicago: Henry Regnery, 1971), 86.

7. *New York Times,* Nov. 17, 1930; Joe Tumelty, "Galloping Ghost Comes to Life! Runs Wild against Yellow Jackets," Frankford Yellow Jackets Game Program, Nov. 27, 1930, Pro Football Hall of Fame; Grange, *Red Grange Story,* 151; Neft and Cohen, *Pro Football,* 77, 79.

8. Whittingham, *Chicago Bears,* 74–75; Halas, *Halas by Halas,* 144–45; Frankford Yellow Jackets Game Program, Dec. 6, 1930, Pro Football Hall of Fame. Grange credited Maxwell with being one of the first sportswriters to publicize pro football consistently, beginning in 1925. Myron Cope, interview with Red Grange, 1974, Pro Football Hall of Fame; "Ex-Irish Beaten by Pro Eleven, 22-0," Dec. 15, 1930, newspaper clipping, Pro Football Hall of Fame; Arthur J. Daly, "Lack of Condition Costly, Says Elder," *New York Times,* Dec. 15, 1930.

9. John R. Tunis, "American Sports and American Life," *The Nation,* June 25, 1930, 729; "Letting the Air out of College Football," *Literary Digest,* June 27, 1931, 40–41.

10. Neft and Cohen, *Pro Football,* 83; Eddie Jacquin, "'Don't Feel Sorry for Me,' Says Red Grange; Alumni Should Get behind Zuppke," Champaign *News-Gazette,* April 26, 1933; "Red Grange Signs again with Bears," July 17, 1934, newspaper clipping, University of Illinois Archives, Urbana.

11. Whittingham, *Chicago Bears,* 75–76; Grange, *Red Grange Story,* 151; Chicago *Tribune,* Sept. 19, 1931; Wilfrid Smith, "Grange Makes Touchdown to Beat

Giants," Chicago *Tribune*, Oct. 12, 1931, and Smith, "Grange Leads Attack; Scores Three Touchdowns," Chicago *Tribune*, Oct. 19, 1931; Daly and O'Donnell, *Pro Football Chronicle*, 8.

12. Richard Whittingham, interview with Red Grange, 1984, Pro Football Hall of Fame; Gallagher, "Galloping Ghost," 97–98; Halas, *Halas by Halas*, 170; Myron Cope, interview with Red Grange, 1974, Pro Football Hall of Fame.

13. Cuneo, "Present at the Creation," 493–94; Gallagher, "Galloping Ghost," 97–98; Carl M. Becker, "The 'Tom Thumb' Game: Bears vs. Spartans, 1932," *Journal of Sport History* 22 (Fall 1995): 219n13.

14. Myron Cope, interview with Red Grange, 1974, Pro Football Hall of Fame.

15. Jim Muzzy, interview with Red Grange, 1984, Pro Football Hall of Fame; Britz, "Of Football and Frontiers," 112.

16. Wilfrid Smith, "Eighty-Yard Dash by Micheleske Brings Victory," Chicago *Tribune*, Nov. 2, 1931; Whittingham, *Chicago Bears*, 76–79; Neft and Cohen, *Pro Football*, 82–83; Benny Friedman, "The Professional Touch," *Collier's*, Oct. 15, 1932, 46; Bob Nelson, "'Other' Grange Looks Back," Champaign-Urbana *News-Gazette*, Sept. 4, 1977.

17. Westbrook Pegler, "Jimmy, Al and Thirty Thousand See Bears Beat Giants 12-6," Chicago *Tribune*, Nov. 16, 1931.

18. Chicago *Tribune*, Nov. 23 (quotation) and 30, 1931; Wilfrid Smith, "Grange Leads Bears to 18-7 Win over Cardinals," Chicago *Tribune*, Nov. 27, 1931, and "Joe Lintzenich Goes across in First Quarter," Chicago *Tribune*, Dec. 7, 1931.

19. Neft and Cohen, *Pro Football*, 83; Jim Muzzy, interview with Red Grange, 1984, Pro Football Hall of Fame (first quotation); Gallagher, "Galloping Ghost," 98 (second quotation); newspaper clipping, Sept. 26, 1932, University of Illinois Archives, Urbana.

20. Neft and Cohen, *Pro Football*, 86. In addition to other criticisms, college football came under attack for the rise in football deaths during the 1931 season. A record forty young men died while playing football; eight of them were college players. "Football Deaths: What Shall We Do to End Them?" *Literary Digest*, Dec. 26, 1931, 25–26.

21. Whittingham, *Chicago Bears*, 80; Neft and Cohen, *Pro Football*, 86–87.

22. Grange, *Red Grange Story*, 152; Neft and Cohen, *Pro Football*, 87.

23. Whittingham, *Chicago Bears*, 81. The NFL championship was then awarded by team owners at the league's winter meeting.

24. "In Other Days, There Were Other Worries," undated newspaper clipping, Pro Football Hall of Fame; Halas, *Halas by Halas*, 170–71; George Halas to Joseph T. Labrum, April 16, 1956, Pro Football Hall of Fame; "Packers Won't Play Spartans to Risk Title," Chicago *Tribune*, Dec. 7, 1931.

25. Becker, "'Tom Thumb' Game," 221–24; Whittingham, *Chicago Bears*, 74; Rathet and Smith, *Their Deeds and Dogged Faith*, 74.

26. Becker, "'Tom Thumb' Game," 216–27, provides the best and most accurate

account of the play-off game. Also see Whittingham, *Chicago Bears,* 82–83; Rathet and Smith, *Their Deeds and Dogged Faith,* 74; and Grange, *Red Grange Story,* 152.

27. Becker, "'Tom Thumb' Game," 216–17.

28. Nagurski and Grange are quoted in Rathet and Smith, *Their Deeds and Dogged Faith,* 74. Becker, "'Tom Thumb' Game," 225; Whittingham, *Chicago Bears,* 82–83; *New York Times,* Dec. 19, 1932.

29. Becker, "'Tom Thumb' Game," 225; Whittingham, *Chicago Bears,* 82–83; "First Use of 'Hash-Marks' in Pro Football," undated memorandum, Pro Football Hall of Fame. Halas is quoted in Rathet and Smith, *Their Deeds and Dogged Faith,* 74. The fourth rule change increased the clipping penalty from fifteen to twenty-five yards.

30. Bill Braucher, "Red Grange Retires from Gridiron to End an Era of the Sports World," Feb. 15, 1933, newspaper clipping (first quotation), and an undated newspaper clipping (winter 1933, second quotation), both in the University of Illinois Archives, Urbana; Becker, "'Tom Thumb' Game," 226; Jacquin, "'Don't Feel Sorry for Me'" (subsequent quotations).

31. From 1929 to 1932 Grange remained a headline player around the NFL and in cities where the Bears played exhibition games. See, for example, Frankford Yellowjacket Game Day Program, Nov. 30, 1930, and "Red Grange in Game Here," newspaper clipping (Milwaukee), Sept. 28, 1930, both in the Pro Football Hall of Fame.

32. Richard Whittingham, interview with Red Grange, 1984, Pro Football Hall of Fame (quotation); Gallagher, "Galloping Ghost," 98; Whittingham, *Chicago Bears,* 84–87.

33. Grange, *Red Grange Story,* 153; James Mark Purcell, "A Legend and a Research Problem: Red Grange of Illinois," *College Football Research Association Bulletin* 2 (Jan. 1984): 2 [part 3 of three-part series]; Neft and Cohen, *Pro Football,* 111.

34. Whittingham, *Chicago Bears,* 87–88; Howard Roberts, *The Chicago Bears* (New York: G. P. Putnam, 1947), 106.

35. Stan Grosshandler, "First NFL Title Game Was Super," *Football Digest* (1973): 56–60, provided by the author (quotation on 57); Rathet and Smith, *Their Deeds and Dogged Faith,* 78, 83; Whittingham, *Chicago Bears,* 88–89.

36. Ken Strong, "From Staten Island to Manhattan, I Couldn't Get Out of New York," in *The Fireside Book of Pro Football,* ed. Richard Whittingham (New York: Simon and Schuster, 1989), 275–76; Whittingham, *Chicago Bears,* 89; Grange, *Red Grange Story,* 154; Gallagher, "Galloping Ghost," 98 (quotation).

37. Whittingham, *Chicago Bears,* 89; Gallagher, "Galloping Ghost," 98; Grosshandler, "First NFL Title Game," 57, 60.

38. Myron Cope, interview with Red Grange, 1974, Pro Football Hall of Fame; Johnny Blood, "At Play in Green Bay," in *Fireside Book of Pro Football,* ed. Richard Whittingham (New York: Simon and Schuster, 1989), 28 (quotation).

39. "Red Grange Signs again with Bears," July 17, 1934, newspaper clipping (quotation), and "Grange Will Open Series of Talks over CBS Stations," Sept. 21, 1934, newspaper clipping, both in the University of Illinois Archives, Urbana.

40. Whittingham, *Chicago Bears*, 89–91.

41. "Talking It Over," Chicago *Tribune*, Nov. 30, 1933; Grange, *Red Grange Story*, 155; Whittingham, *Saturday Afternoon*, 272–87.

42. Whittingham, *Chicago Bears*, 91–92 (first quotation); Gallagher, "Galloping Ghost," 98; "Red Grange to Be Honored at Homecoming," *Illinois Alumni News*, Oct. 1934, University of Illinois Archives, Urbana (second quotation); Roberts, *The Chicago Bears*, 124–27.

43. Grange, *Red Grange Story*, 156 (first quotation); Neft and Cohen, *Pro Football*, 115; Jim Muzzy, interview with Red Grange, 1984, Pro Football Hall of Fame (second quotation); Richard Whittingham, interview with Red Grange, 1984, Pro Football Hall of Fame (third quotation).

44. Whittingham, *Chicago Bears*, 92–95; Roberts, *The Chicago Bears*, 130–31; Walter Fleisher, "Basketball Shoes Prove Big Aid to the Giants on Frozen Gridiron," *New York Times*, Dec. 10, 1934; Gallagher, "Galloping Ghost," 99; Strong, "From Staten Island to Manhattan," 276.

45. *New York Times*, Dec. 5, 1934; Richard Whittingham, interview with John "Shipwreck" Kelly, April 4, 1983, Pro Football Hall of Fame.

46. Gallagher, "Galloping Ghost," 96, 99; Grange, *Red Grange Story*, 158; Paul Zimmerman, "'Positively through This Time'—Red," Jan. 28, 1935, newspaper clipping, University of Illinois Archives, Urbana.

Chapter 11: Finding a Niche

1. *New York Times*, Dec. 7, 1934, June 20, 1935; Zimmerman, "'Positively through This Time'"; Champaign *News-Gazette*, June 20, 1935; Grange, *Red Grange Story*, 165.

2. Red Grange with George Dunscomb, "Little Things Make Big Touchdowns," *Saturday Evening Post*, Nov. 9, 1935, 99; "College Football," undated newspaper clipping (1985), University of Illinois Archives, Urbana; Underwood, "Was He the Greatest?" 128–29.

3. Whittingham, *Chicago Bears*, 96–101; Milwaukee *Journal*, Dec. 22, 1934; "Pro Football Sets Record at Box Office," Nov. 22, 1938, newspaper clipping, Pro Football Hall of Fame; "Football: Doctor's New League Plays to Please," *Newsweek*, Sept. 26, 1936, 30, 32; Rathet and Smith, *Their Deeds and Dogged Faith*, 200; Gerald R. Gems, "Shooting Stars: The Rise and Fall of Blacks in Professional Football," *P.F.R.A. Annual 1988* (North Huntingdon, Pa.: Professional Football Researchers Association, 1988), 11–15.

4. Red Grange with George Dunscomb, "The College Game Is Easier," *Saturday Evening Post*, Nov. 5, 1932, 88.

5. On Grange and the rise of football broadcasting, see Marsteller, "Quin Ryan Says Grange Placed Football on Air." "Taking Football off the Air," *Literary Digest*, July 9, 1932, 35; "King Football Answers the Depression," *Literary Digest*, Sept. 16, 1933, 33; Thelin, *Games Colleges Play*, 60–61; H. I. Phillips, "Hold 'Em, Mike!" *Saturday Evening Post*, Oct. 17, 1936, 25, 97; "Left Wing," "Public Enemy No. 64B: The Football Broadcaster," *The Nation*, Oct. 9, 1935, 405–6.

6. Christian Gauss, "Will the Football Bubble Burst?" *Saturday Evening Post*, Sept. 14, 1935, 45; Grange, *Zuppke of Illinois*, 100 (quotation); George Preston Marshall, "Pro Football Is Better Football," *Saturday Evening Post*, Nov. 19, 1938, 55.

7. On football bowl games in the 1930s, see Whittingham, *Saturday Afternoon*, 236–72; Gauss, "Will the Football Bubble Burst?" 13, 45 (quotation), 48; and "Bloodless Revolution on the Gridiron," *Literary Digest*, Oct. 27, 1934, 40–41.

8. Grange, *Red Grange Story*, 165–66; Chicago *Tribune*, Jan. 28, 1991; Marshall, "Pro Football Is Better Football," 55.

9. Chicago *Tribune*, Jan. 28, 1991; "The President and a Homecomer," *Illinois Alumni News*, Nov. 1940, University of Illinois Archives, Urbana.

10. "Carol Pullen Memorandum," 1957, box 8, Robert Zuppke Papers, University of Illinois Archives, Urbana (first quotation); Thelin, *Games Colleges Play*, 58–59; undated newspaper clipping, Wheaton College Archives, Wheaton, Ill. (second and third quotations); *New York Times*, July 15, 26, 1941 (fourth quotation).

11. *New York Times*, Oct. 14, 1941; Grange, *Red Grange Story*, 167–68; author interview with Richard Crabb, June 15, 1992; Hoffman, "Red Grange."

12. Grange, *Red Grange Story*, 166–67; Loren Tate, "Tatelines," Champaign-Urbana *News-Gazette*, Oct. 15, 1974. Grange told sports broadcaster Lindsey Nelson much the same thing about the insurance business. Underwood, "Was He the Greatest?" 122.

13. Grange, *Red Grange Story*, 168; Thomas Harbrecht and C. Robert Barnett, "College Football during World War II: 1941–1945," *Physical Educator* 35–36 (March 1979): 31–34; "Harold E. 'Red' Grange," University of Illinois press release, Nov. 22, 1955, University of Illinois Archives, Urbana; promotion leaflet for Tele-Visual Production, undated (1944), Pro Football Hall of Fame.

14. Halas, *Halas by Halas*, 234–35; Phil Patton, *Razzle-Dazzle: The Curious Marriage of Television and Professional Football* (Garden City: Dial Press, 1984), 124; Champaign *News-Gazette*, Nov. 28, 1944; Jerry Liska, "Grange Gives up Presidency of New League," Urbana-Champaign *Courier*, June 3, 1945.

15. Grange, *Red Grange Story*, 168; Stump, "The Ghost still Gallops," 146; Chamberlain, "Red Made $50,000 in One Game"; Rathet and Smith, *Their Deeds and Dogged Faith*, 246.

16. Red Grange to Robert Zuppke (telegram), May 2, 1947, box 5, Robert Zuppke Papers, University of Illinois Archives, Urbana.

17. William N. Wallace, "Grange, Galloping Ghost, Reappears for an Award,"

New York Times, Oct. 20, 1974; Benjamin G. Rader, *In Its Own Image: How Television Has Transformed Sports* (New York: Free Press, 1984), 28–31; "Life Goes to a Football Broadcast," *Life,* Oct. 14, 1946, 130–33; Ted Husing with Cy Rice, *My Eyes Are in My Heart* (New York: Hillman Books, 1961), 105–7; Frank Buxton and Bill Owen, *The Big Broadcast, 1920–1950* (New York: Viking, 1972), 223. Buxton and Owen maintain that former Cleveland Indians outfielder Jack Graney was the first prominent former athlete to become a play-by-play sportscaster when he broadcasted Cleveland baseball games in 1932. Grange, *Red Grange Story,* 168; author interview with Merle Harmon, March 11, 1997; "Grange Signs for Weekly Radio Show," undated newspaper clipping (1949), University of Illinois Archives, Urbana (quotation).

18. The first football broadcast on television was a game between Fordham University and Waynesburg State on September 30, 1939. It was followed by the first pro football telecast on October 22, 1939, featuring the Brooklyn Dodgers and the Philadelphia Eagles. Both games were seen only in the New York City area, where there were only about five hundred television sets. Jack Hand to Jim Campbell, Feb. 26, 1974, and NBC Sports press release, Aug. 27, 1975, both in the Pro Football Hall of Fame; Dave Berkman, "Long before Arledge . . . Sports and TV: The Earliest Years: 1937–1947—as Seen by the Contemporary Press," *Journal of Popular Culture* 22 (Fall 1988): 50; Jeff Neal-Lunsford, "Sport in the Land of Television: The Use of Sport in Network Prime-Time Schedules 1946–50," *Journal of Sport History* 19 (Spring 1992): 58–59; Wallace, "Grange, Galloping Ghost."

19. Daly and O'Donnell, *Pro Football Chronicle,* 95; Chicago *Tribune,* Jan. 28, 1991; Grange, *Red Grange Story,* 170, 173; Whittingham, *Chicago Bears,* 139; Halas, *Halas by Halas,* 239–48; Patton, *Razzle-Dazzle,* 32; *New York Times,* July 8, 1950.

20. Rader, *In Its Own Image,* 28–29; Gallagher, "Galloping Ghost," 95; Wallace, "Grange, Galloping Ghost" (quotation).

21. Gallagher, "Galloping Ghost," 97–98; Richard Whittingham, interview with Red Grange, 1984 (first quotation), and Myron Cope, interview with Red Grange, 1974 (second quotation), both in the Pro Football Hall of Fame.

22. Lindsey Nelson, *Hello Everybody, I'm Lindsey Nelson* (New York: William Morrow, 1985), 220.

23. Rader, *In Its Own Image,* 30 (first quotation); *New York Times,* Dec. 2, 1956 (second quotation); Red Barber, *The Broadcasters* (New York: Dial Press, 1970), 97–98; Underwood, "Was He the Greatest?" 120–21 (subsequent quotations); Patton, *Razzle-Dazzle,* 32.

24. Barber, *The Broadcasters,* 237 (first quotation); *New York Times,* Dec. 2, 1956 (subsequent quotations).

25. Nelson, *Hello Everybody,* 218–19; Myron Cope, interview with Red Grange, 1974, Pro Football Hall of Fame; Gallagher, "Galloping Ghost," 98; Grange, *Red Grange Story,* 182.

26. "Greatest Grid Player Seen in Action," Aug. 11, 1943, newspaper clipping, University of Illinois Archives, Urbana; Urbana-Champaign *Courier,* Oct. 20, 1949, April 4, 1951; Heinz, "The Ghost of the Gridiron," 48.

27. Grange, *Red Grange Story,* 168–69; *New York Times,* Aug. 12 (quotations), 30, and Nov. 9, 1950.

28. *New York Times,* Nov. 9, 1950; Gallagher, "Galloping Ghost," 98; Urbana-Champaign *Courier,* Sept. 3, 1962.

29. Grange, *Red Grange Story,* 170–71.

30. Ibid., 172–73.

Chapter 12: A Reluctant Hero

1. Stump, "The Ghost still Gallops," 146; Red Grange to Earl Britton, Feb. 25, 1950, Wheaton College Archives, Wheaton, Ill.; author interview with Richard Crabb, June 15, 1992.

2. Red Grange with Bill Fay, "I Couldn't Make the Varsity Today," *Collier's,* Oct. 25, 1952, 15 (first quotation)–18 (second quotation); Bert Bertine, "Bert's I-Views," Oct. 26, 1952, newspaper clipping, University of Illinois Archives, Urbana (third quotation); Chamberlain, "Red Made $50,000 in One Game."

3. Nelson, *Hello Everybody,* 202, 329–30; Underwood, "Was He the Greatest?" 122.

4. Chicago *Tribune,* Jan. 28, 1991; author interview with Richard Crabb, June 15, 1992.

5. Grange, *Red Grange Story,* 181; Underwood, "Was He the Greatest?" 126–28 (quotations); Jon Nordheimer, "Football Hero Keeps Warm and Shuns Memories," *New York Times,* Jan. 1, 1988.

6. *Congressional Record,* 85th Cong., 1st sess., 10911–12.

7. *New York Times,* July 26 (quotations), Aug. 2, 1957; Rader, *American Sports,* 349.

8. Grange, *Red Grange Story,* 181; Underwood, "Was He the Greatest?" 126.

9. *New York Times,* Aug. 22, 1960; Richard Nixon to Harold E. Grange, Jan. 19, 1961, Wheaton College Archives, Wheaton, Ill.

10. Three scrapbooks of newspaper clippings collected by Red Grange, Wheaton College Archives, Wheaton, Ill.

11. Rathet and Smith, *Their Deeds and Dogged Faith,* 26–30 (first quotation); Arthur Daly, "The Newest Sports Shrine," *New York Times,* Sept. 8, 1963; Ira Berkow, "Conversing with the Galloping Ghost," *New York Times,* Jan. 19, 1982; Underwood, "Was He the Greatest?" 122 (second and third quotations).

12. Undated newspaper clipping (June 1964), University of Illinois Archives, Urbana; Grange, *Red Grange Story,* 182; Michael Davis, "The Galloping Ghost," Chicago *Sun-Times,* Oct. 27, 1983 (quotations).

13. Underwood, "Was He the Greatest?" 122; "In a Hundred Years Never a Back

Like Grange," newspaper clipping, Oct. 5, 1969, University of Illinois Archives, Urbana.

14. Rader, *American Sports,* 258–60; Underwood, "Was He the Greatest?" 128; Randy Roberts and James Olson, *Winning Is the Only Thing: Sports in America since 1945* (Baltimore: Johns Hopkins University Press, 1989), 113–33.

15. Tate, "Grange, Seventy-one, Bright, Witty in Conversation" (first quotation); Jerry Liska, "Halas Pays Tribute to Red Grange," Urbana-Champaign *Courier,* Oct. 17, 1974 (second quotation); Jeff Metcalfe, "The Red Grange Legacy: Statistics Don't Tell All," undated newspaper clipping (Oct. 1974), University of Illinois Archives, Urbana (third quotation).

16. Ruth Weinard, "Thousands Come to See Red's Return to Stadium," *Illinois Alumni News,* Dec. 1974, 16, and Schacht, "A Man No One Could Ever Forget," 16, both in the University of Illinois Archives, Urbana; Liska, "Halas Pays Tribute."

17. Wallace, "Grange, Galloping Ghost"; Weinard, "Thousands Come to See Red's Return," 16; Lon Eubanks, "Illinois Fans Honor a Man and a Legend," Urbana-Champaign *Courier,* Oct. 18, 1974.

18. Author interview with Richard Crabb, June 15, 1992; Jean Moore and Richard Crabb, *Young People's Story of DuPage County* (Dundee: Crossroads Communications, 1981), 1–2; Weinard, "Thousands Come to See Red's Return," 16.

19. Author interview with Richard Crabb, June 15, 1992 (first quotation); E. W. Hesse, "Grange Relives Gridiron Highlights at Fete," Champaign-Urbana *News-Gazette,* Oct. 31, 1978 (subsequent quotations); "National Leaders with Roots in Dupage County," pamphlet distributed by the DuPage Heritage Gallery and the Northern Illinois Tourism Council, n.d.

20. Margaret Grange to Richard Crabb, undated letter (Oct. 1978), Wheaton College Archives, Wheaton, Ill.; "National Leaders with Roots in Dupage County." The other initial enshrinees in the DuPage Heritage Gallery were industrialists Elbert H. Gary and John W. Gates, publisher Robert McCormick, and evangelist Billy Graham. Grange gave a long, detailed interview to sportswriter John Underwood for "Was He the Greatest?"

21. "A Quiet Seventy-seventh Birthday? Not for No. 77," June 14, 1980, newspaper clipping, University of Illinois Archives, Urbana (first and second quotations); Donley, "Happy Birthday, Red Grange!" (third quotation).

22. Carol Lawson, "'Shadow Box' Author Finds New Story in Twenties' Sports Figure," *New York Times,* Feb. 15, 1980; Alex Ashlock, "Grange Center of Scandal Show," Champaign-Urbana *News-Gazette,* March 28, 1982; Chicago *Tribune,* Feb. 4, 1939; *New York Times,* Feb. 4, 1939; Robert Cowley, "The Jazz Age: A Shadow of the Seventies," *Saturday Review,* May 17, 1975, 13–18.

23. Author interview with Richard Crabb, June 15, 1992.

24. *New York Times,* June 1, 1983; Dave Anderson, "Last Roar from the Twenties," *New York Times,* June 12, 1983.

25. Davis, "The Galloping Ghost"; Underwood, "Was He the Greatest?" 136.

26. Nordheimer, "Football Hero Keeps Warm"; Beaumont *Enterprise,* July 25, 1990; *New York Times,* Jan. 2, 1991.

27. Beaumont *Enterprise,* Jan. 29, 1991; Timothy Dwyer, "Football's Legendary 'Galloping Ghost' Dead at Eighty-seven," Houston *Chronicle,* Jan. 29, 1991; Chicago *Tribune,* Jan. 28, 1991; Underwood, "Was He the Greatest?" 135.

Epilogue

1. Peter Williams, *The Sports Immortals: Deifying the American Athlete* (Bowling Green: Bowling Green University Popular Press), esp. 39–56; Michael V. Oriard, *Dreaming of Heroes: American Sports Fiction, 1868–1980* (Chicago: Nelson-Hall, 1982), 36–37; Richard Schickel, *His Picture in the Papers: A Speculation on Celebrity in America Based on the Life of Douglas Fairbanks, Sr.* (New York: Charterhouse, 1973), 7–8, 152–53; Richard C. Crepeau, review of Michael Oriard, *Dreaming of Heroes* in *Journal of Sport History* 10 (Winter 1983): 90–92.

2. Grantland Rice, "The Golden Panorama," in *Sport's Golden Age: A Close-up of the Fabulous Twenties,* ed. Allison Danzig and Peter Bandwein (New York: Harper and Row, 1948), 1; Mark Inabinett, *Grantland Rice and His Heroes: The Sportswriter as Mythmaker in the 1920s* (Knoxville: University of Tennessee Press, 1994), 100–101; Evensen, *When Dempsey Fought Tunney,* xii. For a brief statement of Grange's views, see Anderson, "Last Roar from the Twenties."

3. Richard Schickel, *Intimate Strangers: The Culture of Celebrity* (Garden City: Doubleday, 1985), 23–64, 50.

4. Benjamin G. Rader, "Compensatory Sport Heroes: Ruth, Grange and Dempsey," *Journal of Popular Culture* 16 (1983): 11, 12. Also see Roger Rollin, "The Lone Ranger and Lenny Shutnick: The Hero as Popular Culture," in Ray B. Browne and Marshall W. Fishwick, *The Hero in Transition* (Bowling Green: Bowling Green University Popular Press, 1983), 18 passim, on the point that only individuals within the mass audience can turn a celebrity into a hero.

5. Rader, "Compensatory Sport Heroes," 15; Randy Roberts, "Jack Dempsey: An American Hero in the 1920's," *Journal of Popular Culture* 8 (Fall 1974): 411–26. Roberts makes a similar case with regard to the public perception of Dempsey. Roderick Nash, *The Nervous Generation: American Thought 1917–1930* (Chicago: Rand McNally, 1970), 126–32; Britz, "Of Football and Frontiers," 101–26; John W. Ward, "The Meaning of Lindbergh's Flight," *American Quarterly* 10 (Spring 1958): 3–16.

6. Myron Cope, interview with Grange, 1974, and Richard Whittingham, interview with Red Grange, 1984, both in the Pro Football Hall of Fame; Anderson, "Last Roar from the Twenties."

7. Evensen, *When Dempsey Fought Tunney;* Bruce J. Evensen, "Jazz Age Journalism's Battle over Professionalism, Circulation, and the Sports Page," *Journal of Sport History* 20 (Winter 1993): 229–46.

8. The sled dog Balto became famous in the early 1920s for leading a team that brought the serum to end a diphtheria epidemic in Nome, Alaska. Allen, *Only Yesterday,* 161.

9. Grange, "I Couldn't Make the Varsity Today," 16 (quotation); Ralph Cannon, "The Genius of Coaches," Chicago *Evening Journal,* Oct. 11, 1923. Percy Haughton was credited with reviving Harvard's football fortunes in the 1910s but in 1923 had gotten off to a slow start in his attempt to revive Columbia University's football fortunes. Before he died midway through the 1924 season, however, Haughton had a record of 8-5-1 at Columbia. Michael Oriard has pointed out that historically football has had two narratives, one emphasizing the well-oiled machine programmed by the coach and the other celebrating the individual performer. In general, college coaches were of a high caliber in the 1920s. Some writers focused on the star players of the decade, most likely because they associated them with individualism and the coaches with a corporate structure. The celebration of the individual in an increasingly complex society was a major theme of the 1920s. See Oriard, *Reading Football,* 38–40.

10. "Shall Intercollegiate Football Be Abolished?" was a particularly stinging attack against college football and was summarized in *Literary Digest* about six weeks before Grange turned pro. For a critique of the star system approach to pro football, see John S. Kelly, "Football for a Living," *Collier's,* Oct. 24, 1936, 17.

11. Tate, "Tatelines"; Davis, "The Galloping Ghost."

Index

JOHN M. CARROLL is Regents' Professor of History at Lamar University in Beaumont, Texas. A native of Warwick, Rhode Island, he received a bachelor of arts degree from Brown University, a master of arts in history from Providence College, and a Ph.D. in history from the University of Kentucky. He has written or co-written eight books, including *Fritz Pollard: Pioneer in Racial Advancement.*

Viva Baseball! Latin Major Leaguers and Their Special Hunger
    Samuel O. Regalado
Touching Base: Professional Baseball and American Culture in the
    Progressive Era (rev. ed.)   *Steven A. Riess*
Red Grange and the Rise of Modern Football   *John M. Carroll*

Reprint Editions

The Nazi Olympics   *Richard D. Mandell*
Sports in the Western World (2d ed.)   *William J. Baker*

Typeset in Sabon 10/13
with Aachen Bold display
Composed at the University of Illinois Press
Manufactured by Thomson-Shore, Inc.